A Prisoner of
Martial Law

Jan Mur

A Prisoner of Martial Law

Poland: 1981-1982

Translated by Lillian Vallee

Harcourt Brace Jovanovich, Publishers

San Diego   New York   London

LIBRARY OF CONGRESS CATALOGING IN PUBLICATION DATA

Mur, Jan, 1957-
A prisoner of martial law.

Translated from Polish.
Includes index.
1. Concentration camps—Poland—Strzebielinek.
2. Political prisoners—Poland—Biography. 3. Martial law—Poland. 4. Poland—Politics and government—
1980-   . I. Title.
HV8964.P6M87 1984   365'.45'0924 [B]   84-15648
ISBN 0-15-173088-1

Designed by Mark Likgalter

Printed in the United States of America

First edition

A B C D E

Keep me, O Lord, from the hands of the wicked;
preserve me from the violent men
who have purposed to overthrow my goings.

The proud have hid a snare for me and cords;
they have spread a net by the wayside;
they have set gins for me.

Psalms 140: 4–5

Contents

Map appears on page viii.

Photographs follow pages 76 and 204. All of the photographs in the book were taken by the prisoners themselves. All of the artwork including the sketch on the book's jacket is theirs as well.

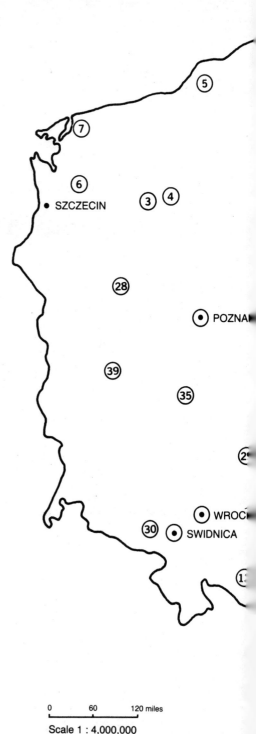

SZCZECIN

POZNAŃ

WROCŁ

SWIDNICA

0   60   120 miles

Scale 1 : 4,000,000

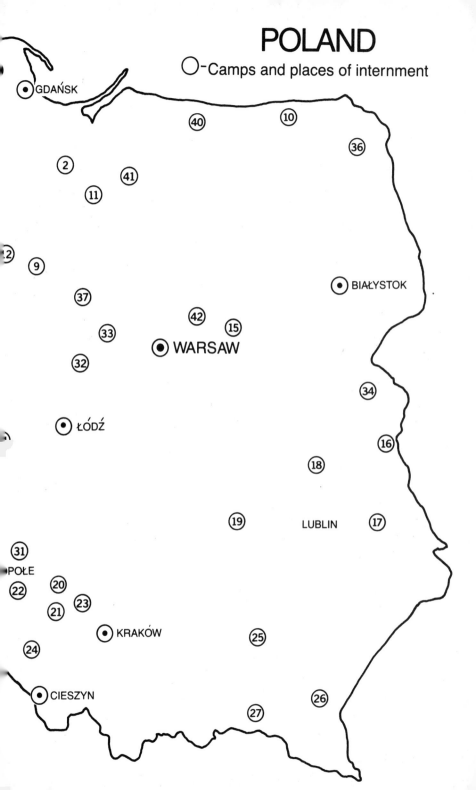

Introduction

Jan Mur was interned in the Strzebielinek internment camp near Gdańsk on December 13, 1981, just as martial law was declared in Poland, and released in early August 1982, four months before it was suspended. His journal covers the period of his own internment as well as the months following it, when he still seems to feel more closely connected to the peculiar world of the internment camp than to the dubious "freedom" he encounters on the outside. Jan Mur is the pseudonym of a young Gdańsk political activist, born in 1957. His choice of name—*mur* means wall—reflects what was for him the central reality of the year he describes.

Jan Mur spent this time in jail as an "internee," not a convicted prisoner. The distinction is central. When the Polish government declared martial law, it also declared an "amnesty." No one taken into custody on the night of December 12/13, including Jan Mur, was charged with any particular crime. The thousands of people seized were therefore not "arrested" but "interned." What this meant officially was that the government considered these people, although presently innocent, "likely to break a law" if they were to remain at large. On the other hand, all those people picked up by the police in the days and months following, while organizing strikes or distributing leaflets, were formally "arrested" and charged with a crime. They were given stiff sentences by military tribunals and confined to regular prisons, far away from the international spotlight. In contrast to the arrested and convicted political activists, the internees, who might be released at any time, were in a very privileged position. They were treated with far greater respect by the prison authorities, who were under special orders to recognize that the internees had certain rights. They were entitled to wear their own clothes (even Solidarity buttons), to receive packages from abroad, and to independently organize cultural and even political events inside the prison. Although there were several instances of force used against them, physical brutality was clearly the exception. Internees were even referred to by the formal "you," a bit of politeness unheard of in a normal Polish prison. Jan Mur describes all these things.

In any case, *A Prisoner of Martial Law* is not just a book about prison conditions. It is a political activist's attempt to think through a year following the collapse of the hopes of millions of people. The astonishing period preceding martial law, from the formation of Solidarity in August 1980 until its violent suppression sixteen months later, is the unstated point of reference for all that Mur talks about. In the Solidarity period anything seemed possible. When I traveled to Poland in March 1981, I traveled to an endless parade of political meetings, mass rallies, and private discussion groups, dealing with issues as diverse as the question of anti-Semitism in Poland, the theory and practice of union democracy, or the proper income of steelworkers as a percentage of the gross national product. It was a period when it really seemed possible that your own activity could help shape the world around you. It was a time not of inevitable change—in fact there was a feeling all along that little had changed yet—but of boundless possibility. The world seemed malleable, there were no absolutes; and it is this very perception that is perhaps the defining feature of a revolutionary period.

Revolutions may be exhilarating, but they are also tiring. By the fall of 1981, during what turned out to be the final weeks of Solidarity, things had changed. Hope lingered on, but it was now mingled increasingly with a tragic sense of despair. All the gains that had been won since August 1980 suddenly seemed to be in jeopardy. Most of the issues that were first raised in August were still unresolved. Even the new trade union law that was to finally and fully legalize Solidarity had not yet been passed. And the economic situation had gone from bad to worse, with shortages of basic commodities and the expectation that things were going to deteriorate still further. When I came to Poland again in September 1981, the words "it can't go on like this much longer" could be heard everywhere, as if they were the refrain from a new national hymn. Some felt things things would change for the better ("because they *must*," I was told); others, perhaps by now a majority, feared they would change for the worst ("because they *must*," I was told again). Often, one person would embody both extreme views. The same people who were telling me ten days before martial law that all was surely lost were telling me seven days before martial law that they expected the Soviets would soon be talking directly with Lech Wałęsa about the formation of a new government.

The ferment of the final days is presented on the very first page of this book. Andrzej Słowik, the leader of Solidarity in the major industrial center of Łódź, a man who had also, until his expulsion a few weeks earlier, been a member of the Communist Party, is presenting the proposal for an "active strike" at one of the Union's final National Commission meetings. What is most interesting about this new kind of strike is that it is not a strike at all. Rather, it calls on the workers in the factories to stop taking orders from the legal administration but to keep production going on their own, themselves deciding the destination of the factory's output. The very consideration of the "active strike" marked a significant raising of the stakes by Solidarity. As Mur notes, this was immediately recognized by the elderly, moderate lawyer Władysław Siła-Nowicki, an old socialist who had been defending political oppositionists in Poland for decades. By considering the "active strike," Solidarity was informing the government that it considered the latter only an annoying obstacle which the Union might yet choose to sweep aside.

There were indeed some people in the Union leadership who began speaking of a "final conflict." They offered concrete, radical proposals leading toward a resolution of the crisis, and glibly threatened the government with a national strike if it rejected the proposals. "Overthrowing the government," a Union activist from Łódź casually assured me three weeks before martial law, "is no problem, if we wanted to. The problem would be what to do then." In the final days some Solidarity locals even authorized the formation of workers' militias to defend the factories as well as the workers who might soon try to run them.

If in retrospect such measures seem to have been unnecessarily confrontational steps or even tragic historical blunders, they didn't seem so at the time. In fact, many reasonable people considered them to be constructive measures. If it were true that "it can't go on like this much longer," then *somebody* must finally do *something* to break out of the morass. For the salient, lived fact of this same fall 1981 was an apparent collapse of the government. The legal government suddenly appeared to be hopelessly inept and utterly helpless. There seemed to be a genuine vacuum of power. It is this more than anything else that drove the union to fatally greater heights. The problem was not that people lost their sense of what was possible, but that they no longer knew what was impossible.

The government knew. Jan Mur and his comrades did not. No matter how intensely people had pondered the real possibility of repression, no matter how imminent they thought it might be, nobody was prepared for the blow of December 13. On that day General Jaruzelski "seized" power (from himself), declared a "state of war" and authorized the internment of thousands of activists like Jan Mur. The revolution had been crushed in one night, because suddenly no one was talking about building any kind of new world. Suddenly nothing was possible. Jan Mur begins his diary in a daze.

This journal of a Polish camp internee should not be read as a "typical" work of a "typical" Solidarity activist, for the simple reason that the union was too healthily heterogeneous to be reduced to a single type. What Jan Mur presents are his own views, according to his own values, priorities, and political assumptions. In his assumptions, his presumptions, and particularly in his silences, Mur reveals quite a bit about himself and about his politics. All this is recognizable to a Polish audience, but naturally remains hidden to an American one. "Moral rectitude," he asserts at one point, "was Solidarity's greatest strength" (p. 32). This emphasis on morality is present throughout the journal. For Mur, the fundamental division in Poland runs across moral lines. The dividing line, in fact, is morality itself, with Solidarity, or society, representing morality and the government its absence. Thus it is not surprising that Mur does not discuss differences among his fellow internees in terms of income, occupation, education, or position of authority. For Mur these are simply not the salient distinctions. If the world is divided along moral lines, it is not divided along class lines. And by virtue of their being interned, his prison mates are all on the same side of the moral barrier. (At least the internees are; Mur's attitude toward the regular prisoners is not so favorable.)

Mur's emphasis on a Christian morality, his belief in the wisdom of the nation: these are component elements of a political tendency that was becoming increasingly influential in Solidarity's final months, and especially in Mur's hometown of Gdańsk. The group, sometimes known as the "national-Catholic" faction, or even as the "Real Poles," was getting very impatient with Solidarity's politics of compromise and sought a more radical break with the government in order to bring about a conservative social order in the future. One of the groups associated with this line was the Young Poland Movement, a Gdańsk-based organization founded in 1979. Mur frequently refers to this movement, usually in a favorable light, although he was probably not a member.

The tendency most consistently opposed to this current was known often as the "social-democratic" tendency, although its politics are to the left of most Western "Social-Democrats." It was represented above all by the veteran opposition organization KOR (Committee to Defend the Workers). KOR was founded in 1976 as a defense group for workers persecuted for participation in strikes in June of that year. (In 1983 its founding members were formally ordered to stand trial on charges of "sedition.") During the Solidarity period, KOR urged the Union to steer clear of activities that it felt would unnecessarily provoke the government. It placed much hope in the self-management movement and sought a moderate socialist social system, with extensive popular participation, for Poland's future.

When Mur talks about KOR, he can scarcely hold back on criticism. He writes that Solidarity ought to have removed KOR supporters from all positions of influence. Significantly, this had largely been accomplished in Gdańsk. But when Mur asserts that KOR "radicalized" people and "undercut the influence of the moderates" (p. 30), he takes a position that he would be hard-pressed to verify, as it seems clearly to run counter to the facts. Interestingly, Mur finds a staunch ally here in the Jaruzelski government, which has been saying the same things about KOR for years.

A personal journal of the sort Jan Mur kept is necessarily a unique reflection of the political life of a country. Yet what's striking is that the same psychological processes Mur reveals at work inside the prison cell prevailed outside its walls as well. The year which Jan Mur experienced in Strzebielinek, I experienced in the cities and towns of Poland, talking with people ranging from underground activists and Party stalwarts to workers and intellectuals who wished only to forget politics. Curiously, developments seemed to be perceived similarly by all, in the way that Mur recounts. There was the initial sense of shock and disbelief, along with the view that the first weeks of "the war" would determine all. As the strikes failed and the shock wore off, a deep depression set in. Jan Mur realized he would stay in jail a long time; those on the outside realized they would live under its shadow a long time. "Nothing can save us," was the sober perception of the new year. And so people turned even more to that one institution that promises the salvation no one can deliver: the Church. Much has been written on Solidarity and the Church. But to an observer, it was clearly apparent that the Church's influence increased dramatically with the imposition of martial law. There simply was no one else left to trust who was neither in jail nor in hiding. Jan Mur's journal entries about the Church are characteristic of the time. At first he trusts the Church completely and tries to ignore or rationalize all signs of its willingness to find a modus vivendi with the military authorities. When the signs become too clear to deny, he criticizes the Church. But cautiously; he's clearly uncomfortable doing so; and, in fact, he wavers, continuing to try to show (to himself) that the Church is on the "right" side. Moreover, for all the misgivings about the Polish Church, one figure remains above suspicion: the Pope. This difficult relationship between political activists and the Church remains up to the present an important part of the Polish landscape.

Finally, Mur's diary presents a picture of the underground. He documents its great success in publishing and distributing oppositional literature, while he implicitly demonstrates its complete ineffectiveness in achieving its stated goals.

Jan Mur mentions many names in his diary and it's impossible to say something about them all. He talks of Jacek Kuroń and Adam Michnik, two leaders of KOR who have still not left jail since December 13. In prison he meets Andrzej Gwiazda, the skilled Union negotiator in 1980 and later vice president of the Union, who has also been in jail ever since. Gwiazda ran against Wałęsa for the post of Union president, and it is surely not an accident that the other two rivals, Jan Rulewski of Bydgoszcz and Marian Jurczyk from Szczecin, both of whom Mur meets in Strzebielinek, were still behind bars in 1984, too. Seweryn Jaworski of Warsaw, Grzegorz Pałka of Łódź and Karol Modzelewski from Wrocław, and Andrzej Rozpłochowski, all members of Solidarity's National Commission, round out the list of those political prisoners who, in 1984, had still not been released since the night of December 12. When their bill of internment ran out one year later, their status was simply changed from "interned" to "arrested," making a mockery of the so-called "amnesty" of December 1981.

Mur once mentions the name of Alina Pieńkowska, a nurse from Gdańsk (p. 24). This young woman, completely unknown in the West, is, in fact, credited by many as being one of the key organizers of the Gdańsk general strike in August 1980, helping to convince the shipworkers to stay out in support of others once their own demands had been won. Mur also speaks occasionally of Zbigniew Iwanow, an engineer from Toruń. Iwanow, besides being a strike leader in 1980, was one of the key figures in the so-called "horizontal movement" within the Party. This movement was one of the most interesting and significant developments of the period. Its aim was to establish regular channels of contact between rank-and-file Party members in different factories and regions, contrary to the "normal" practice where Party cells have contact only with the unit above. The goal was to make the lower Party organs a check on the highest authorities, and to involve the rank-and-file in policymaking. Taken together, the horizontal movement constituted the most innovative internal opposition in a Leninist party since the Trotskyite Left opposition of the 1920s.

Inspired by a prison lecture series given by a fellow internee in May 1982, and aroused by the ensuing debates, Mur finally discusses seriously the political views of his comrades. And it is not at all surprising that the person whose lectures provoke such thoughtfulness and such constructive controversy was Krzysztof Wyszkowski. Wyszkowski is one of the most interesting, perceptive and courageous figures of the modern Polish workers' movement. One of the founders of Solidarity's precursor, the Free Trade Unions, in 1978, Wyszkowski was the person to whom Lech Wałęsa came when Lech decided that he, too, wanted to get involved. Once Solidarity was formed, Wyszkowski drew back from active involvement, although the editor of the *Solidarity Weekly* persuaded him to join the paper's editorial staff. Wyszkowski, in fact, did not even join Solidarity! He was wary of all mass organizations, especially those that are always convinced they are right. He felt that the best service he could render the new Union was to be an incisive critic, to say what needed to be said rather than what people wanted to hear. The impact of his interventions are clear from Mur's account, although Mur seems a bit too anxious to note Wyszkowski's remarks when they are critical of KOR, and not when they are critical of other tendencies.

Mur's *Journal* is filled with many other persons and events. Sometimes his anecdotes touch on politics here in the West, as when he cites the letter from a Solidarity émigré living in France, who writes that Solidarity's only real support comes from the Left, since the Right is too naturally conservative to support something as radical as Solidarity. Mur tells us of prison guards with their doubts and of workers with their lack of doubts; of priests trying to help the cause and of other priests trying to impede it; of underground activists pushing onward and of others giving themselves up. There emerges a picture of a society in flux living through a very difficult year. It is a society that resolutely tries to salvage some of the hopes and lessons of the past and slowly work its way toward a new but uncertain future.

—*David Ost*

Camp Journal,
Poland: 1981–1982

Preface

The only instinctive defense is memory, the written record, the attempt to appeal to the Tribunal of the Future, the hope for a fair judgment. Perhaps this hope is illusory. Perhaps time and subsequent events will so cover our tracks that my voice will be lost among the many other voices clamoring for justice. But at least it will not fade from my mind nor be dissolved by eventual waves of doubt. It will be preserved in concrete form, as something which I shall be able to look at and something which I should never forget. There really was such a time.

This diary of an internee is made up of fragments of daily notes, written in an internment camp in Strzebielinek, not far from Żarnowiec in the district of Gdańsk, and it was later continued "in freedom" and made up of messages smuggled from prison. The stuff of the diary is everyday experiences, events, scraps of readings, reports and news that made their way into the camps by various routes. The photographs were taken by us, the prisoners.

I believe that many records of this kind have been kept since martial law was declared. Someday, when these written records are put together, they will constitute full documentation of this period, of this crucial turning point.

J.M.
Gdańsk, January 1983

Prologue

A Journalist's Account

Gdańsk. Grunwald Street 114, fourth floor, meeting room of the National Commission of the Independent Self-Governing Trade Union (NSZZ) "Solidarity," December 10, 1981, 10 A.M.

The Presidium* of the National Commission is late in beginning its deliberations. Antoni Tokarczuk, the secretary of the Presidium, announces that Lech Wałęsa will take part in a press conference, but Wałęsa himself has not yet arrived. Tokarczuk, as secretary, initiates the proceedings, which move along sluggishly. The television crew from Solidarity's Bureau of Press and Information (BIPS), which has been admitted to the proceedings, has

---

*The Commission's executive.

nothing to record. It packs its equipment and leaves. Wałęsa runs in. Journalists squeeze into the small room along with Wałęsa, but after it is confirmed that there will, in fact, be no press conference right at that moment, they go into an adjacent room.

The Presidium once again takes up deliberations. After those present acquaint themselves with the situation in specific regions, someone proposes an "active strike" as the Union's response to the deadlock in talks with the government. An "active strike" means, practically speaking, a Union takeover of the economic apparatus in several of the country's voivodeships.* This idea, as worked out by the Łódź chapter, is presented by its chairman, Andrzej Słowik, who uses a large wall map to illustrate his points. The plan anticipates continued but selective production of foodstuffs. Further discussion reveals the multiplicity of cooperative ties, which would have to be maintained, even perfected, for this plan of action (a show of "how Solidarity works") to yield the desired results. Wałęsa does not seem convinced. Słowik insists, arguing the weariness and discouragement of the people, who would finally like to do something. Something that everyone could understand. Something useful, normal. They had come to this conclusion in Łódź after discussing all the possibilities for action. The Union's decision not to participate in sensational protest actions, and the impasse in matters concerning the Union's access to television and overall economic reform, drastically reduce the Union's room to maneuver. Sensing this situation, Łódź is aggressively imposing a positive (in their opinion) method of action which translates political slogans into practical terms: here are working people, people disillusioned with the lack of competence and good will of the authorities,

---

*Województwo, an administrative district in Poland.

people who in the face of the deepening economic crisis are taking matters into their own hands.

Władysław Siła-Nowicki, an attorney and adviser to the Union, gives a dramatic speech. He explains that this is a plan of action without historical precedent. He draws attention to the great risk involved in an active strike, which, in case of failure, would draw sharp criticism from society. He talks about an idealistic approach to a complex economic reality. Słowik will not budge; he lets everyone know that he will present his proposal to the National Commission tomorrow.

Wałęsa, who has come to Gdańsk directly from talks with representatives of the Episcopate in Warsaw, obviously wants neither quick nor radical solutions. He makes it understood that the time of instant and stunning victories is over. He outlines a broad program for strengthening the Union. Wałęsa's conciliatory approach, the more mature approach overall, is aimed at introducing broad changes into all social strata, together with that of the ruling elite. Wałęsa's approach obviously does not harmonize with the fractionalizing propositions put forth by individual regions.

The meeting of the Presidium, which was to work out a strategy and an agenda for tomorrow's national meeting, ends with no binding resolutions.

Finally the promised press conference. It is evident that it is important to Wałęsa. Anticipating questions, he begins with explanations and something like an apology for the Radom statements, which have been the cause of media attacks on the Union for several days now.

"Get this down accurately," he says. "The people must understand us. When we say 'confrontation' and 'fisticuffs' this does not mean a fight in the literal sense of those words. We have no tanks nor do we want them. Our words are straightforward, and though they may sound brutal, let the authorities look to our intentions, not grab at what we say. . . ."

The last two days, the final hours:

The meeting of the National Commission in the Gdańsk Shipyard (December 11–12) turned out to mean two days of silence from Wałęsa. The basic conflict that had been coming to a head for many months demanded some kind of resolution. There were two possibilities: backing out of the hard line taken by the Union in Radom, or supporting it and sharply formulating a series of actions that could eliminate the government obstacles to long-awaited changes due as the result of August. Deliberations moved in the direction of supporting the Radom position, despite attempts made by a group of advisers of the Union to stop this move, which argued a real confrontation with the authorities. Before 10 P.M. on the second day of deliberations, there was an attempt to get approval of this resolution. Events, however, had already moved beyond the historic main hall at the Gdańsk Shipyard.

The Account of a Worker from Regional Headquarters in Gdańsk

Around 5 P.M., we picked up the following order on a receiver that was tuned to the frequency used by the police in the Tri-City (Gdańsk-Gdynia-Sopot) area:

"Everyone drive to base. Leave the detained behind. Everyone return to base." From this moment on, we listened regularly and taped the messages. Around 7 P.M., we began to pick up reports made by police personnel (using cryptonyms such as "Karpaty," "Rysy," "Himalaje," "Tatry" and "Pieniny"*). After 10 P.M., the "base" ordered its personnel to "assemble on Kartuska [Street]." In the meantime, a column of police vans approached from the direction of Gdynia. There were about sixty of them. One of the Union cells from Słupsk informed us of

---

*All are names of mountain ranges.

a long column of ZOMO (Motorized Units of the Citizen's Militia) vans heading in the direction of Gdańsk. This report was confirmed by a taxi driver who had seen the same column and had driven to the Shipyard with the information. Around 11 P.M., Konrad Marusczyk, the vice-chairman of the region, came to regional headquarters with the information that he had called the *wojewoda** but had not been able to reach him. So he had called the police chief, Lieutenant Jerzy Andrzejewski, and had asked him why there were so many police in the city. The chief had answered that Operation "Three Rings" was being executed. Marusczyk had then asked which ring was for Solidarity. He received no answer.

Around midnight we began to transmit, by telex, the information that phone lines had been cut. Of the three telexes in operation, only one was still working. We asked the Gdańsk Health Department to send us an ambulance so that we could safely drive into the city. We drove in the direction of Przymorze and another group, in a taxi, got to the tram turnaround on Kartuska. The information was confirmed: city police units in full riot gear were assembling in various parts of Gdańsk.

We picked up the following police report in the area: "001 has barricaded himself. He has two big dogs." The response was: "Break down the door." When we heard the information about the dogs, we realized that it was one of our colleagues who had barricaded himself. He worked at regional headquarters and lived close by. We drove over to Sobotka Street to confirm what we had heard. It was confirmed. At a distance we heard the wild barking of Karol Krementowski's dogs, and the people in neighboring buildings were banging something against the windowsills. As it turned out, the dogs saved Karol. He managed to escape the raid.

---

*Highest authority in the voivodeship; district prefect.

First Account: Worker from the National Commission

We kept the National Commission people, who were deliberating in the Shipyard, up to date on the concentration and distribution of police units in Gdańsk. About 11 P.M. we got word about the attempted arrests of people from the Young Poland Movement. Gradually all telephone and telex lines were being cut. Gas station attendants were informing people that they had received orders prohibiting them from selling gas. We felt that something truly extraordinary was happening. Journalists observing the deliberations speculated on the subject. The National Commission, however, wanted to complete its deliberations at all costs. It was late. All the items on the agenda after the vote confirming the Union's position toward the situation in the country were shortened. None of those present was impressed by the news in the corridors about the concentration of police force or by the officially read letter, appealing for moderation and patience, from Primate Józef Glemp to Wałęsa. When he ended the deliberations around midnight, Wałęsa informed those present that communications were being cut and that people were being detained. He gave no instructions. Everyone left. The Shipyard was not obstructed. The majority of the members of the National Commission reached their hotels without difficulty. Some of them drove directly to their home regions, others went to the train station. We drove to Regional Headquarters along with a few colleagues. There were several persons who remained there on normal night duty. Reports about arrests in the city were multiplying. According to this information, Anna Walentynowicz and Leszek Kaczyński had been detained. Around 1 A.M., I drove to Zaspa to Lech Wałęsa's apartment to inform him about these incidents while my colleagues headed for the Hotel Monopol in Gdańsk to inform those who were there from the National Commission. I went back to Lech's house around 2 A.M. and he said: "Don't panic, maintain calm and wait until morning. It is difficult to judge the new situation at this point." The members of the National Commission reacted in much the same way. When we got back, we listened to the radio news. There were short, three-minute news items about the Front of National Unity, which, according to the broadcast, was enjoying wide support. A few minutes later, police vans drove up to Regional Headquarters and ZOMOs spilled out, surrounding the building. We turned on the theater spotlight, which was on the balcony, to light up our attackers and their loudspeakers. One of us shouted out to the neighbors: "Fellow Poles! We are being attacked by the police! Help us!" That didn't last long. They cut off our power source. We repeated the call for help through a bullhorn. In a moment the entire upstairs was blue with police uniforms. We offered no resistance. They took our i.d.'s.* One of the plainclothesmen accompanying the police announced that as of midnight, martial law was in effect and that the army had taken over the government. We were taken downstairs and loaded into vans parked in front of the building. We were driven to police headquarters in Pruszcz Gdański.

Second Account: Worker from the National Commission

Around 4 A.M. we were led into a waiting room. The tables were arranged in the shape of a horseshoe and there were photographs from police and ORMO (Volunteer Reserve of the Citizens' Militia) life in the voivodeship of Gdańsk and the township of Pruszcz Gdański on the

---

*Dowód osobisty: Polish i.d., really an internal passport, without which a citizen is a legal nonentity.

walls along with police banners. One policeman stood at the door, and two sat at the tables. There was a television set in one corner. We were very tired, time seemed to drag on. I lay my head down on a table and fell asleep. I kept waking up every few minutes. We were called out one at a time for questioning. Each person that returned told those that had not yet been questioned what it was the police wanted to know and what kind of questions they were asking. We quickly realized that they were taking only personal information and asking what a given person was doing in the office of regional headquarters. We began to talk to the police who were guarding us. We found out that martial law had been declared at midnight. What was going to follow, no one knew. The sergeant was the most talkative. At first we exchanged mere cursory remarks, about the uncertain situation, etc., and then we began to talk more "ideologically."

"I don't believe anyone anymore," said the sergeant. "Tell us, gentlemen, what really happened in Radom?" He took our newspapers from us, saying that he collected them. Someone explained to him that when you run a tape on the radio you can select fragments in such a way as to completely change the meaning of what is being said. He nodded. By this time, several of us had already undergone a second questioning. The questioning was done in a very individualized way. Some of us were threatened, others were made to understand that they could be released relatively quickly. There was just one condition: signing a declaration (of loyalty) form. The declaration form read: "I declare that I give up all activity detrimental to the interests of the PRL (Polish People's Republic) and that I commit myself to abide by the legal order." A date and a place for a signature followed. In this short text there were at least two catches: the words "I give up" meant that one had conducted such activity before signing the declaration. The second catch, "committing oneself" to abide by the law in a situation where any kind of decree could suspend specific articles of the constitution, not to mention the penal code or other laws regulating the legal order of the state, was sheer madness. Everyone in our group refused with the exception of one older man, who was immediately and ostentatiously released in our presence.

A young internal security (UB) officer about my age questioned me. He proposed that I sign, claiming that he had no reservations about me. "It's just that, well, you understand, we have to protect ourselves" and he pulled a declaration blank out from under his notes. I refused to sign it. He shook his head with feigned concern. "You are making things unnecessarily difficult and complicating your predicament. This is only a formality. I have to have this in writing immediately, you understand, such are the requirements and regulations." When I refused again, he asked what I intended to do after being released. I said that I intended to meet with my family and then to find myself a job. He acted rather routinely toward me but was very courteous. Then he gave a series of short speeches about the erroneous politics of Solidarity, about the complex situation in the country, and each of these he would conclude with the question: "Isn't that true?" I kept silent. He finally said, that if I didn't sign the declaration, I would probably be interned. For how long, no one knew. A week, a month, three months. . . .

We were sitting in the waiting room again. About 11 A.M. we turned on the television set. An announcer in military dress informed viewers that there would be a speech given by General Wojciech Jaruzelski, the chairman of the Military Council of National Salvation (WRON). First the national anthem, then the words "full of concern and bitter regret" about the declaration of martial law. After Jaruzelski's speech, there was a break and then the program was repeated at 2:20 P.M. Two sons of bitches dressed in military uniforms adorned with "model soldier" pins took turns reading detailed injunctions. Curfew had been introduced, the activities of the trade unions suspended, and certain articles of the constitution, dealing with the inviolability of the body and other civil liberties, revoked. Certain branches of the economy were militarized, telecommunications were cut, and military tribunals and summary courts were decreed into being. War, martial law, but who exactly was the enemy? We, the defenseless, the labor force, or society? It was not yet clear how the people would react. This was, after all, a special time, the eleventh anniversary of December 1970, and there was little time left until the holidays.

They must have been very afraid. All telecommunications networks were disrupted and the publication of almost all newspapers and magazines was suspended. Only one station was allowed to broadcast on the radio and television. There was censorship of all correspondence and telephone eavesdropping sanctioned by special decrees.

Sunday was passing, and a normal work day was nearing; what was going to happen? Were they really counting on some kind of support from the people or only on fear and terror? What kind of conclusion did they anticipate, what kind of resolution of this surrealistic state of war with society did they envision? There was no concrete program put forth in all the declarations, decrees, and resolutions. The general thrust was that citizens' rights were being restricted to the maximum, all the mechanisms of democracy were being violated and a system of autocratic rule was being imposed so that "order, harmony, and quiet" could reign. When that happened, civil liberties could gradually be restored. At the same time, WRON declared the implementation of a whole package of reforms. In these circumstances, the contradictions of dialectics seemed to be the result of ironclad logic.

Toward evening the police shared some bread and sau-

sage with us, then led us, one by one, to the canteen for
bigos. * The television was on constantly. Military scenes
were followed by a whole series of news programs which,
in turn, were followed by a war film (Red Rowanberry)
with lots of shooting. Many of the policemen came over
to watch the film: they were all pale, tired, and seething.
Talking among ourselves, we came to the conclusion that
the authorities were overworking them to make them
angry and aggressive. I said that aloud later on, and one
of the police officers hurriedly agreed: "The sons of
bitches are goading us, they do nothing but goad us all the
time." It was clear during our stay that the police themselves were divided. The police officers from the acade-
mies were young, tall, and a little impersonal; the almost
always silent ZOMOs were the ones most reminiscent of
automatons; and the plainclothes security police were obviously distasteful to the police in uniform. It was easiest
to strike up a conversation with the ordinary policemen,
as they made up the most individualized group. After the
film, we lay down on the floor, covering ourselves with
our coats, but we barely had enough time to fall asleep.
Around 1 A.M. we were told to get ready to leave. It was
already Monday. After a two-hour trip in a transport van,
we arrived in Strzebielinek around 4 A.M. on December
14.   . . .

While this was happening, people from the National
Commission and Solidarity experts and activists were
being arrested.

Lech Wałęsa is taken into custody: The First Secretary
of the Communist Party in Gdańsk, Tadeusz Fiszbach,
and the *wojewoda* of Gdańsk, Jerzy Kołodziejski, ap-

---

*Traditional Polish dish made of sauerkraut and assorted meats, known as
"hunter's stew."

peared at Wałęsa's apartment after 2 A.M. They proposed that he come with them to have a talk with Wojciech Jaruzelski in Warsaw. Wałęsa refused and insisted that all those detained must be released before any talks could begin. At this point both government representatives left to convey Wałęsa's position to the authorities. In the meantime, a special "combat" squad armed with crowbars arrived at Wałęsa's door and demanded entry. As a result of negotiations carried on through the closed door, it was decided that the squad would be let in only after the government's emissaries had returned. Around 3 A.M., Fiszbach, Kołodziejski, and the major of the special combat unit appeared. Fiszbach and Kołodziejski talked to Lech, while the major calmed Mrs. Wałęsa, who was in a very advanced stage of pregnancy and quite upset. Wałęsa was left with no choice and went down to the waiting car. In the morning a plane took him to Warsaw. There he found out that he was being interned. It was not until January 26, 1982 that he was presented with a bill of internment and an official internment number: 182.

Third Account: Member of the National Commission

Around 2 A.M. in a room in the Grand Hotel in Sopot where I was spending the night, the phone rang and I heard the word "Police." I looked out the front window of the hotel. I saw a scene straight out of a film: falling snow, trees, thick cordons of police, and, in the front driveway, a column of military field vehicles and police transport vans. My friends, who had windows facing the beach, saw police cordons stretching all the way to the sea. The police were dressed in surrealistic outfits complete with helmets and shields. The building was crawling with police. In about a half hour, several police and two plainclothesmen came to my room. Our i.d.'s were checked; we were handcuffed and then led out, each of us accompanied by a pair of ZOMOs. The vans stood right next to the stairs. Everyone from the National Commission that I saw was handcuffed, others were not. We were seated in the van with two policemen between each of us. When detained, we were shown neither a bill of internment nor an arrest warrant. Nor had any of us requested to see them because we realized what was going on.

We were transported to ZOMO barracks on Kartuska in Gdańsk. There we were led to a hall in the basement. There were a couple of dozen people down there already: Rulewski, Sobieraj, someone from Radom. Each minute brought new transports. We were lined up against the walls and ZOMOs, armed with hand guns and howitzers, stood in between us once again. There the handcuffs were removed. One by one our names were called and we were led out of the hall for questioning. Conversations were forbidden but we exchanged remarks all the same. After a while transports of women arrived.

I was called into a room where there were a couple of *ubeks** waiting for me. They asked me what I had on me. I had a statute book and some papers connected with Union matters. They were not at all interested in that. They did not know what to do with me after that and did not ask any more questions. After a few minutes of exchanging remarks among themselves, they returned to me and asked: "What's going to come of this?" "We'll know on Monday," I replied. I left with the impression that they were more frightened by the turn of events than we were. Several times they repeated that they did not know what all this was about and that they had been called to the barracks on an emergency alert. This was a group quite different from that which had arrested us at

---

*From the initials (UB) of the internal Security Police (*Urząd Bezpie-czeństwa*), now the SB (*Służba Bezpieczeństwa*).

the hotel. I was then led from the large hall to a waiting van. Among the twenty people who rode in the van with me were Kuroń, Rulewski, Sobieraj, Jaworski, and Onyszkiewicz. We were not told where we were going.

We experienced one indescribably difficult moment when the entire column of vehicles came to a halt in the forest. It was only after we had figured out from the shouting of the drivers that they were lost, that certain persistent associations vanished. The country roads were covered with snow and the van got stuck a few times in the drifts. We arrived in Strzebielinek at around noon. It was December 13.

. . .

The arrests of the remaining members of the National Commission in the Hotel Monopol took place in similar fashion. Those who went directly to the train station even though it was quite late, or those who had their own cars and set off for their home regions, avoided arrest. Some of those waiting for late trains that day watched from the train station as the police raided the Hotel Monopol.

Similar individual arrests took place throughout the night in the Tri-City area, but the course and scenarios of those arrests varied. The so-called "operational" groups often tried to trick their way into individual homes or apartments. The most frequent strategem was "a visit from a colleague from work with important news for your husband," or delivering a telegram. In cases where the trick fooled no one, the doors to the apartment were broken down and, regardless of the family situation within, the person appearing on the police list was taken away. There were incidents of persons being arrested and toddlers being left behind alone in empty apartments. Neighbors, disturbed by the brutality of these procedures, often helped by taking the children into their homes. Some women suffered shock and miscarriages as the result of the events of that night. Not everyone was presented with a bill of internment; most of those detained were not even told where they were going. Some were handcuffed, others were not, at random. Those detained before 3 A.M. in Gdańsk were usually transported to an assembly point in Pruszcz Gdański, where, after a few hours, they ended up in Strzebielinek. The first internee of the camp was Leszek Kaczyński, a lawyer and jurist.

You ask me: Did they beat you? Did they give you anything to eat? Did you sleep on concrete floors?

Let me answer you in this way. Imagine loving a woman and being very possessive of her, and then imagine that she is raped and you are not far away but you are not allowed to move because the General has issued a decree. You had a home, your own home, the one place where you felt safe, and then you watched while they kicked and broke down your door. And it fell in: the door which you always locked to feel safe and at home, and a shifty-eyed *ubek* and his uniformed buddies walked in. Well, this is certainly no tragedy, you can live with it, except that, well, it's as if they had done it to your girl. From then on your apartment is no longer your safe and beloved home. So I answer: No, they didn't beat us.

They took you and you drove through your hometown at night, squeezed in between two of those who took you from your home (the *ubek* sat in a more comfortable seat in the front). You passed columns of armored vehicles and you were not able to see if there was an eagle painted on them. And when you finally saw the eagle illuminated by a streetlamp, the whole thing became sadder though less terrifying than before. Or: you rode in the van for a few hours and didn't know where you were going. The guards, separated from you by a wall of bars, also knew nothing and kept quiet. And when the van stopped, you thought: what a shame that I have not had time to do more in my life. So this is how it will end. . . . But someone outside suddenly cursed loudly and the van set off again. You were ashamed of your thoughts, but they had already come into being. You felt fear close on your heels. So I answer: No, they gave us something to eat, normally, the way they do in the can.

You were a free man (if in your life up to then, you had had the courage to be so), your face was your own, and the lines of your fingertips were your own secret. But they decided to label you, to stick you into their index file, to describe and remember you. They jotted down a few notes about you. Well, dear fellow, they took each of your fingers, one by one, and pressed them in ink and made prints of them on special government forms. Your hands stopped being yours. Your face was photographed from three sides. Have you seen the concentration camp files in Auschwitz? There you were photographed for the simple reason that you existed, simply because you *existed*. And so I answer: No, we did not sleep on concrete floors.

SMALL INTERNED FORMS

Just about everyone is writing something. Pages from the diary of an internee. This is all right, it's just that December is a bad time of year. Apparently they take them away when you leave. The regime is terrified of words. It kills workers and the poets are afraid. Here poets must be brave. We are, all of us, poets.

The Journal

SUNDAY, DECEMBER 13, 1981

And so I am in prison—why? For what reason? What crime did I commit? I lie on my bed and constantly ask myself these questions. My companions in misfortune ask the same ones. No, I cannot forget this. All of this must be described. Not from a distance in the future, but now, every day. Something in the form of a diary, a conversation with myself. This has to make up for being separated from my loved ones. For how long? But first I should reconstruct a chronology of events.

It is after midnight and I am on my way home from the National Commission meeting. I wonder along the way if I shouldn't just disappear somewhere and not go home. But then I ask myself why I am afraid. The most they can do is detain me (for the first time) for forty-eight hours. Surely they want only to frighten the people connected with the Union, because, in the end, no one can govern this society without listening to its voice. Seeing no unusual police activity on the way home, I finally relax.

At home we have guests who are already sleeping. I eat my evening meal in peace. After two days of listening to the National Commission's deliberations, I am exhausted. I fall asleep immediately. The doorbell wakes me up. In answer to my question, "Who's there?" I hear "Police." And, indeed, I see three uniformed policemen and one plainclothesman through the peephole. I tell them to come back in the morning. They immediately try to break down the door. I open it. They burst into the entryway and surround me. At first they are aggressive, then they calm down a bit. I demand an arrest warrant. In answer, the plainclothesman, who seems to be in charge of this raid, tells me that I am being detained on the basis of some unknown Article 42. He adds that I am not being arrested but being interned. He shows me the bill of internment. I read in it that I am to be interned at Strzebielinek or Czarne. I get dressed, gulp down a little milk, and my wife gives me a bit of bread, a toothbrush and toothpaste. I am told that everything else must be left behind. I slip my watch into my pocket anyway. My horrified children and wife look on, as they lead me out.

They take me away in a cold *Nyska*.* First we drive through the city, passing regional headquarters, where there are a lot of police. Then we turn onto Słowacki Street. I look at my watch: it is almost 4 A.M. During our trip, a young police officer tries in vain to start a conversation. I think that we are heading for the airport. I relax when we turn off at the Tri-City exit. I think then that we are going to Wejherowo. We drive through it, however, and into a forested region where a road sign with the word "Piaśnica"† flashes by. After a two-hour ride

---

*Brand name of van, small truck.
†Site of mass executions of Poles in the fall of 1939.

during which we lose our way and get stuck in the snow, we drive up to a high wall. At the entrance, the sign reads: "Penal Institution/External Division of the Wejherowo Prison in Strzebielinek." There is a high, gray wall with watchtowers in the corners, searchlights, and machine guns. My "guardian" leads me into a large room. They take my picture from three sides. They take prints of all my fingers and both palms. They tell me to sign this. I'm dazed. While waiting for whatever was coming next and later when surrendering my things (I have to give them everything I have including my watch), I see familiar faces. I do not remember their names. Finally, I am led into a courtyard surrounded by a high chain-link fence that ends in rows of barbed wire. Beyond the fence are five one-level pavilions joined by a corridor. There are bars in the windows. In the guard booth I am assigned a cell. I happen to see a doctor on my way there. He asks, "Don't we know each other? I can't recall." The guard leads me down a long corridor, on both sides of which are cells. There are twelve. The corridor begins and ends with a grating that reaches the ceiling. The key rattles and in a minute they have me locked behind a door that is covered with a heavy sheet of metal, or perhaps the entire door is steel. There is a row of bunks along the wall, in which are two barred windows. At first I think that I am alone, but then I spot a friend whom I had been talking to a few hours ago. Things perk up. Our cell is filling up fast. By evening we have a complete set of sixteen people, a real tower of Babel: workers, an engineer, a teacher, lawyer, journalist, secondary school student, and various Union activists. Through the window, we can see women being led in. We recognize Grażyna Przybylska-Wendt and Alicja Matuszewska, both of whom are from the Presidium of the National Commission. There is Wiśniewska from the Department of Intervention, Krystyna Pieńkowska from Teachers' Solidarity; Halina Winiarska, an actress from the Wybrzeże Theater; Joanna

Gwiazda, Joanna Wojciechowicz, and the diminutive Alina Pieńkowska.

The first meal, tea, is at noon. Later, pea soup. Our table setting, if one can call it that, is two aluminum bowls, a mug, and spoon. We wash the dishes in a sink which is right next to the toilet in one corner of the cell and divided from the rest of our "apartment" by a partition.

DECEMBER 14, 15, 16: MONDAY, TUESDAY, WEDNESDAY

Slowly we are getting used to our new environment. Prison authorities, as we are slowly finding out, exist on a few levels of initiation. The warden of the penal institution, who holds a major's rank, can make decisions regarding everything: toilet paper, cigarettes, toothbrushes and the amount of stools for each cell. The remaining matters, such as the required routine, our status, appeals of the internment orders, and so on are the domain of the police spokesman relegated to the affairs of the interned by the district commander of the police. We hear that the police spokesman is timid, and demands that everything be in writing to the district police commander. He avoids making any independent decisions. He introduces himself to someone as "Captain Maciuk, M.A." It seems that he is an *ubek* known in the Young Poland circles, because he personally directed searches in their apartments. His new job is certainly a promotion. The guards that watch us are also organized according to a definite hierarchy. This is obvious during our walks outdoors. The guards let us out of our cells, but in the courtyard they have nothing to say. The ZOMOs decide how we are to move around (there are marked routes for walks) and how long the walk is to last. This matter becomes a source of conflict immediately because sometimes the walks last fifteen minutes and at other times a half hour. According to rumors about the regulations, it would appear that the walks are supposed to last an hour. It seems that the ZOMOs shorten them at will.

The first walk was on Monday. We all went out. The guards and ZOMOs showed us the circle in which we were to move. We could run, throw snowballs at each other, walk—whatever anybody wanted to do. The only restriction was that we weren't allowed to get near the people running on the opposite side of the square. So we shouted to one another and exchanged a little information, but we shouted mainly to raise our spirits. The ZOMOs pretended not to hear. It was clear that they did not know what their attitude toward us should be.

The first assignment that we gave ourselves was to make a list of all those interned in Strzebielinek. Thanks to contacts made during our walks, through the Judas window* and through written messages left on the walkways or thrown through windows, in a little while we knew that a large group of members of the National Commission were locked up with us, as well as other Union activists from various strata of the Union membership in the Gdańsk and Słupsk voivodeships. Together there were around 200 people.

We quickly came up with a few plans to avoid the rigors of prison life and to make contact with other cells, that is, to organize a life that was as free as possible. There were all kinds of ideas about how to survive and not to soften and sell out. On Tuesday we had a list of demands ready and delivered to the warden's office. No one wanted to submit to the routine of a penal institution. The first serious clash came in the evening of the second day

---

*Small opening in the cell door.

when our guard told us to carry a stack of our neatly folded coats out of the cell. We protested. "We have not been given due process, and so we are not obligated to abide by prison rules. We demand to be informed of our status, and we demand to know the rules for the interned. Until these demands are met, we follow no rules."

The guard tried persuasion, but he got tangled up in his own arguments. On the one hand, he was our guard, on the other, he was powerless. "Gentlemen, this is how we are accustomed to doing things, it has always been this way. . . ."

The next day, the guard on duty simply posed a rhetorical question, "You are not returning your coats?" "No." He shut the door.

On the third day the Black Major, chief of the guards and warden of the institution, appeared. He stood in the doorway of the cell and a few of his men stood behind him. "Gentlemen," he said with a sweet smile, "please do not make things difficult for us. You are a very difficult cell, why all the resistance?" and he pulled a bench up to the door. We repeated our arguments, adding that surrendering our coats was an unnecessarily repressive measure. We used them to cover ourselves. It was cold and damp in our cells. The major listened with a smile on his face at first and then gradually his demeanor became more somber. He was risking his authority by carrying on this exchange in the presence of the guards. Then suddenly he refused to talk any more and interrupted our explanations, saying dryly: "Well, then. You won't put them out?" "No." "Well, then, thank you. I will remember this." And turning around, he slammed the door of the cell.

The confrontation with the major upset the cell. A heated discussion erupted on the wisdom of being stubborn in so petty a matter.

"I don't know," said J. "I personally could have given

mine up. The line of my resistance is elsewhere. Coats are probably not worth the battle."

I disagreed. The battle for coats, our first victory in the camp, was psychologically significant. The incident with the major, however, had brought out the rather characteristic range of positions. Cell mates who swore "not to surrender a single button" began to waver after the warden left, slamming the door behind him, a neat move straight out of a book of guard pedagogy. Some believed that aggravating relations in this way was senseless, that, after all, it was no big deal, putting the coats out and now, you'll see, they'll show us. . . . In the end the majority decided that if the guards insisted on the coats again tomorrow, we would give them up without resistance. And in fact, the next day when the guards asked for the coats, we folded them on the bench and put them in the corridor. In the morning, our coats were returned, but they kept the bench, which was replaced with stools. We were fighting for our coats and surrendered them, and they were fighting for the bench, which made an excellent battering ram when left in the cell (as was proven in a neighboring pavilion). The affair with the coats ended.

That was just one of the fronts on which we did battle. We fought for ourselves with many much smaller actions. Many useful talents surfaced in these circumstances. It began with painting posters which we then pasted to the cell door. Most of them arose on the occasion of the anniversary of December 1970. We were also getting ready to organize a demonstration during our walk on December 16. We were supposed to stand in the middle of the courtyard and sing a hymn, "God, Protector of Poland,"* and the Ballad of Janek Wiśniewski.† During

---

*Boże, coś Polskę.
†About the seacoast bread riots of December 1970.

the singing we were going to hold signs that read "Let no one shoot at us again," and "December 1970—we remember." Our illustrations bore religious and patriotic symbols. The Gdańsk monument to dockworkers who were killed was painted on one sign. Later it turned out that similar activities had been planned by other cells without our mutual knowledge. Not knowing this, we began to call the various cells on our camp "telephone," that is, on the radiator pipe, and to tell them through the window about the arrangements. The guards probably heard our conversations and told the warden, who spoke to us that evening over the loudspeaker (called a *kolkhoznik*) and announced that all demonstrations with signs were forbidden and by force of martial law were subject to strict prison punishment. This announcement sounded rather funny in a prison cell. In the end, after talking it over with a few cells, the warden agreed to allow commemoration of the anniversary with the singing of religious songs. We did not want to stand on the square with empty hands on that day, however, so we decided to make red and white flags. This was no mean feat. At one point Janusz simply took off his sweater and then his white undershirt. We tore a fairly even rectangle out of the undershirt and colored the lower half red with the stub of a crayon that was left behind in a cabinet. We tied string to both sides of the flag so that each of our sixteen cell mates could hold it. When it was our turn to take a walk, we gathered in a circle, and opening our circle we unfurled the flag and stood in a row facing the pavilions, from which our friends watched. After a minute of silence, we sang the national anthem and the hymn "God, Protector of Poland" together with our fellow prisoners from both pavilions. The ZOMOs and guards reacted in a variety of ways. Some of them moved discreetly aside, others smoked cigarettes and did not react to the words of the anthem but simply stared at us menacingly. We felt strong, stronger with each line of those songs, and they knew it.

We spent our evenings in the cell, arranging our abode. We made a cross from slats torn from the tables. The Christ figure was made of ordinary hemp twine normally used for packages. Below we affixed a picture of the Pope. Under the cross on the wall hung our flag with a piece of black mourning ribbon attached. At 11 P.M., all the cells in both pavilions sang "All of our daily cares" through the open windows. We said an "Our Father," "Hail Mary," and "May They Rest in Peace" for those who died in December of 1970.

After lights out at 11 P.M. we would return to the analyses and discussions that we had carried on from the very first day. We discussed what had happened, what we could have done to avoid the catastrophe, and whether or not the Union's strategy and the tactics of the Union's last moves were without reproach.

These were merciless analyses. We began with the assumption that the blind, brute force that had been used against us could not absolve us of our mistakes.

There are those who claim that one of these mistakes was the political burdening of the newly formed Union with the activists from the old opposition groups, especially from KOR.* As early as August during the strike some of them had apparently agreed to retire from activity in the new Union. The most devoted of them seemed to understand that this had to be done, saying that the next step for the good of the cause should be "climbing onto the pyre," in order not to provide the suspicious authorities with pretexts. The matter of old activists was not an easy one. They doubtlessly had a moral right to

---

*Komitet Obrony Robotników, committee first established to defend workers involved in the Radom disturbances in 1976.

exist in the new circumstances. Earlier, when they had spoken out, the great majority of so-called "decent" people did not have the courage to express their own opinions. Many did not even take the effort to analyze the world in which they just so happened to live. They lived a semiconscious life, squirreling away life's small achievements, scraping together a little here, twisting things around a little there, dealing, lying, avoiding the children's questions and pushing them away if they caused problems with their inquisitiveness. The others decided to take a stand characterized by great personal sacrifice: they decided to go public with their moral reflex, with their evaluation of the authorities' behavior. They offered society an active stance and revealed the king's nakedness, which others did not want to see because it would interfere with their own comfort. How human it is that when the time came, they hesitated to move into the wings. Nor was it easy to remove them or suggest that they leave. Who was supposed to do that?

At any rate, Solidarity was not a movement guided by political or tactical considerations. Poland seemed to us to be a country that could accommodate all of our viewpoints. Intentions counted and moral considerations were placed above all others. It would have been immoral to remove those who were there at the beginning and prepared the new perspective when quite a few of us were suspended in lethargy. Yet, in the specific conditions of the post-August months one often felt the disturbing presence of these people. Sometimes they influenced others with their mere presence, radicalizing their views and undercutting the influence of the moderates, who were ready to compromise. Perhaps one should have risen and, despite the regret, fought for the removal of these people from the Union. Because we had such a miraculous thing in our hands, such a splendid instrument for making all those changes awaited by successive postwar generations in Poland. It was our generation, the one that reached a certain threshold of professional and political maturity, that succeeded in articulating those expectations and writing them down in the Gdańsk Accords. Where then lay the mistake?

It is true that beginning with August of 1980, the UB (Security Police) set to work on drawing up a proscription list; that the most active persons among us were watched and followed; and that provocateurs were introduced into the Union. All this is true. But there were ten million of us and another ten million behind us. The Union, however, was divided. Wałęsa's position, which had been making its way with difficulty into Union documents and pronouncements, was clear. Another elemental current grew in strength, feeding on the successive short tensions caused by the various provoking moves of the authorities, who defended their monopoly and had not an ounce of confidence in the social maturity of the people, insulting them in their official television news broadcasts, the most hated propaganda programs. And this is why the people reached for the television with such fury, this is why they wanted to bind and gag the mouth that was goading dockworkers into a murderous frenzy and insulting their feelings of dignity and justice.

I return in thought to the first Solidarity convention in Oliwa. The second round of discussions began with the matter of access to the television. Wałęsa's first and probably symptomatic mistake was to side with those delegates who took an uncompromising stance: it was determined that the reporting aspect of television coverage would either be in the hands of the Union or it would not be there at all. On the other side of the barricade, there were intensive discussions as to the shape and makeup of the reporting crews. These discussions ended with the conclusion that members of Solidarity were to comprise part of the television crews. Recognizing their participation as no guarantee against propaganda manipulation, Wałęsa, to the approval of most of the auditorium, announced that the convention would take place without television coverage! The spontaneous ovation in the auditorium drowned out the voices of journalists and observers who doubted the wisdom of what was happening and realized that a dangerous precedent was being set. Solidarity, which from its inception in the shipyard had been open to every type of public medium, independently of the intentions of the various media manipulators, was strong by dint of argument and faith in the people who were communicating its message to society. And now, this very same Solidarity, instead of playing with an open hand, was passing into a stage of direct head-on confrontation. These were battles waged not to determine moral rectitude, which was Solidarity's greatest strength, but to vie with the opponent in arguments of an administrative nature. This was a dangerous novelty, a weapon from the opponent's arsenal, an opponent well versed in this kind of competition. Playing this way, we could only lose. And lose not only the fragmentary transmissions of the Solidarity Congress to the multimillion masses, even though the transmissions were cut, incomplete and full of lies, but also to lose something that was incomparably more important: the awareness that delegates must be publicly accountable for their statements. When the seething cauldron of the Solidarity Congress was removed from television coverage, the social lever that restrained the statements of individual delegates stopped functioning. "Live it up, dear little soul, for there is no Hell" is how that contest (who can formulate the most radical program postulates?) began in front of the delegates, the sole audience. The delegate from television-radio circles in Gdańsk also voted to eliminate Gdańsk television from the conference hall. This was a position contradictory to the real feelings of those circles which, up until that time and in spite of the various difficulties, were successful in creating programs and gaining a certain amount of public confidence. These people drew a sharp distinction between local television and that from the much-criticized Warsaw stations.

It was probably a matter of trying to raise the prestige of the Union's television station, which was in the process of organizing itself and had its own equipment. Yet even though the Union's crew was capable of filming its own material, its access to the official airwaves was uncertain at best. It was sheer naïveté to think that, by bringing matters to a head, one could force significant concessions from the opponent. Television was certainly one of the last things that the ruling elite was inclined to let out of its hands. In such circumstances, one had to take what was given and maneuver around in that small margin of independence.

The Union members themselves were not very consistent in their attitude toward television. When a young journalist from Gdańsk TV ignored the order prohibiting filming of the negotiations and filmed (with the help of a hidden camera) the moment when election results were announced, the same people who wanted the TV thrown out of the conference room in Oliwa were divided in their opinions as to whether or not the journalist acted responsibly from the point of view of the good of the public. I think that the majority was glad that the election results were shown on a local channel, even though they said nothing. Yet the journalist was asked to leave so that there would be no violation of the Union's resolution not to admit cameras. I did not share the general feeling that, at last, the Union was making its own decisions and that the great propaganda machine, television, must come to terms with it. The real concern should have been to inform society, and not to show the result of the Union's confrontation with television administrators who were acting on the behalf of the authorities.

This coming to terms with our conscience (that we had moved too fast, wanted too much right away, that perhaps we had lacked humility and certainly patience, that we did not see the limitations and reserves of good will on the other side) is further obstructed by the radio "reptile paper"* which, right after the General's speech "full of concern and bitter regret," poured out a gutterful of calumny and lies about Solidarity. This convinces those who had claimed all along that the Union's mistakes were not so important; that it was the authorities who, from the moment of signing the accords which were forced on them, were ideologically bankrupt and were just waiting for the opportunity to get even with the whole movement. In the evening, there was another WRON communiqué from a loudspeaker in the corner. It was about hands outstretched to society, about understanding. Someone turned off the speaker without a word.

On the third day, we were allowed to write letters to our loved ones.

THURSDAY, DECEMBER 17

In the morning news broadcast a list of the interned is read. It is incomplete. We complete it aloud. On the radio lists, there are no women. We do not know the fate of those who left Strzebielinek three days ago. We get a brochure with regulations for those temporarily arrested as opposed to the requested regulations for the interned. We are to abide by this in camp.

The bridge players among us cut a deck of cards from wrapping paper. There is also a chess set in our cell and a tournament is taking place. Someone is washing an undershirt and underwear in the toilet, underwear that has not been washed since our arrival. We walk around

---

Gadzinówka, instrument of government propaganda, usually quite vicious.

and sleep in the clothes in which we were taken from our homes.

During the evening news broadcast we hear that seven people have died in the Wujek mine in Katowice. They died yesterday on the anniversary of December 1970. A terrible gloom descends upon the cell. That unforgettable date, commemorated in the Gdańsk Monument to the Fallen Dockworkers, seemed inviolable. It was our contemporary relic. Having it in our hands, we felt safe. And this is where they struck. We expect the worse, a Russian invasion. And then our destiny is sealed. In the evening we pray for the deceased. Everyone goes to the window, even nonbelievers.

SMALL INTERNED FORMS

Playing War

The boys did not mean to kill anyone. They herded a few thousand people into camps and the rest were inducted into the army. They trampled democracy in order to restore it. They began their battle for peace in the streets. They killed accidentally. A mistake in the show. A work accident.

"The dead cannot be brought back to life," writes *Trybuna Ludu.* * The tragedy could have been avoided. Why are they trying to bring about a civil war? After all, we have machine guns. You are madmen. The authorities will not retreat. You are just pretending. If you want to take care of dirty business, take that and that and that! Why have you lost your instinct for survival, where is

---

*The People's Tribunal, the Communist Party newspaper.

your animality? You are tightening the noose around your necks with your own hands. Seven dead miners threaten the peace of the world.

People! Fire.

. . .

Today our cell received some money and a few small personal items from the depository. The watches are your responsibility, the warden said. He doesn't want any complaints if something disappears. He emphasized that the criminals run their own little economy. *Wypiska.* *
This is the opportunity to buy items that can supplement our usual ration of bread and margarine: liver sausage, meat loaf, onions, apples, tea cookies, or dill pickles. And what is even more important is that we can buy soap, detergent, shampoo (two bottles per cell), and razor blades (!). They inform us of the right to file an appeal of the internment decision. It turns out that many of us have not even seen the document which is responsible for our sitting here.

I drew myself a calendar on the wall next to my bunk. Just up until the end of the year for now. I marked Christmas Eve and Christmas with a circle. Deep in my heart, I hope that perhaps I will be with you for the holidays. I think about you, about the children, all the time. I wonder how you are managing and if you already know where I am. I sent you a letter, will it get there?

---

*Best described as a prison charge account that allows the internee to purchase otherwise unavailable items. Relatives could pay into this account for the internee, and each time he or she made a purchase, that amount would be deducted from the account.

FRIDAY, DECEMBER 18

I write another letter home before noon. This isn't easy. I cannot write what I would like to. Nor do I want to worry them. Today it is extremely cold and that is why the walk is limited to forty minutes. The ZOMOs, who are bored and get cold during our walks, wanted to shorten the outing even more. After a while we figured out that the guards were searching our cells during the walk periods to find out if we were burrowing a tunnel to neighboring cells. Apparently such a hole was made in Cell 35, occupied by Tadeusz Mazowiecki, editor in chief of the weekly, *Solidarity*, and adviser to the Union, and Krzysztof Wyszkowski, the secretary of the editorial board of the same weekly. As punishment they were transferred to another, exclusively criminal, pavilion.

Today we were in the chapel for the first time, that is, in the cell that has been made over so that mass can be said in it. There is paneling on the wall behind the altar where a picture of the Black Madonna* is mounted along with a reproduction of the signature of Primate Wyszyński. To one side of that hangs a crucifix. On a wall mat next to this is a large photograph of the Holy Father. On the altar were a priest's stoles and two candles. A few rows of benches.

We rearranged the furniture in our cell. We moved the bunks which had blocked the windows to the opposite wall. During the evening head count, the guard told us that rearranging the furniture was against regulations. The furniture could be moved only after having received the warden's approval. We said nothing. We have better ventilation now and a good half of us are smokers. Our

---

*A reference to the historical painting at Częstochowa which depicts the Virgin as dark-skinned.

daily routine slowly establishes itself: after our morning repast and awaited walk, there is peace and quiet in the afternoon. Some of us sleep, others read books from the prison library, play chess, write letters, or teach one another foreign languages. We try to prepare something edible from our store of extra foods. Most of the time this turns out to be bread and margarine with onions. The food here is awful. We get soup (if one can call it that) for all three meals and it is always outright repulsive. The daily money allotment for food per person is 25 *zlotys* and the warden claims that he can do no better for that amount.

Military marches and news broadcasts blare from the *kolkhoznik,* also known as the chamber pot. The declarations of Solidarity activists who cut themselves away from Solidarity's old line are also broadcast. The declarations of Zdzisław Rozwalak, the chairman of Regional Headquarters in Greater Poland, and Wojciech Zierka, chairman of Solidarity in Słupsk, elicit the most comments. We consider their pronouncements their personal defeat and a betrayal of our common ideals. Someone who was present in the Shipyard in August 1980 and remembers what was being fought for cannot participate in this type of propagandistic swindle. Who then were these colleagues of ours? How did they get these people willing to do such dirty work over the airwaves? And in a series of programs that are supposed to render a "real" picture of Solidarity? One of the main roles in this production is played by an unknown, lisping editor, and the level of falsehood in reasoning is worthy of the worst kind of propaganda.

The cell also got word that Piotrowicz from Słupsk had been released. We heard that he had signed a declaration stating that he would not speak out against the constitution or the leading role of the party. Apparently they are also releasing others. We associate the release of Słupsk activists with Zierka's declaration. This is obviously the reward for cooperating with the local CROW.*

SATURDAY, DECEMBER 19

Today we learned that the Gdańsk refinery is surrounded by the army. Apparently the workers have threatened to blow it up if the army tries to storm its way in. We have also gotten details about the street battles in Gdańsk (December 16 and 17). The situation in the shipyards and ports of the Tri-City area is unclear. The rumor is that the dockworkers will not return to work until December 21. That is also when the plenum of the Central Committee of the PZPR† is to convene.

I have grown accustomed to the thought that I will have to spend quite a bit more time here. The holidays will be the most painful. O that my loved ones will be able to stand this heavy burden of current everyday life.

A stormy discussion raged today when after 6 P.M. the warden announced that tomorrow is the deadline for filing an appeal of the internment decision. Some of us feel that no one should write an appeal and that all of us should stick together so as not to confirm the legality of our imprisonment here. Others believe that all opportunities should be taken advantage of, even cynically, in order to get out of here to continue our activities. How should we act: romantically or positivistically? We are learning to read between the lines of the loathsome radio news

---

*English translation of the Polish acronym for the military government, WRON.
†*Polska Zjednoczona Partia Robotnica*, Polish United Workers' Party.

broadcasts. The communiqués about strict curfew hours for specific voivodeships and cities are a good indication of where people are still resisting.

December anniversaries remind us that we must resist the use of force; we are subconsciously working within the postwar tradition marked by the years '56, '68, '70, '76, and '80. We will add the year '81. We have very little room to maneuver, and we cannot allow ourselves to be drawn into prison routine. How should we act? We recall models of organizing life in POW camps. As there are those here who have survived POW camps, we do not have to come up with new ideas. Someone has the idea of organizing a camp postal system that would function outside of the three-tiered system of censorship applied here against us. The most important thing seemed to be the making of rubber stamps. We looked for rubber everywhere. We said that one man was taken from his home at night without winter boots and consequently could not go out for walks. Shortly thereafter they brought us an old pair of shoes from which we tore the heels. When the rubber stamps were finished, we made ink from black shoe polish, iodine, or ballpoint pen refills. We stamped our notebooks and the clean sheets with stamps were passed on to other cells, where no time had been wasted, either. Other materials served equally well—linoleum, for example.

A system of camp "phones" allowed us to organize collective action, such as evening singing or pounding on doors. The last of these became another ingredient of our rebellion. At the beginning we used any old pretext to pound on the doors, but after a while, opinions once again grew polarized. Some of us thought that we should establish good relations with the guards, who were not really responsible for our predicament. Others believed that the enemy was the enemy regardless, and that we should be ruthless in our actions, pounding as much and whenever possible. After a few days of pounding, the moderates won out in our cell.

The struggle to survive depended, first of all, on the ability to stay in good physical shape. This was quite difficult. Each person reacted to the experience of internment differently. Finding common goals was possible only for moments at a time. The time that passed no matter what, the monotony of day after day spent within the confinement of the same cell walls, the uniformity of the passing days, all of this was very debilitating. Some are obviously fading. They lack the humor and energy that they had during the first days of internment. There are those who show no desire to take their walks, and they can sometimes sleep through the entire day.

Thirty-one members of the National Commission are interned in Strzebielinek. Six of the fourteen members of the presidium are included in that count. People whom I had usually seen "in flight," in action, sure of themselves and their causes, suddenly looked quite different, close up, during our walks. If I wanted to play psychologist, I could say that they seemed ashamed of what had happened and of the situation in which we all found ourselves.

I discover a shade a resentment in myself, irrational, but there it is. A while back, despite the various reproaches that one could level at the leadership, everybody avoided criticism. The truth was that Solidarity had been fraught with heavy confrontations. Many of these people had overworked themselves in round after round of negotiations with government representatives who stacked obstacle upon obstacle against the Union. Their emotional resilience had been worn down. To criticize them then meant to weaken the Union. Now, when the die has been cast, there is more hesitation; can one burden them with the mistakes that followed? We, after all, elected them, and if they did something inappropriate, well, then, they had only acted with the risk that accompanies every action, and in this case an especially complicated one: blazing an untraversed "third road," the first such experiment on a world scale.

Outside my window on the walkway are the people from the front line: Antoni Tokarczuk and Karol Modzelewski, the latter showing another side, completely unknown to the Union: full of empathy and concern for his younger colleagues to whom he had been somewhat inaccessible, as if he wanted to get closer to them. Modzelewski is an experienced prisoner and warns us against hastily undertaken hunger strikes. The calm Stanisław Wądołowski, vice-chairman of the Union, is there; the more nervous and frisky Jacek Kuroń, an advisor; and Janusz Onyszkiewicz, the introverted press spokesman for Solidarity at the Congress, whose thin, bent figure runs around the camp compound. He seems to be absorbed only in running. Maybe there was an element of nonchalance in his famous "press conferences" from the Congress. There is also Jan Strzelecki, a well-known sociologist, who reflected aloud in an interview in March '81 about whether or not Solidarity, that national Christmas tree on which everybody had hung their unrealized hopes and aspirations, that little tree loved by everyone, could withstand such a great burden . . .

A few months later, during the August celebration of Solidarity's first anniversary, Wałęsa spoke of Solidarity a little differently: "Solidarity is a ship afloat and I, her chairman, sit at the helm. Today I have just one concern: that the ship should continue to stay afloat and neither smash itself nor sink. If the ship stays afloat, then all of us who are on deck, all strata of society, will slowly be able to take care of our affairs. But the ship must stay afloat. . . ."

The guards ask at first which one is Rulewski. Not all the faces are widely known. Jan Rulewski, chairman of Regional Headquarters with a seat in Bydgoszcz, with his boyish bearing, is speaking in the same tone he used at the Congress and to the police in Gdańsk. He has a carefree manner of saying that which others restrain in themselves but gladly listen to. The names and figures of people from the Union's last phase: Grzegorz Pałka from Łódź, Józef Patyna and Ryszard Błaszczyk, both from Silesia and members of the National Commission's presidium.

SMALL INTERNED FORMS

Deeper Still

Prison is beginning to pressure my brain. A terrible pressure that makes every word and mental image difficult to grasp. Time to jump the next hurdle. Hop! I jump into myself. Less and less room, though, here in my rib cage.

SUNDAY, DECEMBER 20

It was exactly one week ago that I arrived here. I am spending Sunday, the day I like so much, alone, in spite of all the hubbub in the cell. I tune out, but I also try not to think about you all the time. I am sorry that I have to run away from you, but here a person has to lock himself up and not show his feelings. Perhaps this is dangerous, but necessary nevertheless to preserve one's personality. Everything here tries to destroy you. The sentinels, guards, ZOMOs, and the cynicism of the warden and the police spokesman.

Today the first visitors got here. The mother and sister of a friend in Cell 6 came to visit him. ZOMO sentries stopped them about a mile and a half from the internment camp. They were driven to the camp in a jeep, given a receipt for the things they brought, and sent back. They were not allowed to see their relative, only the package and a note got to the cell. Another internee was called to the visiting room, where he received a torn parcel and cigarettes. He never found out who brought them.

We are absorbing, like it or not, some prison savvy. The accumulated know-how of the prisoners comes in handy here. A few days ago we knocked the thick panes out of the Judas windows. In this way someone passing by in the corridor of the pavilion can get in touch with us merely by lifting the outside flap or throwing in a message. There will be no lack of opportunities. Each person that walks by to go to the chapel at the end of Pavilion III has such an opportunity. Those that are being taken to the doctor, going to watch TV at the allotted time, or going to the library take advantage of the guard's momentary lapse when his attention is drawn to our intentionally distracting pounding at the other end of the pavilion.

Today someone threw us a sheet of paper with a song written on it. Many songs are being composed in camp. We didn't like this one. Somebody said "Listen, we have to be straightforward about this, this isn't a text under which I would want to sign my name."

A discussion arose concerning the attitude to be taken toward that current of thought in Solidarity which, instead of constructing a program, had taken up "painting the bear" and had given no quarter in argument to any opponent. This did more harm than good to the Union, although it was clear that "people gagged for decades have to make up for that forced silence and falsely imposed unanimity." All kinds of caricatures of Brezhnev appeared in the various bulletins and these were quite offensive to the workers in the Russian consulates who kept track of that kind of publication. Our propaganda machine and the media in Socialist countries exploited this later on. They did not need to search for counterarguments and bypassed the important documents and fragments of programs that were coming into being at that time. Instead, they conducted a pseudo-polemic, and easily struck back at the Union. These attacks, in turn, divided the various sectors of society that were disoriented by this turn of affairs.

We understand that, sitting here, we are responsible for the image of the Union that will be composed by our overseers, who observe us every day. The high standards set for ourselves could not always be upheld by everyone. Temperaments and varying beliefs entered into play here.

Today is the deadline for appealing the internment decision. At the beginning, no one wanted to write an appeal, but now there are two very distinct positions being taken on the issue: some speak in favor of taking advantage, on sheer principle, of the limited but functional law; others feel that there is no sense in creating the illusion that the law exists. I decided to write an appeal of the internment decision which accused everyone of the same thing: "undertaking activity resulting in social anarchy in the voivodeship of Gdańsk, according to Article 42, decreed on December 12, 1981, in reference to the preservation of the State and public order during the time of martial law." When some of us decided to write appeals, a guard showed up around 5 p.m. and said that the warden could not receive our appeals in the absence of the police spokesman. Nevertheless, we gave them to the guard and composed an additional document confirming the fact that these appeals were tendered. Everyone in the cell signed this document, just in case the warden tried to outmaneuver us.

In Cell 6, four of our colleagues are holding a hunger strike to commemorate the miners killed in "Wujek." The fourth and last one to join the hunger strike quit after one day.

The state of the camp today is 197 internees plus 35 prisoners who assist the staff.

MONDAY, DECEMBER 21

In the camp, there is still one group of people with whom we maintain constant contact. These are the doctors, who in a certain sense also represent the authorities. They say when the walks are taken, and it is on their recommendation that people get sent to the prison hospital. We go to the doctor often. Every day at least a few people from our cell pass through the doctor's office. This is partially the result of the epidemic of colds caused by the dampness in the cells and the frightening increase in stomach and heart ailments. A visit to the doctor's was also a good time to pick up some adhesive tape, paper, ink for the rubber stamps, thread, or scissors. While waiting for your appointment, you could exchange information, and find out from the inmates (who had contact with the plumbing teams that had to come to the camp constantly because of the incessant breakdown of the water pump) what was happening in the Tri-City area. After a while each of us had an impressive supply of vitamins, medicines, cough syrup, and pills and medicine for indigestion.

In spite of the prevailing strictness regarding communication, I was able to get information about where I was to my family by taking advantage of various opportunities. As confirmation, I received my usual socks along with a little information about how things were at home. In this martial madness, this was not an isolated incident. We got news we had been waiting for, losing sleep all the while: about the birth of a child or the fate of children left behind alone on the night of the arrest. This raised our spirits and indicated that people were beginning to organize themselves.

TUESDAY, DECEMBER 22

At seven A.M., the guard who did the head count rattled the door as usual to wake us. The *kolkhoznik* was broadcasting a press conference held by Jerzy Urban, the government's press spokesman, and Wiesław Górnicki, known up to now only for his journalism. The number of interned was reported as being around 5,000 people, some of whom had already been released. Those remaining in "isolation centers" have freedom of movement within, the opportunity to hold classes on subjects pertaining to Polish culture, to receive correspondence, and the right to visit with their families, and so on. One could conclude from the conference that we are staying at vacation resorts, in which life is organized according to specific regulations set up for the interned. Of the pile of falsehoods that we have had to listen to since our internment, these last lies drove us into a state of unadulterated fury. All of the cells began banging on the doors at almost the same time. The guards went crazy. We all demanded to see the police spokesman. After a little while, the guard told us that beginning at noon, the warden would visit the cells to conduct talks. Around 1 P.M., however, the guard returned and said to send two representatives from each cell.

We quickly wrote down all of the demands discussed earlier:

Because our earlier demands have not been met, we repeat them:

(1) The creation of a group of internees who would have the right to move freely in the camp compound

(2) The facilitation of free contact between cells (in keeping with the statement of the government spokesman) and freedom of movement

(3) Continued access to a minister

(4) The facilitation of written contact with families, including:
   a) the return of letters stopped by censorship
   b) a description of subjects banned from correspondence

(5) The printing (in local papers) of a communiqué containing the names of the interned and the places of internment in order that families may take advantage of their legal rights to visit the internees

(6) A meeting with a competent representative of the military regime with the purpose of delineating the basis and term of internment

(7) The regulation of living conditions so that they meet the demands of all the cells

This day, December 22, 1981.

As it turned out similar demands had been prepared by other cells.

I was a member of our delegation. We were led to the reading room of our pavilion, where delegates from other cells were already waiting. Already present were: Karol Modzelewski, member of the National Commission; Andrzej Sobieraj, chairman of Regional Headquarters with a seat in Radom; Zdzisław Złotkowski, vice-chairman of Regional Headquarters in Gdańsk; Lech Dymarski, member of the National Commission; Konrad Marusczyk; and Stanisław Wądołowski. The police spokesman, Captain Eugeniusz Maciuk, and the prison warden, Major Franciszek Kaczmarek, were seated at the table. The conversation was really like talking to a wall. Captain Maciuk simply repeated everything that we already knew, emphasizing that there were strict regulations against contact with the other cells. The delegates from the cells tried every available argument to convince him that opening the doors in the cells during the day is the norm in camps for the interned.

"Mr. Commander," (yes, this is how we addressed him), "there are two nonsmokers in our cell, older men. They have constant headaches because of the smoke," someone argued. Another said that isolating people who had never been in prison, and who, in addition, felt completely innocent of the charges, was very detrimental to their well-being and was arousing a lot of indignation.

Captain Maciuk just shrugged his shoulders. "Those are my orders. Let us wait for the new regulations, which are supposed to arrive this evening. Tomorrow, gentlemen, you can get acquainted with them and then we will see how that matter is regulated. Until then, not a chance."

There were also a few humorous dialogues:

"Are people allowed to visit us?"
"Yes. Once a month. Only the immediate family."
"And do our families know where we are?"
"I don't know."
"May families from other voivodeships come to visit? There are people here from Silesia and central Poland."
"Of course they may."
"Will they receive permission? As you know, travel within Poland is banned."
"I don't know. Maybe they won't."

And on and on in a circle. After a few minutes it was clear that this talk was going nowhere. We demanded a meeting with a competent representative of the military regime. Captain Maciuk replied that he would like that as well because he had had enough of our questions. He also said that he had contacted his superiors in this matter and they had refused his request.

"Well, gentlemen, you know how it is. I listen to orders, not to what comes over the loudspeaker. The government spokesman's message contained many serious inaccuracies. Perhaps he had been inadequately informed."

So we demanded a rectification. No response. Someone said that many of those interned had not yet even seen their bill of internment and are imprisoned here with no legal cause. Captain Maciuk expressed surprise.

"That's impossible. The warrants were probably left at the place of arrest."

"You mean to tell us that you do not know how we were arrested? No one showed anyone any warrants, it was kidnapping. Doors were broken down and people were taken as they were. No one told us where we were going, or why."

"Gentlemen, please lower your voices. I have jotted this matter down and will look into it immediately."

This was typical. Captain Maciuk "jotted down" all the problems which were the result of obvious violations of the law or negligence of basic procedure. That is all that he could do. On the other hand, when he was accused of being a machine that simply carried out orders and could not take care of any problems in a humane way, he became infuriated. He stood up and announced: "You gentlemen have no idea how much I do for you. You have to be blind not to see this. Why? I won't explain it you now, gentlemen. Maybe someday you will understand."

Perhaps he was partially right. It was true that from the beginning of our internment, the routine which we were supposed to follow as temporarily arrested persons was not upheld too rigorously. It is another matter that this situation was comfortable for both sides, because the authorities, by not enforcing the routine, also did not fulfill that which they were supposed to do. They did not, for example, immediately notify our families of our whereabouts.

Andrzej Sobieraj gave a more elevated speech: "Mr. Commander, we are not criminals. We were incarcerated illegally. We are trade unionists, Poles, who want to pull our country out of the morass into which the authorities have sunk it. You must realize that sooner or later we will get out of here and we will continue to work for the cause. You must realize this."

Captain Maciuk received this speech with a nod of the head. The matter of letters came up again at the conclusion of the meeting. Antoni Tokarczuk asked: if he would write that he was going crazy in here, would censorship consider that a personal or government matter? Captain Maciuk answered that it is probably a personal matter, but that it would be better not to write such a thing. Andrzej Gwiazda, on the other hand, tried to explain that from a purely personal standpoint, the most important thing for us now was news about the course of strike action throughout the country, because that determined whether or not we would be set free.

The meeting lasted close to an hour. In the end someone proposed that it become a tradition. To that Maciuk replied that he had arranged it on his own responsibility and that he might have to suffer the consequences for that decision. He agrees, however, to meet with us again tomorrow to discuss the new regulations that are to arrive this evening.

We left with practically nothing. The only advantage was the exchange of information between the representatives of the various cells. We found out that Union advisor, Dr. Jan Strzelecki of Cell 33 was released last night. Today at 5:20 P.M., Tadeusz Mazowiecki was set free, apparently as a result of the personal intervention of Primate Glemp.

The following message was distributed to all the

cells either through the Judas windows or during the walks:

Listen. Yesterday a commission from the Ministry of Justice appeared in camp. They conducted the first talks. With Rulewski among others. Your assignment is to glean and disseminate information from the meetings conducted with people from your cell.

A few days ago the UB set up an office in camp. They call people in for talks during which they try to convince people to sign the declaration of loyalty forms. In addition to proposing that internees sign the loyalty oath, they also openly invite some of our colleagues to collaborate with them. I guess they assume that one means the other.

Yesterday we watched the television news broadcasts, from the first program to the last. A pretty grim picture. We also learned from the radio that there are over two thousand miners on strike in two mines, and that they are being held underground by terrorists.

Yesterday, while preparing our demands for the police spokesman, we realized that no matter how just and right our demands were, it was unrealistic to think that they would be met. We could not even count on their being taken seriously or answered. By the process of elimination, we came to the conclusion that the only way out was a hunger strike. We decided on that because the holiday season, so full of liturgical meaning, was nearing, and because we could not spend those holidays with our families, most of whom did not even know our whereabouts. Both as a sign of protest and as a show of unity with our families, we would undertake a strict fast during the Christmas season beginning with Christmas Eve.

SMALL INTERNED FORMS

Wałęsa Speaks in Our Cell

I foresaw all the possibilities. I wish you a good holiday season at home. He said those words after December 7 and right before our internment. The Chairman knows. The audience listens. There will be no confrontation or perhaps only a verbal one. Our arguments are stronger. It has to be good for the people. The cell listens. The guard turns off the light.

WEDNESDAY, DECEMBER 23

We received a copy of the State Council's declaration of martial law. At noon, the cell representatives were once again called together for a meeting with the police commander of the voivodeship. Practically the same group of internees as yesterday assembled in the same reading room. Jacek Kuroń was also present this time.

Our "guest" turned out to be Colonel Ring, a spokesman for the police commander. One of the assembled remarked that it was this colonel whose name appeared on the majority of arrest warrants in recent years in so-called "political" cases. He was an older, rather short man with bulging fish eyes that show us a piercing look. Whenever he lacked an argument, he automatically began shouting. He was in a big hurry and kept getting up to leave. Whenever that happened, Major Kaczmarek would also get up with the colonel in order to be able to hand him his coat before he got out the door.

His speech was short. He asked that no one interrupt him, and looking down at a card, he announced that because of martial law, the penal institution in

Strzebielinek has been militarized and that the recommendations of our superiors, from the guards to the warden, should be regarded as orders. Insubordination will be severely punished. It would seem from his version of the regulations, that we are not allowed to maintain contact with one another. We will be immediately released "when the reasons for our internment are invalidated or when martial law is suspended." Of course, the cases of those who appealed to the Minister of Internal Affairs will be studied by a special commission. There is no use in counting on the publication of a complete list of the interned in either the central or regional press. He gave no reasons for this decision. Correspondence is subject to censorship; only writing about personal and family matters is permitted. All social matters are taken care of by local prison authorities. If there are questions, he is ready, but make them short.

Right from the start, the colonel made the worst possible impression on us. The tone and contents of his little speech were full of an obvious hostility toward us. He tried to frighten us, but that did not work at all. He got furious when we laughed at some of the things he said. Once again we reminded him of Urban's statements about letters, and contact between internees in the camp compound, and then we described the methods used to take us from our homes: breaking down doors and what amounted to kidnapping. In answer to a specific complaint voiced by one of us, he said: "You, Sir, are not going to tell us how to do our work!" In spite of the terrible tragedy of this admission by the chief of the security forces in the voivodeship of Gdańsk, who without a smattering of shame supports the brutal methods of his subordinates, we all laughed.

Andrzej Gwiazda tried to say something about a violation of the law, but Kuroń interrupted him. "Don't try to unmask something that wears no mask."

We realized that this briefing was going nowhere, and

we began to talk among ourselves to take advantage of the opportunity to contact representatives of other cells. We also quietly discussed our decision to go on a strict fast during the holidays. Karol Modzelewski was decidedly against this.

"We couldn't do anything worse than to go on a general hunger strike. They'll simply separate us and we will have achieved nothing. Our job is to survive this, and not get sold. Now others are struggling in our places on the outside." Those who had any prison experience shared Modzelewski's opinion.

After about twenty minutes, Colonel Ring got up and left. We also left right after that. In the cell we discussed the meeting. Now everyone was convinced that attending any more meetings like this last one was pointless. The behavior of the most seasoned internees, Kuroń, Modzelewski, and others who had been imprisoned before, attracted our attention. They demanded improvements in areas pertaining to social, sanitary, and hygienic conditions above everything else, knowing that the "ideological" talks never brought any results.

In the afternoon, we had our first meeting with a chaplain, Lieutenant Colonel Tadeusz Błoński, the parish priest of the garrison church in Gdańsk-Wrzeszcz. He was visibly agitated by his position and it certainly was not an easy one. On the one hand, there were we, suspicious of everything that the camp authorities gave us; and on the other hand, the chaplain, who, as it later turned out, had also been warned about the possibility of court-martial in the event that he should convey any information from us to the outside. He was also led to believe that there were informers among the internees who would notify the authorities of any false move. We, in turn, heard about special groups that were supposed to have infiltrated various opposition circles by dressing up as priests bringing pastoral aid. We then had to make our way through this wall of mutual suspicion, in order to be able to create something like normal conditions for future meetings. Because of these suspicions, the internees demanded documents from diocesan authorities verifying the chaplain's office. He had such a document to show us, we could see it with our own eyes. This was one of the sadder incidents in camp. This was a classic *ubek* mechanism for sowing mutual suspicion. In the chapel, the priest gave us collective absolution and distributed communion. We also got the special wafers* for Christmas Eve. We hope that he will come tomorrow and say mass in the chapel. We requested prayer books and the Old and New Testaments. Apparently the Gdańsk bishop, Lech Kaczmarek, intends to visit us and the Gdańsk Curia is preparing packages.

Finally, after ten days of sitting in prison, we got our prison underwear (all of it was a gray-buff color), shirts, and rubber sandal-slippers, a few sizes too big. Once again we were not taken to have a bath, apparently the water pump has broken down. There was no alternative: we had to wash our hair in the toilet bowl. We heated the water in pickle jars with a small heating rod and then we helped each other wash up. Everyone wanted to get clean.

We already have the names of 180 people interned in Strzebielinek. It turns out that there are a few secondary and trade school students among us, some of them barely seventeen years old!

**Opłatek:* Christmas wafer shared among family members on Christmas Eve.

SMALL INTERNED FORMS

Martial Law for the Holidays

We are afraid to have you appear, O Star of Bethlehem!
What will happen when you flare up, what will happen?
War is all around us but in your light will the enemies of
that army and those police and those generals forgive
them when sharing the wafer or will they swear revenge?

THURSDAY, DECEMBER 24

Christmas Eve. One of the most beautiful days of the
year. I realize that this day and the following ones will be
especially difficult for my family. I have never been away
from home at this time; it was always a time for coming
together. Will they be able to bear this? Will they break
down? It is probably easier for me to endure this state as
I take part in it every day, I am written into it along with
so many others. I can also guess about our eventual fate
from the behavior of the authorities and guards. They, on
the other hand, know nothing. They can only guess, as
they probably do not believe the propaganda.

Yesterday and today visitors have confirmed this. From
them we found out about the situation in the Tri-City
area, about the way martial law looks (tanks; street, bus,
and tram searches; checkpoints at toll gates; closed factories; patrols in the city). We know, too, that in spite of
the assurances of camp authorities, our letters are not
getting through to our families. Officially, no one knows
where we are. Neither the city or voivodeship police
offices, nor the public prosecutor's office know the names
of the interned. Everyone gets sent to the security police,
even from police stations.

We received the regulations for the interned dated December 20, 1981 (the date was inserted by hand). They were signed by the Minister of Internal Affairs. From the regulations we can conclude that they can do what they want with us: we are subject to disciplinary punishment, searches, and censorship, and our "violations" can result in arrest. We are allowed one visit per month and then only for an hour. We can receive two packages per month at a weight "not to exceed three kilos* including the wrapping," and so on. In some ways, this set of regulations is considerably worse than the regulations governing those temporarily taken into arrest.

Preparations for Christmas Eve have been underway since morning. First we bought a tree from the prison authorities and fixed it to a stool. We put a can of water under it and later set our little factory of Christmas ornaments into production. We tore newspapers into more or less even strips from which our specialists made various types of stars and ornaments. These ornaments and candy received in packages all appeared on our holiday tree. Our Christmas Eve supper, which was made up of presents from home, was at 4 P.M. When the supper began, the chaplain and the warden, Major Kaczmarek, came to offer us their holiday greetings. We shared the Christmas wafer with them and also with the guard that accompanied them. The warden and guard were taken aback. When we broke the wafer and exchanged wishes, each of us had tears in his eyes. Something new was taking place in camp. Some kind of mutual solidarity, a feeling of unity and brotherhood. Even just a few days ago, those words rang of the great program to rebuild our society, but now those words possessed their primal and elementary meaning: man's relationship to man. We were discovering the man in ourselves again and not just a great political pro-

---

*Three kilos = 6.6 lbs.

gram. We were getting to know each other again through reminiscences and conversations about our loved ones. Here, too, within these prison walls, we felt the profundity of the carols. We sang all the ones we knew, and then we reached for the children's prayer books written by Father Tymoteusz that we received today from the chaplain. At midnight we listened to Midnight Mass over the *kolkboznik*. Our spirits were lifted by the Primate's Christmas oration.

We wrote a Christmas letter to Lech: "Today, on Christmas Eve, breaking our wafer, we share it with you. May this symbol of unity give you the hope which we draw from the birth of our Lord and which you especially need at this time. We will get through this! The Interned. Strzebielinek. Christmas Eve 1981." Into the envelope we put the Christmas wafer which we had broken and shared. Will these wishes reach him?

Throughout the day preceding Christmas Eve, people, mainly from Słupsk, were being released. All of them had been called in by the security police. Some admit that they signed loyalty oaths, others say that they refused.

SMALL INTERNED FORMS

They Intern

One of the Christmas carols was rewritten. Now it is about us. That is how the birth of Jesus got mixed up with our imprisonment. We listened to the Primate shout at Herod and bless the united shepherds. Then we were reminded of St. Stephen's death and the priests imprisoned in Auschwitz who would not deny their faith. And no matter who comes, do not sign your name. And the tidings were that they are fighting on, that they have not sold out. The game of mobilization turned out not to have a trump card. The people played with hearts.

FRIDAY, DECEMBER 25

First Day of the Christmas Holidays

We have our own radio! It is probably the most primitive Polish transistor in existence, but it nevertheless allows us to pick up all the Polish language broadcasts from western radio stations. What a change in atmosphere! At last we know what is going on in Poland and the world! It is easier now to make sense of the information from our families.

Reagan's statement about Poland and the request of the Polish Ambassador in Tokyo, Zdzisław Rurarz, for political asylum in the United States have made quite an impression on us. We knew about Rurarz's friendly attitude toward Solidarity from Solidarity delegations who visited Japan in May of last year. Someone heard a fragment of the speech made to the United States Congress by another Polish Ambassador, Romuald Spasowski, who also refused compliance with WRON and, instead, asked for asylum in the U.S. These are hard blows dealt to the regime. And they confirm the fact that even those from within immediate government circles who have a vested interest in the government do not want to turn another loop on the roller coaster of history in the company of this crew. This raises our spirits. At the same time, I voice my personal suspicions: I cannot forget that these words are being spoken by people who had the "better half" of the deal, certainly much better than the lot of the average Pole, and they took advantage of their positions by hiding their reservations under the table. Now, despite the drama of their decisions, which is perceptible in the formulation of their statements, they are still "ahead" in the sense that they are in a better position than we are. The price we pay is real. But perhaps we should not judge things in moral categories, but rather in categories of political impact.

The information we get about the reactions to martial law in the West are totally different from that which is served up by Polish Radio. Meanwhile our families are bringing us the first news of Lech: that he is on a hunger strike, that talks are being conducted with him on Rakowiecka,* and that he is in touch with the Episcopate through Father Orszulik. A little hard to believe is the news that he is calling for a general strike. We calculate that in the face of the overwhelming odds on the side of WRON to annihilate any form of resistance, such a call could only end in defeat. It seems to us that the current situation has created the necessity of working out new ways of doing battle for the rights acknowledged in the Accords, but no one here knows yet what they will be.

We are getting eerie information that three people died in Gdańsk during the last few days of street fighting, and that scores of people have died in Śląsk, some reports mention figures up to 100. In Wrocław, supposedly, the detained are being held in tents in one of the stadiums. And apparently those arrested after December 13 are not being "elegantly" led to prisons as we were. Some have to "run the gauntlet." People are being arrested who had nothing to do with "big politics" and worked in small plants and factories. It has become obvious that some of the arrests are being determined by personal vendettas. We conclude that the security forces could not have had an intimate knowledge of whole groups of people and that especially in the smaller institutions they are being

---

*SB headquarters in Warsaw.

helped out by local party activists and common swine, who want to get back at their former colleagues. Apparently there are also rumors circulating about the internees in Strzebielinek, that we are being kept in terrible conditions, that some of us are wounded, that we have broken arms, legs, or that ears have been severed, and so on. The point of this obviously controlled dissemination of rumors is to frighten families, organized groups, and society at large.

Someone slipped us the second issue of *Our Bars*, edited by one of the cells and dated December 24. It contains a carol and the hymn of the interned as well as holiday greetings from the editors: "We wish you courage, and faith in God and people." The following inscription was included: "We implore Thee, O King, born beyond bars and prison walls." The issue ends: "This issue was wrapped up on December 23, 1981, and the editors were locked up on December 13, 1981."

A new saying has appeared in camp: "The CROW* will not conquer the Eagle." Today, out on our walk, we took advantage of the abundance of beautiful snow this winter, to make snowmen. One wore an officer's cap and the other one had large protruding ears. We had some good laughs and fun over the both of them, and that evening the ZOMOs worked quite methodically to destroy the figures. Well, and that is what it was all about . . .

Things have certainly relaxed in the cell as a result of the visits and being able to get the news through the radio. The mass which the chaplain said also raised our spirits, especially when the thirty of us belted out a Christmas carol. We made a pretty good choir. We often discuss the current position of the Church. We all recognize that the Church has become quite active. The most important

---

*Acronym for the military government.

thing is that the Church supports the newly forming solidarity with the families of the imprisoned and interned. The priests help, encourage, and refer families to individuals who can help them with specific problems. The Church is organizing a network of aid and material self-help for families of the interned. Yesterday we received packages from Evangelical and Roman Catholic churches in Düsseldorf by way of the Gdańsk Curia. In the letter that was contained in every package was the following: "Guided by the close relations we have with the Archbishop of Gdańsk and the awareness of the current difficulties in obtaining foodstuffs in Poland, we are sending you this package. The packages which we are sending to the inhabitants of Gdańsk were bought with money donated by the parishes and inhabitants of Düsseldorf."

SMALL INTERNED FORMS

Packages from the Priest

A black St. Nicholaus appeared, and he turned out to be the chaplain. He brought thirteen mysteries in identical cartons. After singing a carol, each of us opened his package and out flew cheeses, chocolates, sticks of margarine, containers of cocoa, and bottles of oil. This is the third day that we are eating and eating from them. Whenever someone visits us, we go BAM, and send a package to freedom.

SATURDAY, DECEMBER 26

The Second Day of Christmas

Yesterday we sang carols until late into the night, and after that we sang everything that we could remember. Beginning with the first day of the holiday season, we have not been accepting prison meals, nor are we saying that we have begun a strict fast. This is our own private affair. We do not want to give cause for creating a sensation.

Today again there is no water in the cell tap and, well, no baths. A doctor has visited us and he, of course, supports our demands in this matter. The fire department is distributing water from cisterns and the water is dirty and rust-colored.

From time to time, someone out on a walk steps up to the window and takes advantage of the momentary inattention of the ZOMOs. This time it was Andrzej Gwiazda, who tried, in his own way, to cheer us up.

The discussions about the situation in Poland and in the vicinity of Poland are endless. It looks like WRON will not win society over to its side. The people are distinctly turning away from any authority stemming from the party. As a result of this there may be a dramatic conclusion, perhaps the collapse of the government and Soviet intervention. Then our predicament will be unenviable. As "dangerous" people we will turn out to be as much of an obstacle to someone on the outside as we have been to WRON. What that could mean we can well imagine. What would happen? We could be transported out or maybe right here on the spot. The most militant activists feel that we should be prepared for such an eventuality. We try to reconstruct the topography of the camp and the surrounding terrain. We try to figure out how Strzebielinek is laid out, and where the forests that come up to the walls lead. We think about the possible behavior of the guards and the ZOMO reinforcements. During the walks some of us try to feel out the mood of the guards. Looking at each other we wonder if we will be life-and-death opponents if the time should come . . .

SUNDAY, DECEMBER 27

From visitors we find out that there is a persistent rumor in the Tri-City area that many of the internees in Strzebielinek are wounded. Tadeusz Mazowiecki is reported to be among the deceased and Kuroń and Michnik are being tortured, according to even the radio broadcasts from the West. These rumors infuriate our guards: "What? Why, Mr. Kuroń is healthy and all in one piece, and Mr. Mazowiecki is certainly alive . . ." To us these rumors seem to be the intentional work of you know who. None of the information about the hundreds killed in the streets or kept in tents has been confirmed. During mass, the chaplain announced that a bishop from Gdańsk would visit us in the New Year.

In the evening we listened to Haig's statement: that the Soviet Union is ready to intervene as never before in Poland. Later he reflects on how to treat Jaruzelski: as a man who decided to declare martial law to offset the possibility of Soviet intervention, and therefore as a patriot, or a conscientious executor of the Kremlin's orders? Haig admitted that he had not yet formed an opinion, although he tended to move in the direction of the latter.

The news agencies are giving important information about Archbishop's Luigi Poggi's visit to Poland. On his way back to Rome, in Vienna, he told the Pope about the results of his conversation with Jaruzelski who apparently said that "Poland would neither return to the state of affairs before August of 1980, nor to that before December

13, 1981." Poggi was supposed to have received information to the effect that there were forty camps for the interned, and that the internees would slowly be released, with a few exceptions.

TUESDAY, DECEMBER 29

In the afternoon members of the National Commission were called out of their cells. Gwiazda, Onyszkiewicz, Kuroń, Sobieraj, Dymarski, and Tokarczuk were called out first. Then Rulewski, Wujec, and Modzelewski. Altogether about sixteen persons are to be transported elsewhere. Their escorts are numerous and armed, as we can see through our window. We shout our farewells through the open window. Everything seems to indicate that the authorities want to have the so-called "politicals" close at hand.

Today's radio news at 8 P.M. and especially the bits of information from news agencies in Cuba and Turkey were constructed in such a way as to fit the excesses of the Polish junta as well. These selections sounded so unbelievable that we all interrupted whatever we were doing and listened intently. And just as a few minutes ago, when a report on the strike in the Piast mine was cut off, so now again someone interrupted this broadcast. Was it possible that something was still "rattling" in the militarized radio committee?

THURSDAY, DECEMBER 31

New Year's Eve is spent preparing a supper for all of us. There is no lack of canned fish and meats, cheeses, and there are even fruit juices. At midnight we wished each other well, and later over coffee, the rest of the pastries, and smuggled bottles of champagne and vodka, we did our usual talking and singing.

We write down the most important information from the radio news broadcasts and pass them on to some of the other cells. We decide, however, that this type of note-taking can easily be picked up during a search, and we begin to pass the information on during our walks or to those who pass by our window. It is true that the ZOMOs try to chase them away, but we are always successful at getting a bit of news through anyway.

And there certainly is a lot of news to pass around. We get news about the organization of a charitable commission at the Episcopate as well as about committees for the defense of the interned in Warsaw and in other cities throughout Poland. A similar committee was organized in Gdańsk. Lech Bądkowski, the editor in chief of the weekly "Self-Government," is at the head of that committee. Similar committees have been organized abroad at the initiative of well-known Poles who have lived in the West for years, such as Czesław Miłosz or Leszek Kołakowski, or those who found themselves abroad when martial law was declared, such as Stanisław Barańczak. Not only are politicians interested in what is going on in Poland, but trade unionists are interested as well, especially in countries visited by Lech Wałęsa. The western media continue to show interest in Wałęsa. Most recently, *Time* magazine announced Wałęsa "Man of the Year for 1981." He found out about this distinction after being interned. The last prisoner to be so honored was Gandhi in 1930. Many appeals are issued in defense of Solidarity.

The unexpected, short trip to West Germany made by

Prime Minister Mieczysław Rakowski received a great deal of attention from politicians all over the world. Everyone knows that during Rakowski's talks with Hans D. Genscher, the latter demanded a speedy resolution of the abnormal situation in Poland and the release of all those arrested and interned "for prolonging trade union activity after December 13." Later Rakowski denied western press reports that he had assured the West Germans of a speedy amelioration of martial law. Currently the political leadership in Poland has no clear idea of how to resolve the problem of Solidarity: one group proposes transforming the union into an institution entirely dependent on the party, another predicts Solidarity's liquidation.

We listen carefully to every bit of news having to do with the statements of the Pope and the Polish Episcopate. On Wednesday (December 30), during his last public audience of the year, John Paul II included a fragment of the Primate's December 13 proclamation and supported the position of the Polish bishops who stated that martial law violates the indispensable rights of each human being and so the Church must oppose it.

This and other information was transmitted to us on our little primitive transistor with batteries attached to its exterior. We were able to widen the transistor's range by placing it on the radiator. Because the waves would often vanish, only listening to the repeated broadcasts for several hours could give us a picture of the news for that day.

New Year's Eve was also memorable because we could take a bath, or rather, a shower, for the second time since our incarceration. At the same time we received fresh washcloths, which we used for towels. After days spent in filth, under dusty blankets with suspicious-looking stains, this brought us great relief.

SMALL INTERNED FORMS

The Year Will Last Only One More Hour

And then there will be another. The bars will not
    come down.
Nothing will change. What should one do in the last
    hour
of the old year? Some people play, others talk,
this one reads, that one thinks. As usual, we curse
just for the heck of it, out of habit.
A little spider takes a walk, the door is locked.
My head begins to hurt. It becomes large and heavy.
I wrote the history of an illness. The minutes pass,
there are only fifty left until midnight. In the cell
that means more and more smoke and my swelling
    head.
Eighty-two. My twenty-fifth.
Greetings to you, New Year, from my cell. A few
    days ago
Jesus was born to us, and there is room for you here
    as well.
There are a few free beds here. The only things that
    are free.
And what of the old year? He will remain. Like a
    bitter tea
stain at the bottom of a tin cup.
Be friends with one another. The little spider has
crawled across the wall.
In the hallway, shouting, shoving.
Everything is blurring, the card games, wrinkled
    newspapers
and unwashed dishes, a conversation about something
    that happened
long ago and thoughts. Thirty-five minutes more and
    so long.
So I wish myself
survival.

FRIDAY, JANUARY 1

Today I finally had a visit. Those closest to me came. I also finally found out what has been happening at home. All of our discussion in the cell about the possible signing of loyalty oaths, along with the somewhat weaker support of the Church, that such a signing under duress has no binding power in a legal sense, not to mention a moral one, all of these speculations were undercut by my child's question: Daddy, *you* won't sign one of those declarations, will you?

I realize that our stay here has no real end in sight, especially when I observe the development of the situation in Poland, particularly in the Tri-City area. I know that I will return to an altogether different world, in which there may not be a place for us in the new model of society. People are saying, and probably not without cause, that some of us will get family passports to emigrate. I do not want to leave. I would like to live and work here in Poland, but will I be able to? It is common knowledge that things are being done to make it impossible for us to work at our old jobs. It is not unreasonable to expect that we may have to get training in other professions. Nothing surprises me anymore. I would be surprised if the reverse were true.

SATURDAY, JANUARY 2

In the afternoon the third meeting of delegates from the cells with the assistant warden of the camp, Captain Wojciech Biegaj. Along the way, we decided that the only thing to do at this meeting is to organize a group from among the interned to represent us before the camp authorities. The meeting began, however, with a presentation of the internal camp regulations. Opinions were divided: some of our colleagues felt that the regulations were an attack on the rights traditionally belonging to the interned, and, disregarding parliamentary form, accused the speaker of using methods reminiscent of Nazi concentration camps. To others these accusations seemed exaggerated.

These were not simple matters and we had different opinions as to how to judge them. People with a wide and differing range of personal and professional experience suddenly found themselves in the same camp cauldron. There were quite a few people that had a legalistic approach to the existing societal structures and were attached to them. It also seemed obvious to them that even under the present circumstances it was necessary to find solutions that were acceptable to, as we say, both sides. Unfortunately, the system here gave no opportunities to set up this kind of cooperation. That is why they could not find support for their quite idealistic imaginings. They struggled with themselves, and they tried to oppose those who clearly saw a division into camps: we versus them. The first basic dilemma had no solution: to impose war which no one knew how to wage and no one could win. There could only be mutual losses.

The rest of the meeting was led by the police spokesman Maciuk, who announced that from today on these regulations would be strictly enforced especially in the area of administering punishment: no visitation with families, a ban on correspondence, transfer to isolation cells, and so on. He also declared that the interned have no rights whatsoever regarding representation of others, and that in all cases each person may speak only for himself.

SMALL INTERNED FORMS

The Third Talk with the Warden

He announced the return to regulations and walks along prescribed circles. Earlier he had encouraged collaboration with the SB.* He is most likely a devil. Certainly a devil. But a skittish one: he is afraid of ordinary water and breaks pumps. A devil from the hell of the Reds using language that leaves me dumb.

SUNDAY, JANUARY 3

Today I am a prison employee, that is, one who cleans the cell. I washed the floor, the bathroom area, scrubbed the toilet bowl, and washed the dishes. This took a lot of time. Our cell was a mess because we stayed up last night until 3 A.M. Around midnight my cell mates woke me up to tell me that Rakowski's son had asked for asylum in West Germany. A clearer indictment of the father's actions would be hard to come by.

The new authorities do not have the confidence of the people, and that is why they are feverishly searching for allies that could give even the semblance of their having a base of influence in society. And that is how the creation of the Citizens' Committees of Salvation† ought to be viewed as they are nothing other than the old Front of National Unity with a new label. The way in which they were formed indicates what they are. The authorities want to resurrect structures which are anachronisms. It

---

*Interchangeable with UB, Security Police or Secret Service.
†OKON.

is pitiful that during the last year and a half the authorities have learned only to oppose the aspirations of the people. Solidarity, on the other hand, is not blameless. Of course now is not the time to flagellate ourselves for mistakes, but it is the time to deepen our awareness of the complexity of the changes which should take place in Poland. And we cannot run away from the issue of a clear statement of our position toward the Soviet Union. For without the Kremlin's assent to reforms in Poland, not to mention its geopolitical interests, it does not seem that the road chosen in August will be an easy one. Polish society no longer wants to wait. It wants to decide its own fate.

A very dangerous period is beginning for Poland, especially after the announcement of price hikes. Even the guards are beginning to wonder what will happen next. Because there is no organized force in society which is capable of opposing the predicted price hikes in conditions of martial law. The worst human traits will begin to surface, especially aggressiveness in the battle for existence and along with that a contempt for any type of moral reservation.

SMALL INTERNED FORMS

The First Sentences

They are giving sentences of five, seven years, and are depriving people of their rights for more or less half of that. For leaflets, for strikes. And how will they punish those who do nothing but hate?

TUESDAY, JANUARY 5

Yesterday we received presents from the Primate's Committee for Aid to the Interned. These gifts supplement our prison diets. Stomach ailments, so common because of prison fare, finally stop bothering us.

Last Sunday one of our colleagues fainted during mass and the whole incident was painful because we could not get him out of the chapel. A guard finally opened the chapel door, but only after prolonged pounding, and then we got our colleague to a doctor.

Those moments of meditation in the chapel help us get through our drab everyday life. At such moments I am very close to you. In my prayers I ask God to watch over you. They give me the strength to endure while time moves relentlessly on. It is easy to see that this is a time of anxiety, but also a time of deep personal reflection.

All the news blaring out of the *kolkhoznik* inevitably maintains the obligatory propaganda line: to split society away from Solidarity. First there was an attack on KOR,* the KPN† and NZS‡ which had allegedly been steering all the Union's activities and had formulated its program. In recent days there is a clear attack underway on the intelligentsia, especially on those who formed the core of Union advisers and experts. It seems that the point is to convince people that the worker element in Solidarity is one thing but that quite another is the vicious, intellectual element. It is now being suggested that the worker element ought to occupy itself with "purely worker" issues, such as benefits, vacations, the department of safety and hygiene, that is, with the sharing of the carrot, by cutting itself off from the diabolically represented intelligentsia,

---

*Committee for the Defense of the Workers.
†Confederation of Independent Poland.
‡Independent Student Union.

who "wanted to trample on the heads of the workers to reach for power." As if it had not been a mutual discovery. As if these two groups were not made up of people gathered around a common goal, needing one another, and for the first time in so many years . . .

Today's communiqué about the abolishment of the Independent Student Union proves that the authorities are in a hurry. Rakowski was not mincing words when he said during talks in West Germany that WRON does not have the support of any social group, not of the workers, peasants, intelligentsia, students, or of the Church. Therefore, we have to act quickly, he had said. And that is why they sought talks with the representatives of all trade unions, including Solidarity. Nobody knows, however, who the people are that have agreed to do the talking. One can assume that they will go all out to find people who are willing to cooperate and that they will bypass the established Union officials. This will lead to internal divisions with the Union between those who want to take advantage of any opportunity which martial law offers and those who see no sense in any kind of collaboration with the current government. Those who see no sense in cooperating with the government will remain engaged in illegal activity.

SMALL INTERNED FORMS

A Fairy Tale for New Year's Eve

The princess awoke in a milk bar, ate her buckwheat groats, and went downtown. She was stopped by a patrol, militarized and interned inside out by one of the combat groups in the field. After that she was sent to work at the railroad station where she recognized seven dwarf extremists, who to disguise themselves were without caps. Together they published a bulletin, "Wild Strawberry Solidarity," in which they wrote that martial law was the bastard of the Party. Days passed and the dwarves were caught one by one. The Military Council for National Salvation locked them up in matchboxes for many years. In the end, the princess was left alone and pregnant. Suffering from insomnia, she edited successive issues of "Wild Strawberry Solidarity" at night at the switch block near Kluczbork. There the little prince found her and gave it to her full blast out of his automatic rose. In self-defense, of course.

The Moral: Sleep, princess, apparently it is still too early.

Epilogue: After some years, the Government Council issued a decree announcing the resurrection of the princess.

Finale: And nothing came of this except that seven dwarves were granted amnesty on this occasion.

THURSDAY, JANUARY 7

We have spent all day talking about yesterday's "bombshell," the television interview with Marek Brunne, the last press spokesman for Solidarity. We all have the same thoughts. He got duped. They scared him and he showed a political naïveté and lack of character which are unforgivable in someone of his position. No need to waste any more words on the subject. So long, Marek . . .

There was a blizzard on Tuesday night. We thought that we would be snowed in and that the chaplain would not be able to get through. He did though. There was a

The main gate at Strzebielinek. All photographs were taken by the prisoners themselves.

The east end of the camp, showing the administration building.

A watchtower.

The mess hall.

View from a cell window.

BELOW: Przemysław Fenrych, the only member of the Primatial Social Committee, posing for his ID picture.

Awaiting treatment at the hospital in Wejherowo.

A group of the internees.

Inside one of the cells.

The camp doctor (woman) conversing with internees.

Stanisław Wądołowski, Vice Chairman of Solidarity.

Taking a walk.

Henryk Szabała, a philosopher from the University of Gdańsk who suffered a heart attack in the camp.

Young internee, Zbigniew Pilachowski.

LEFT: Leon Stobiecki, a factory metalworker.

RIGHT: Announcement for a literary discussion, "What Next?" to take place in cell no. 30.

LEFT: Stefan Korejwo, a member of the "Camp Council," delivering a lecture.

Our Lady of Strzebielinek (upper left), an adaptation of the famous Black Madonna, was painted by the internee Antoni (Antek) Szymkowski. Note the barbed wire on the frame. This photograph was taken in a church in Gdańsk whose rector was a chaplain in Strzebielinek.

The camp chapel. Note the improvised cross.

Making stamps.

A collection of stamps. The one in the center commemorates the imposition of martial law on December 13, 1981. The other two commemorate the anniversary of the Polish Constitution (May 3). Note the sign of "Fighting Poland": the P with an anchor; note, too, the eagle with the crown: a symbol of old Poland.

A collection of Solidarity stamps.

ABOVE: *Tank with the words "peace race," the name of an officially sponsored race.* LEFT: *Note the crow, a representation of the Polish government, WRON.*

transport of new prisoners today, and among them a colorful personality, Tadeusz Szczudłowski. So we get some new information about the situation in the Tri-City area, as well as in the Gdańsk shipyard. People from Słupsk are still being released. The entire pavilion was allowed to take a walk at the same time. This year's winter is beautiful: maddeningly white, regal. We dream of skiing, downhill runs, mountains. We walk in the narrow grooves cleared on the walkways.

We talk about the situation at the universities. The abolishment of the Independent Student Union thrusts the more active students into the conspiracy. The intimidated ones will return to their studies and small stabilization. For them that period lasted a very short while.

Yesterday they took Staszek Wądołowski. Where did they take him? Rumors have appeared about releasing greater numbers of internees. We all know that a selection will be made. There will be those who will leave and those who will face trial for so-called "political activity" in the Union. The rumor that there is an informer in each cell returns like a boomerang.

FRIDAY, JANUARY 8

The twenty-seventh day in camp. Again four members of the National Commission were taken away. All of them are from Silesia: Ryszard Błaszczyk, Józef Patyna, Jan Lużny and Michał Mąsior. We think that they will either be transported to a place close to Warsaw, which would indicate the authorities' intention to re-initiate talks with the Union, or, for the convenience of local security forces, they will end up close to their homes and dossiers. Something is going on at any rate.

Patyna has bad luck. Today, right after his departure,

his wife, who had found out where he was only after a great expenditure of effort, appeared. She returned home with nothing.

Stabilization in our cell: they put up shelves with hangers, and the sick are returning to camp after their hospital "cures." It looks like we'll be here a bit longer. It is only now that we are able to appreciate the quality and conscientiousness of the care afforded us (in spite of the primitive conditions) by the doctors who commuted to the camp from Gdańsk. Medical care has been taken over by prison employees.

SATURDAY, JANUARY 9

Our moods oscillate between hope and doubt. We pay special attention to the actions and statements of the Church. The Polish Church has sharply opposed the government's order to forbid members of Solidarity to hold public office. Primate Glemp's homily on Three Kings' Day also demands a normalization: he calls for the release of the interned and the initiation of talks with Solidarity. Within the last few days there was a conference of bishops, who issued a statement on the subject of the situation in the country. No details yet. At the same time, the Solidarity underground has announced that it would begin talks with the authorities, but only after the suspension of martial law and the release of the internees without division into better or worse. The official figures claim that 5,900 persons are interned, and that 5,100 are still in "isolation centers." In the West, the unofficial assurances of the Polish authorities—that the interned will be released with the exception of those against whom proceedings have already begun—are receiving wide coverage. Apparently the authorities also proposed that the

Church should "intern" Wałęsa in one of its monasteries. The Church, however, refused.

There is news that two district Party secretaries, Żabiński ("super-cement") of Katowice and Fiszbach ("super-liberal") of Gdańsk, have turned in their resignations.

The camp radio announced that punishment was administered to three colleagues for conversing, during a walk, with the inhabitants of another cell through the window. Two received so-called "first warnings" (!), and one got isolation, but the sentence was suspended.

The stores of food from packages and home are depleted. We will have to return to the prison menu.

SUNDAY, JANUARY 10

We always await Sunday with hope and animation. During the visits there is an influx of information which must last us the whole week. We also wait for Sunday masses (unfortunately, Polish Radio has not been transmitting masses), during which we hear information about the activities of the Church. We also participate more in the liturgy. Our colleagues take turns reading fragments of the weekly lesson, or prepare the intentions of the mass. We listen carefully to all the messages from the Episcopate. We pay special attention to the statements of our Pope. Today, as the western radio agencies reported, the Pope sharply condemned the junta's actions. Primate Glemp gave a sermon in a similar tone. His meeting yesterday with Jaruzelski added nothing new.

The prison kitchen received a shipment of foodstuffs from the diocese of Chełm. I note the following for the record: we received 100 pounds of sugar, two sacks of Dutch tea per person, and 100 pounds of powdered milk to add nourishment to our morning milk soups.

Our faith falters occasionally, even our faith in those closest to us. We are afraid that our tracks will slowly be "covered with sand," because slowly life in Poland is returning to normal, people are getting increasingly weary, depressed, and occupied with taking care of their basic daily needs. Less and less room for us . . .

The state of the camp today: 138 internees and 33 regular prisoners. The guards are made up of about 30 ZOMOs and 24 prison functionaries as well as the police spokesman, the warden, his assistant, and a woman officer, a lieutenant from the SB.

MONDAY, JANUARY 11

More politics. We have noted the shameless tone of Vice Premier Obodowski's statements made at the press conference for western journalists. He said that if Reagan denied Poland economic aid, then the brunt of the reform will be thrust onto the shoulders of Polish society, and the authorities will not suspend martial law in the near future. How's that for laying out the cards! Bravo.

From time to time we hear about the actions of colleagues that one way or another have found themselves in the emigration. Most recently they fought off the temptation to create an émigré Solidarity Union, which could have given the authorities cause to disband the Union. They obviously feel and understand what is going on in Poland. The West has decreed January 30 a day of solidarity with Solidarity.

A strange relocation of our colleagues is taking place in camp. It all happens in the best *ubek* manner. A guard appears and tells those whose names are read from a list to pack up their things. They pack everything, down to the last pin, say good-bye to their colleagues, and prepare for departure. Many say good-bye not knowing when they will see their cell mates and colleagues again, and leave word for their families. We wonder about their destination. When they are already out in the corridor, the guards point them to a door, usually that of a neighboring cell. And how can we forget who we are dealing with?

TUESDAY, JANUARY 12

My Beloved Ones: Today makes it one month that I have been sitting in here. The most difficult month of my life, a very painful month, wasted, but not lost. I realize more and more what you mean to me, and from far away I still feel responsible for you. This marks the beginning of the fifth week of martial law. How many more will there be?

Today during our walk we once again returned to the subject of yesterday's relocation of people. The talk about the way in which the relocating was carried out leads me to reflect on the very meaning of the word "solidarity." It turns out that the "new" colleagues who were thrown into other, partially inhabited, partially empty cells because of released internees, were not received as they should have been. There were incidents of people switching furniture around so that the new cell mates got the "worst" bunks, they were given the worst locations in the cell, and just generally received unenthusiastically. The Church is right, after all, when it speaks about the need to rebuild hearts and minds, not just organizations. We noticed that these manifestations of mutual animosity were noted with satisfaction by the prison authorities. In their reckonings of conscience, they probably note that even *we* are incapable of maintaining a high level of moral and decent behavior. I feel, however, that this accidental and diverse group of people that we are is able, despite the abnormal conditions of isolation and confinement, to create that familial climate that was mentioned by Czesław Miłosz during his memorable visit to the Gdańsk shipyard. Here in camp, in spite of incidents such as the ones I have mentioned, there is a good deal of mutual contact. Of course, it could be even better . . .

I return in my thoughts to the conference masses and the sermons given by the ethical mentor of Solidarity, Father Tischner: "Our problem is neither political nor economic. It is a problem of conscience and that is what must guide all of our work. We could lose everything, but we will win if our actions are rooted in the conscience."

And more from my notes: "Tomorrow depends on today. We feel the gaze of our fellow Poles upon us. Will we be capable of changing our Polish hopes into reality? The trees of hope have many lovely blossoms, but the more important thing is the root system. The time has come to set roots. It is amazing how close our works about *work* have come to the Gospels. You can take bread away from man and he will still be able to endure a great deal if he has hope. We were chosen by our hope, she chose us. That is how a vocation begins. John Paul II has said that one of the characteristics of work is that it brings people together. There is an inner logic to work. Work is, first of all, understanding. But the spirit of work is solidarity. It is a blossoming of the meaning of work rooted in logic."

How does one convince people to understand Solidarity in this way? If we could even approach such a level of ethics and build a moral force in ourselves, we would be inaccessible to any power that tried to strangle our movement. There were many splendid moments that we experienced together and those moments are our capital, our strength, and the people are still living off of it.

Our insatiable desire for the presence of our loved ones, for as many visits as possible, is somewhat egotistical. In order to see us for that hour, our families must undergo quite an ordeal. First there is the matter of getting permission to leave the Tri-City area. Then there are transportation problems, especially from Wejherowo to Strzebielinek, which are off the beaten track. There is only one morning bus which gets to the camp at 8 A.M. It is almost impossible to catch if you are coming from the Tri-City area. There is a train, but it stops in Rybno, which is over a mile and a half from the prison. The roads leading from there are impossible to traverse because they are covered with great mounds and drifts of snow. That leaves the taxi, which can cost from 500 to 2,000 złotys depending on the amount of time the driver must wait. If, after that, they make it to the camp, the guards keep the families waiting in lines for hours. Sometimes for three or four hours, which is torture beyond the endurance of most children.

On the other side of the gates, that is on our side, there is a whole series of "surprises" that await us when a visitor is announced. Depending on the makeup and dispositions of the guards and ZOMOs, we can be searched or even completely undressed. People react to the latter in a variety of ways depending on their psychological resilience and personal sensitivity. There have been instances of internees' refusing visitors because of these preliminaries.

Just as in Poland, so in our camp so-called "operations" took place. These actions revolve around the upsetting of some established habit or accepted order of being, which in the course of the "operation" turns out to be criminal. One such custom observed from the first days of internment was the individual decoration of the inside of the cell door. The door became the calling card of the people in the cell. We hung quotations from *Trybuna Ludu* and *Żołnierz Wolności*, our own slogans, stickers advertising former Union events, and other graphic compositions.

There were a variety of things in these compositions, from a silhouette of the Gdańsk monument to dockworkers killed in the December 1970 strikes to actual "wall" newspapers. We would add and improve our wall decorations as inspired. Yesterday, during roll call, they began to tear down all of these compositions. We suspect that the idea for the operation was born somewhere "higher up."

There are various attempts being made to contact us. Józef Duriasz and Jolanta Strzelecka from the *Solidarity Weekly* went to Urban and got permission to organize help for interned journalists and to get a pass that allows for visits. Duriasz showed up in Strzebielinek with this letter/pass, but police spokesman Maciuk would not allow him to see even a member of the editorial board, Krzysztof Wyszkowski. There is news that Tadeusz Mazowiecki, the chief editor of the *Solidarity Weekly* who was here in camp for a while, is now in Jawór near Drawsko. That is also where some of the participants of the Congress of Polish Culture are interned.

WEDNESDAY, JANUARY 13

We are getting more and more letters from our families. I thought today with envy about the colleague who, in addition to a visit, also got a letter. Constant contact is needed in order not to succumb to the debilitations of camp life. The entire prison routine is geared to destroying one's personality and to reducing the prisoner to the level of someone grateful for the opportunity to bathe or wash clothes. Prison life imposes a low and basically debasing hierarchy of affairs upon man. Contact with the outside world turns this order upside down and one has to reconstruct it. A Sisyphean labor. I pity the functionaries the most.

I think that life as it is now actually favors the thinking through of certain family matters. It creates caesuras, opens new chapters, which we have a chance to refill with life. I miss our conversations. It is hard to believe how many things have been left unexpressed. After all, I still know nothing at all. Things about which we had stopped talking and other things which eluded us during the course of those accelerated days and daily struggles.

This second part of my notes I owe to a lucky coincidence. We got ahold of a night lamp for our cell. Because of this I am no longer condemned to think my evening thoughts in the dark. I can read, and, of course, write, even letters. Letters, after all, are all the rage these days: today letters to the general were read on television. Every few days we get to watch television, but we would do just as well by limiting ourselves to reading *Trybuna Ludu*. We have gotten into the habit of reading that paper and working out a common viewpoint. If not for the contact with the people here in camp, we could come to the conclusion that everybody in Poland thinks the same way in keeping with recommendations from above. If homogeneity of viewpoints is what the authorities are after, and if our release is subject to our changing our colors, then I am afraid that it will take the authorities forever using this kind of propaganda.

Our lives are undergoing a stabilization: there are even propositions from those higher up that we take over the responsibilities of cleaning and distributing meals in a few of the pavilions. This is supposed to be in answer to our demands. We imagined things a little differently. We are ready to take over these responsibilities, but only if they are accompanied by an equal bundle of rights. And they will not agree to that.

More internees released from camp. This time four of

the older men were discharged, including Henryk Napie-
ralski from the National Committee (Bydgoszcz) and
Zdzisław Kobyliński, a member of the presidium for the
Strike Committee in Gdańsk in August 1980. I wonder if
they really went home.

SMALL INTERNED FORMS

Peace reigns in the country again. It is green outside.
In spite of the constant snow. In spite of limited strength.
Meeting the people halfway, they inducted them into the
army. People are on trial now in summary courts. These
were people who thought that we should trust our enemies. For us this is irreversible history. For history we are
dispensable. Did we make a mistake? When? We think
about this in each cell. They do what they want with us,
with all ten of us. Mr. Major came and shouted that we
do not want to return our jackets. They take you to a
doctor, and are supposed to return your watch. Over the
loudspeaker they play music that muffles the echoes of
footsteps. Your game is a thread, the flashing police light,
a snowball hitting a wall. When you read a book under
the window, the shadow of the bars makes it hard to read
some of the words. In the evenings, romantic heroes run
around in our heads, with our wives and children they
emigrate from the books and pictures to our heads. The
guards and doctors know nothing according to regulations. Neither do we.
Freedom is a chapel, a walk, sleep. Prison, is it in us?
In some it is.
I must not hate.

SATURDAY, JANUARY 16

Last week we returned to our forgotten habit of singing during walks. In the meantime, thanks to the singing talents of Szczudłowski and the incredible memories of some of our older colleagues, our repertoire has been expanded. We added the old insurrectionary hymn, "O Lord, who art in Heaven . . ." which has now become the camp hymn.

When everyone had become familiar with the words of the hymn and when we sang it well together, we sang it in the chapel during mass. The chaplain was deeply moved. From that time on, feeling the power of the hymn, we sang it on visitation days, often with a group of us standing right across from the prison gates. The hymn carried well over the prison wall and bolstered the spirits of those standing and waiting to be let in to the visitation hall. Our ironclad repertoire on such occasions was "God, Protector of Poland" and the "Hymn of the Interned." All the groups out on walks sang these hymns in turn so that the concert lasted during the entire time that there were visitors and became another form of communication with our families. During visitation, some of the internees out on walks would come to the window of the visitation hall and flash a V-sign before the guards would chase them away. The prison authorities tried to interfere with the singing by using, among other things, ZOMO troopers, but that did not work.

The ZOMOs were a separate problem in camp and a part of the "ideological front" which ran through all the situations in which we found ourselves. The ZOMOs were housed, right from the very beginning, in the first two cells of the pavilion. They lived in conditions not differing very much from ours. They had, however, their own canteen with a buffet and television set. They had their own kitchen and also differed from us in the amount of food that we got. Strzebielinek, just as other penal institutions, raised its own pigs, which, paradoxically enough, were very well fed because of the awful food which was served us (most of our food ended up in their troughs). After a pig was slaughtered, we were given the fatty scraps while the chops and other edible sections were reserved for the ZOMOs. They ate practically as well as at home: butter, sardines, various kinds of canned goods, cheeses and jams. Jerzy Urban's memorable statement that the "government will somehow feed itself" was certainly the rule here. The food gifts which made their way to camp from the Church were appropriated by the communal prison kitchen. This allowed for various kinds of "transfers," especially of the more attractive items such as coffee or canned pork. The canned pork would be distributed in such a way that there would be one can for every two internees while each ZOMO got one whole can. But these are mere irritating details.

The neurological meeting point of the two worlds, that of the interned and that of a detachment of ZOMOs, were neighboring cells in the first pavilion. The ZOMOs met their match. The ZOMOs had a "singing group" of internees for neighbors, and it happened to be the group with the best repertoire of patriotic hymns and legionnaire songs. The assignment of the buffer cells was to "bear the camp standard high," to demonstrate the power of the spirit, and to hold their ground. The loud evening prayers and the singing that went on for many hours were quite a contrast with the life-style of the ZOMOs, who, after the first period of mobilization, were quickly demoralized by the monotonous routine of camp life. They took advantage of various opportunities to get beer, wine, or vodka somewhere in the vicinity despite the ban on alcohol. There were constant tensions between the internees and the ZOMOs. Those internees who had to deal with the ZOMOs on a daily basis complained that the ZOMOs acted provocatively and crudely towards them by making noise until late at night and insulting them with cutting remarks when they went out for walks. Only from the very beginning did the ZOMOs make up a homogeneous group. After a little while we began to differentiate between them. It was only the uniform that gave them the appearance of a monolith.

Yesterday we had another *wypiska:* we were able to buy a portion of blood sausage, headcheese, lard, butter, onions, tea, matches, and cigarettes. Together it all cost 420 złotys. We melted all the lard in a bowl and added the onion and the last three apples. We borrowed a small burner from the prison workers, who had set themselves up quite well. Practically all of them were multiple offenders and they knew how to move about the prison world with ease. There were no problems that they could not solve. The electric burner reminded us of an electric chair, and at any rate, was dangerous to use. A terrible spiral, threatening to shock the user at any time, was spread over an overturned iron stool with scant insulation. An equally risky instrument was an electric heating rod that we got from them, a so-called "cement mixer" which boiled water in a large jar in one quick minute. The immersion heater was two thin steel-cutting saw blades isolated with string and when we turned it on, the lights went dim in the whole pavilion. We began complicated negotiations with them for construction of additional "lighting fixtures" in our cell. Afterward, the cell was covered with a web of electrical wiring leading to night lights made from old cans. We did not inquire about where they got such closely watched items as sockets and light bulbs. At any rate, the night guard from the third pavilion spouted profanities every day because someone would always steal his light bulb. After a while he gave up and sat in the dark in his booth or he would go to the corridor between pavilions where the entire night shift could be found playing some mean poker.

TUESDAY, JANUARY 19

In the Tri-City area, after the resumption of work by the shipyards and the large factories, relative quiet returned to the country, and that gave the SB a chance to complete their operation of interning people who had avoided arrest in December. People taken to camp straight from questioning became our new colleagues. Among them were two journalists that increased an already long list of people from that profession. We have journalists from radio, television, the Union and Catholic presses, as well as quite a few people employed in Solidarity information agencies.

We compare fragments of the reports made to an American Senate commission by former Polish ambassadors Spasowski and Rurarz with our own analyses. They would seem to hold up, especially the sections having to do with the already existing plans of settling accounts with Solidarity. There are old, sometimes six-month old, addresses and names of workplaces on the internment lists. This would mean that the lists were prepared as early as August of 1980. The final fragment of Wajda's film, "Man of Iron," which enraged party viewers with its supposedly unjust evaluation of the intentions of the authorities (the scene where the *ubek* driving away from the shipyard threatens "We'll get even yet") turned out to be quite accurate.

From a superficial analysis it would seem that the people who occupied first place on the list were people from former opposition circles; secondly, militant strike activists; and thirdly, Union officials and experts. After these came journalists and anyone representing Solidarity in any way.

FRIDAY, JANUARY 22

Our immobility quickly led to symptoms of increased frustration and depression, not to mention various illnesses. First nervous disorders, then heart and stomach ailments, and, finally, rheumatism.

From the very beginning of our internment, we realized the need to organize some kind of sports activities. It was not easy. The cells in which there were, at first, sixteen persons, then between ten and thirteen, were limited because the small space was crowded with eight bunk beds, stools, and tables.

At first we smiled indulgently at those who, no matter what the weather, ran a few laps on our walkway. Later others joined them. These certainly were not ideal conditions for running but that one hour spent in such intensive exercise turned out to be very relaxing. Some of the internees were capable of running ten kilometers, that is, fifty laps around the walkway. This type of activity was not possible for everyone, however, and that is why we did other kinds of exercise every day: self-defense moves, kneebends, push-ups, and arm wrestling. We would also pull the matresses off the beds and practice forward rolls and yoga positions. There was not enough room, however, and we asked to use the empty cells in the second and third pavilions. We were able to get permission to use one of the cells for exercises. The next day the authorities forbade us to use the cell, saying that we might get concussions and that an instructor was needed for this type of activity. It turned out, however, that the nicely cleaned cell was a good place for the ZOMOs to put a Ping-Pong table. After a great deal of discussion, we were able to get the cell back. We can play Ping-Pong but only according to a special schedule: each cell gets a half hour.

SUNDAY, JANUARY 24

Yesterday there was a great deal of housecleaning in camp. The prisoners were chased out to shovel snow from the courtyard and to dig access roads in the meter-high snow from the gates to the entrance pavilion. We helped them with this work, and found out that the prison authorities are expecting a visit from a Gdańsk bishop.

Early this morning we listened to mass and the Primate's sermon on the radio (the last mass was broadcast on Christmas Eve and the sixteenth of this month). The words of the Primate also boomed into the courtyard outside from loudspeakers set in the windows so that those on a walk could listen to the Primate's homily. We have listened to his words very attentively from the very beginning of martial law. We have not known him for very long. He came after Stefan Wyszyński, who could not be there at the most difficult moment. We are afraid that Glemp may not be able to fulfill our great expectations. This time, however, his words were much like Wyszyński's. There was concern, opposition, and hope. We feel that we are a real part of that Church when it speaks to us this way.

There is quite a holiday in camp: the bishop-suffragan from Gdańsk, Kazimierz Kluz, arrived in the company of a youthful and energetic priest, Stanisław Dułak, who is familiar to us from masses he said during the strike in the Gdańsk shipyard. Together with our chaplain, they have said three masses, for both pavilions and for the regular prisoners. During his homily, the bishop said that negotiations for this visit had lasted forty days. After the masses, he visited practically all the cells. We talked about the position of the Catholic Church in general and the Polish Church in particular regarding the current situation. He explained certain strategical aspects of the Church's activities: the Polish Church acts directly for the Polish people; the Catholic Church at large had undertaken to show the complexity of the Polish situation in the international arena. John Paul II's involvement in this matter is considerable: his prayers during the Wednesday audiences and his reminding people of Poland's importance to peace in Europe and of the role of Solidarity, about which he said "Solidarity belongs to the common heritage of working people in my homeland. . . . I place Solidarity in the common treasury of all people. It is a part of the common good, common justice and common peace."

MONDAY, JANUARY 25

Today, for the first time since the introduction of martial law, the Sejm—in which Polish society has registered a vote of "no confidence"—is meeting. It was in the "defense" of the Sejm, among other reasons, that martial law was declared. So what can we expect from it? Maybe a miracle will happen. The Sejm surprised us once before when, before the second round of the Solidarity congress, it managed to take an independent position, in concordance with the feelings of the people, in the matter of workers' self-government.

Underground publications—bulletins, flyers, and appeals smuggled in from the outside—are beginning to circulate in camp. We got the eighth issue of a Gdańsk bulletin, which published a complete list of the interned in Strzebielinek. Apparently these lists are also known abroad, in France, for example, where additional copies of them are made.

People say that Andrzej Gwiazda escaped from Białołęka, and that he hid for a while in Gdańsk, but apparently was caught again. A peerless example of a conspirator is Bogdan Borusewicz. Legends are circulating about his escape from a raid in December supposedly made by jumping off a roof. They say he got away in his pajamas with the police firing at him as he escaped into a nearby wood. Just like in mystery novels. Not everyone shares his style. Many of us feel that a person should attempt to act within the framework of legal structures and possibilities of persuasion. We hit on the project of a letter addressed to the Sejm's Commission of Justice, but the course of that Sejm session, especially the cynical statement made by Deputy Janusz Przymanowski, deprives this project of all meaning. We also conclude from Jaruzelski's speech that there will be no room for us in his homeland; he said that no one would interfere with those internees who would like to emigrate. This is a confirmation of the earlier, we thought unlikely, rumor about deportations. Karol Małczużyński was shouted down, and the applause of the auditorium indicated unambiguously that this is a Sejm obedient to the junta.

While we were absorbed with the large problems of Polish parliamentarism, the guards were conducting their own little politics regarding the internees. Today they told us that we are using too much electricity with our night lights and the immersion heaters we use to make tea. In keeping with the warden's orders, the pavilion electricity will be shut off at ten o'clock. There was an uproar! Przymanowski, deportations, and now this. We began to bang on the doors. A long empty corridor resonates so unbearably that there is no way that the guard can stand sitting in his booth. We also have a hard time standing the din, but the battle is a sports event and the winner is the one who can stand it the longest. This method is probably beneath our dignity, but an internee hasn't much of anything left to work with. To put it briefly, our "automatic reaction" took them by surprise and they turned on the electricity.

TUESDAY, JANUARY 26

And how is one not to believe in the simplest solutions: the result of yesterday's pounding was today's meeting with camp authorities, Major Kaczmarek and Captain Biegaj, who made the decision not to turn off the electricity. As of today the lights are on legally. Yesterday's pounding woke the families of all the prison functionaries who live in a nearby camp building. The major had been called all the way from Wejherowo to decide personally about turning on the electricity.

Today in our cell, a few people were called in for questioning. The thread that joins all of camp life is the steady stream of questionings conducted by the *ubeks*. The *ubeks* are not very conscientious types: they show up at odd hours, sometimes before, sometimes after, noon, and sometimes early in the evening, when they are least expected. Usually they sit down in the pavilion reading room and spread out their papers, from under which they pull a "loyalty form" when they feel the appropriate moment has come. Our guards wink at us and say "They're here" and we understand what they mean.

Some of them work routinely, knocking off one point after another, according to a list of questions and subjects which they are supposed to discuss with the offender. But there are proud people among them who let the internees know unequivocally that Poland owes it to them that Party hustlers have not yet torn the country apart. According to the *ubeks*, the Party people end up somewhere in the West or in the Jewish lobby which still has cushy jobs in key Party positions. Jaruzelski is a marionette and, just between us, they say, we must look for forces that will pull this country out of the quagmire that it is in. We are given to understand that the straightest road to repairing the Republic would be collaboration with the *ubeks* and that all other independent ways of rebuilding society are a waste of time: they control everything, they know everything, and if one is indecisive, there will be problems. They talk about Solidarity as if it had never existed. According to the opinion of one of the *ubeks*, the government will destroy the Union through democratization of the country and by raising the standard of living. Then the Union will not be necessary to anybody. In political issues, they distinguished between real Poles, which is what they were, and the Commie-Jews, who unfortunately make up the liberal current in the Party. That is why there is no agreement as to the direction of proposed reforms, and there is a stalemate in the government. After pronouncing these crazy viewpoints, they usually left with nothing. Yet they were always perfecting the "loyalty forms," so that they were as easy to swallow as candy-coated pills. For us, however, the issue was whom we were signing the pact with, but they could not understand that.

The notion of having political responsibility for the country was certainly a new element in the *ubek*'s pronouncements. They displayed this new patriotism, creating the illusion for themselves that they were more than brooms in the hands of their overseers, who wanted to sweep all notions of how the country should be governed (except for that proposed by the government) out of the heads of the people. The fact is that the SB had never had as much power as it did after the declaration of martial law on December 13. They seemed to control everything on a massive scale: eavesdropping, censorship of all correspondence and conversations, infiltration of professional circles, and collaboration with informers eager to dispose of competition in their fields. Unfortunately, the star of the Gdańsk Party Secretary, Tadeusz Fiszbach, grows dim here as well, because in the first days of martial law, when he still thought of extending his stay in office, he personally supervised the internment of potentially troublesome Union activists who might have threatened to strike. There was no lack of collaborators with the security forces on each rung of the Party ladder. It was not without reason that the *ubeks* who would come for talks were greeted in the pavilion with the song: "Two inseparable sisters are we, the Party and the SB!"

Although they posed as an independent political formation, no one seemed in a hurry to help them establish a "new order." After all, they were not the only pretenders to power. There were the army personnel and the somewhat illegitimate group of old, disillusioned orthodox Party activists, that is, ideological cavemen whose resuscitation no one expected. All sorts of people were pushing their way to the top, according to the local press: unsuccessful docents, centuries-old journalists from Comsomol newspapers, and strange "cultural activists" from Gdynia.

I should note, just for the record, that the prison commission, which was visiting us to take down our remarks concerning various matters, did, in fact, visit one cell after which they decided not to visit the remainder.

WEDNESDAY, JANUARY 27

Today four new internees were brought in from Słupsk. They are rather strange types, so-called "golden boys," as we determine from their answers to our questions, who up to now have dealt mainly with selling hard currency. In exchange for these, another group of internees was released, among them was Tadeusz Kruża from Tczew.

THURSDAY, JANUARY 30

We have drawn up the final version of our letter to the Pope. We feel that our recent experiences and genuine attempts to erect a certain moral order gives us the right to turn to him:

"Our Beloved Holy Father!

Throughout our country there is the hope that the lies told about us are impossible to uphold. Your voice and prayers come to us across borders and through prison bars. They are a great comfort to us. We thank you for your testimony of truth on our behalf before the world.

You know that we were led by the great hope for a better life in our homeland. Many paid the highest price for this.

From the camp in Strzebielinek we direct these thoughts and prayers to you. Do not forget us, those deprived of freedom and those who must undergo even more difficult trials. May God invest you with great strength so that you can support us and help us to return to the path of hope.

Joining together with you in prayer, we wish to inform you of the will of the people to have you make a second pilgrimage to your homeland in August 1982.

Strzebielinek. January 30, 1982. The Interned."

For technical reasons, only a few dozen colleagues signed the letter; the remainder refused, fearing some sort of trap.

Today is world solidarity day with Solidarity. I wish I were able to fly to see how many candles were lit here in Poland and around the world. We turned off the lights and at about 10 P.M. put the candles which we had been saving especially for this occasion in the windows. We also made torches from newspapers. Our singing of the hymn and "God, Protector of Poland" resounded in camp. In answer to this, the power was cut off.

We listened to western broadcasts about the events of that day until late into the night.

TUESDAY, FEBRUARY 2

Forgetting about the old discussions of the reason for, and effect and duration of, a hunger strike, three cells of the third pavilion went on a hunger strike this morning. It all began this morning with individual declarations that were handed to the guards that assist with the distribution of breakfast.

Various motives were supplied. They were usually quite specific as, for example, the appeal for release of internees whose health had seriously deteriorated. Other motives were: pure solidarity with the interned and sentenced, as well as a general protest against everything that had been done to the people since December 13. The hunger strike is supposed to take place in waves, that is, some of the cells will begin earlier and afterward others will join in. We are considering limiting the hunger strike to seven days so as not to wreak irreparable physical harm on those who are already quite weak. We hear that a wave of hunger strikes is supposed to wash over all the camps in Poland. This will be an entirely new form of unity for us.

At the other pole of events, an interview with the Minister of Justice, Sylwester Zawadzki, appears, in which the minister discusses the reasons for internment and the eventual conditions of release. Citizen Minister of Justice feels that it is entirely normal that another citizen, imprisoned without any kind of officially formulated charge, should turn in, to an *ubek*, a declaration of loyalty form, in which the internee accuses himself, promises to behave, and gives up all Union activity. This is how the Party partner completes his dialogue with the most serious representatives of the people.

The initiation of the hunger strike prevented sick colleagues from leaving camp to go to the hospital in Wejherowo. After the departure of the highly trained doctors (who were often specialists) from the Tri-City area, the local prison medical staff could not assure the internees adequate medical care, and, what was worse, did not want to make important decisions regarding methods of treating the ill. The camp doctors began sending patients to Wejherowo for consultations and treatment, and for us it was a chance to catch a second wind, through the accounts coming back of how the outside world looked in its second month of martial law.

The sick were transported to Wejherowo in keeping with prison ritual: in a paddy wagon, a "Beetle" with an armed guard of five to six uniformed men for every two sick internees. These were the first opportunities for direct and more private contact with ZOMO people. When they got to know us and were in the van alone with us, they would curse martial law and complain about their lot. They justified their being in the police by saying that they had been seeking higher wages and the quick allotment of an apartment. Many of them, they said, did not expect this turn of events nor that they would be used to break up Solidarity. These moments of frankness would pass quickly, however, the minute they were back in full formation as an escort with the leader of the convoy, in whose presence there were no such admissions. Occasionally, it also happened that they themselves (wanting to shop in Wejherowo) would take an internee along and make it possible for him to phone home, or even visit a friend if he lived somewhere along the way. We had to admit that we had never expected this from ZOMOs and, after hearing the first accounts of such incidents, we looked at our guards with new eyes.

The ZOMOs treated the trips as a chance to get some alcohol and to make the acquaintance of salesgirls in the surrounding small towns. They obviously tried to model themselves on cowboys or cops from American movies. Neat uniforms, holsters slung low, practically on their thighs, field jackets . . . The "apartheid" mechanism was activated: they were the rulers, the privileged, those who were beyond the reach of the law. The new situation gave them power that went to their heads. We felt their headiness and we opposed it in camp during our walks by demonstrating scorn for them as lackeys and prison beaters. Most of the clashes between us broke out because of their arrogance. There was no fear psychosis in camp and their entire outfits were of no use in intimidating us. We did battle on a moral plane, and in that arena they had very little to say.

During one of the return trips from the hospital in Wejherowo, the ZOMOs overdid it on the cheap wine in one of the local bars, and the leader of the convoy, an unsavory, strawberry-blond fellow with a tendency to hypertension, drank himself stiff. Because he fell out of the van with all the symptoms of "seasickness," he was not able to cover up the incident. The camp authorities decided to drag the entire matter out into the open and investigate. As a result, they questioned the sick internees who had been taken to the hospital, hoping to exploit mutual hostility between the ZOMOs and internees. This time, however, they were mistaken: the internees declined to cooperate in any way, reasoning that the morals of ZOMOs were beyond the boundaries of their concerns. They told the major that he would have to fend for himself.

FRIDAY, FEBRUARY 5

A moment ago there was a terrible night row in camp.
A young boy, seventeen years old, was taken away from
Cell 33 and put into an isolation cell for six days as punishment. He was a hotheaded fellow from the group of
"poster boys"* from Regional Headquarters. He's a
tough one, has to prove himself all the time, and so is easy
to goad. During our walk, he went up to the open window of one of the cells to talk. Chased away from there
by one of the ZOMOs, he threw them a remark. They,
in turn, informed on him by writing up a report and
consequently, the major decided to punish him. He probably did it reluctantly because Artur Pisarski, called "the
minor," always aroused everybody's paternal feelings.
But the major found himself between the anvil and the
hammer in this case. The young ZOMOs, who did not
share the Major's sentiments, put the matter to him
sharply. One of the cells began negotiations in this matter
with a so-called "educator" to whom it was proposed that
the punishment be withdrawn, at least for the time of the
hunger strike. It was already the fourth day of the fast and
the additional punishment in isolation could prove too
much for the young boy. The counselor acknowledged
the justness of the arguments but he could not change the
major's decision. Artur was put in solitary confinement.
The third pavilion protested immediately by banging on
the doors with whatever was at hand. In a moment, the
entire camp had joined in. The banging went on for two
hours with fifteen-minute breaks, but we finally gave up
because many of our colleagues were already in their
second day of the hunger strike and there were also many

---

*Pisarski was one of the younger members of the "Poster Brigade," which
plastered Gdańsk with posters, signs, and graffiti. The Brigade's activities are
described later in the journal, on pp. 267–69.

sick internees. The camp radio warned us of ZOMO retaliation and of the consequences of martial law provisions. The loudspeaker blared: "Internees! Are you sure he's worth the price?" This was a little funny, a little grim, especially since armed ZOMOs had been let into the corridors of the pavilions. We were a hair's breadth away from a confrontation. This young man with bad nerves is such easy prey that he is really defenseless. Every reaction of his could run afoul of camp regulations or some decree. We fear for him.

It is already well past midnight and so another day of fasting has begun for me and a few dozen colleagues. I could never have imagined that I would have to fight for my basic human rights as a man in this way. Yet the system found a way to force me, a man guided by rational appraisal of issues, people, and circumstances, to qualify as an opponent, "an anarchist," to accuse me with its aggressive propaganda, and to force me to this irrational but only remaining means of defense. Unless I become a passive puppet, taken from my home, transported, "interned," fed and waiting until the owners of my future assent to my release.

Of course, I have no illusions about the fact that for them this is something ridiculous and meaningless, unless, of course, it results in medical complications. As the warden, Major Kaczmarek, says: we are hurting ourselves more than anyone else. Yet in order to regain some respect for ourselves, we had to do this. This is a dialectics applied in opposition to a system based on force, a system to which we have no alternative. As in the old saying: he who sows the wind, reaps the whirlwind.

The long stay here, violently and dramatically begun, crystallizes certain personalities. The weaker ones, the outsiders, suddenly appear to be the strong and wise ones. The rabble-rousers drop out of sight or their dynamism leaves them. Reevaluations, new choices. An entirely new consciousness evolves: cleansed of emotions, seeing past mistakes, alert to new information, and full of self-knowledge. This is the advantage. This prison university, and our doctoral studies come right after our August diploma. The authorities are training me to be a specialist. I myself would not have made this choice.

SUNDAY, FEBRUARY 7

A visit from the bishop of Chełm, Marian Przykucki, who is accompanied by diocesan priests and our chaplain, becomes further confirmation of the Church's commitment to the issues which concern us. During mass, the bishop reminded us that this period of being apart is the occasion for an inner renewal. Here we can and should concentrate on matters pertaining to man's ultimate goal in life. We should not waste this time, which, in a certain sense, was "bestowed" upon us. These words reveal a new perspective, and change the way we look at our daily life here in camp. The diocese of Chełm feels especially obligated to care for us in all ways. Even though we received formally instituted help from the Gdańsk Curia, we also received individual food packages from Pelplin. The camp in Strzebielinek is in the diocese of Koszalin, but the internees come mainly from the Tri-City area, which is divided between the dioceses of Gdańsk and Chełm. Now during the hunger strike, we have received more food than ever before and so we pass most of those packages on to our families.

The Dutch Red Cross also sent us packages with sanitary aids.

TUESDAY, FEBRUARY 9

We have received Lech Wałęsa's bill of internment along with his own handwritten comments:

I did not sign the original. It was handed to me on January 26, 1982, at 3 P.M. I would not be surprised if they started attributing various absurdities to me. Fabricated, of course, together with the false testimony of drummed-up witnesses. Local and world opinion was deluded into believing that I was not interned, while the bill was written on December 12, 1981, and given to me on January 26, 1982. You should use this as an example to further undermine the credibility of the undertaking, and I ask you to make it known to the public. This partner never was and never will be honest. That is why we cannot take even a single step backward and we cannot lose even one person because that is what They are after. Please make this example of Their method known to the public.

                                        Wałęsa, January 27, 1982

This letter appeared in the French newspaper *Le Monde* and resulted in the authorities' withdrawal of permission for Wałęsa's meeting with visiting priests. Father Alojzy Orszulik, who said mass for Wałęsa every Sunday, and Father Henryk Jankowski from Gdańsk were forbidden to see Wałęsa.

Yesterday they finally suspended the remainder of Artur's solitary confinement.

Because of our participation in the hunger strike, there have been more problems with prison authorities. On Sunday, one of our colleagues, Józek Wyszyński, an older and sickly gentleman with a kidney ailment, received word on the seventh day of his strike that his wife was waiting to see him. She was supposed to have brought with her an important document concerning his health problems. The information was needed by the prison doctor. Because he was extremely weak, two colleagues wanted to escort him to the visitation hall. The guard, not knowing what decision to make, called the major, who, we were told, was supposed to have said: either the internee mobilizes himself and gets there by himself, or we take away his visitation privilege. You have to understand how an internee waits for a whole month for the possibility of meeting with loved ones, to understand the reaction to such a pronouncement. Wyszyński's cell reached its boiling point, threatened to protest, and demanded to see the major. He came to the cell to tell the internees that Wyszyński's wife had already been sent home. That is how the interned are punished for an action which does not fit in with prison regulations. "Concern" for those on strike was rather specific. There were even days when there were no doctors in camp, and many internees were already feeling quite weak.

An important result of the hunger strike was the feeling of a growing bond between the internees and the overcoming of all the petty resentments that had sprung up during the weeks that we had been all together. United by our common effort and by our decision, which almost all of us upheld, we became more sensitive and gentle with one another. We were also acquiring a feeling of moral strength and the consciousness of basic goals for which we were fighting as the Solidarity Union. This was a clean operation and so all the more attacked and questioned by the authorities, who would suggest that some of our colleagues were eating on the sly. This was untrue. The few who decided to quit the strike were put in other cells "officially" or at their own request so as not to demobilize the rest of their cell mates. We did not hold it against them, but we did see to it that they did not eat right under our noses because that magnified our hunger. We drank only tea or water.

After seven days of fasting, and in keeping with our agreement, the first of the groups to begin the fast stopped their hunger strike at midnight. It is very strange to return to eating. You begin with a cracker, dipped in water. Usually, and this was confirmed by the doctor's scales, the hunger strikers lost weight at a rate of about one kilogram (2.2 lbs.) or slightly more per day. Altogether from seven to ten kilos for the week of the strike.

FRIDAY, FEBRUARY 12

On February 10, eighty-five people were taking part in the hunger strike. It was also on that day that a series of vicious radio programs with the participation of a certain Irena Chociewska-Puciatowa, who had worked in the legal counseling section of Regional Headquarters in Gdańsk up until March 1981, were first heard on the airwaves.

SATURDAY, FEBRUARY 13

At night yesterday and today, the windows of the cells were illuminated by votive lamps to mark the passage of the second month of martial law. We commemorated this anniversary in our own way: yesterday at 10 P.M. we banged on the bars and doors of the cells. Guards went through all the cells of the camp afterward to check the condition of the bars and doors after the concert.

We have to admit that the camp is probably the last scrap of "free" land in the entire voivodeship. We wear our Solidarity pins and various other badges, some of which were made here, others which were left over from the activities of the monument construction committees in Gdańsk, Gdynia, and Poznań. The camp has also become a center for gathering information from the radio, smuggled letters, the underground press, visits with family members, indirect contact with the new internees, and workplaces. The *ubeks*, prison guards and workers and even the prisoners themselves were unintentional information banks that involuntarily signaled bits of information regarding the attitudes of the authorities. There were, therefore, various sources from which we could skillfully reconstruct the whole picture. Our grasp of the situation often surprised our visitors.

The authorities still lacked a way of getting out of the impasse which they had created for themselves. One could see a wavering in the two basic tendencies that alternated with one another: they would either want to allow for limited Union activity, under their control, or they would want to strengthen the apparatus of repression, which led to the creation of an underground. We suspect that the street confrontations on January 30 were provoked by the representatives of the "hard line" tendency in the government, who needed the street violence as pretexts for their position at the Madrid Conference and for the anticipated Party plenum.

The authorities are still compromising themselves, not just with their decision of December 13 but also with the way they are implementing martial law among specific social groups. The *apparatchiks*, who, for the first time in the postwar history of Poland experienced genuine fear that their painstakingly built system was giving way and that the mechanism protecting their careers and promotions (which had seemed so certain and lasting) was beginning to falter, are now having their revenge. Now they want to pay us back with interest for that moment of fear and uncertainty. It is true that they will (as it said on the posters that they had printed, "fight as if they were fighting for the independence of Poland") fight for the "socialism" that means a high standard of living and stability for them and for their families. They have the tacit support of their entire clientele, which has learned to live and move in that schizophrenic world which it has created for itself and which fears the proposals of a self-governing society, where one would have the inconvenient job of coming to terms with one's conscience. It is easier to commit small swindles and wink an eye to let others know that they should not take this socialism so seriously. They come to an easy understanding with WRON which seeks any kind of formal support and tangible evidence of the benefits of its takeover.

Eight of our colleagues applied for emigration papers, and the camp authorities are releasing other individuals. Today another group of five people (from Gdańsk and Słupsk) was brought into camp.

The attitude toward the internees and the official declarations about the conditions in which the internees find themselves are well illustrated by the case of our colleague, Konrad Gajewski. He had been trying to get out of camp on a temporary pass for a long time because he had a child at home that was deathly ill with cancer. The authorities demanded some verification of the child's condition, and when it was provided, questioned its authenticity. It was only after an accidental meeting between the chaplain and Gajewski's desperate wife that a resolution to the matter seemed possible. After many pleas, including that of the Church, Gajewski was released. He got home just in time for the funeral: the child died two days after he left camp.

Many of our colleagues are awaiting news of the birth of their children. And it doesn't always get here in time. This is how the wall that divides us has grown and one would have to get rid of one's memory to accept the cynical propaganda declarations of an alleged understanding.

TUESDAY, FEBRUARY 16

For many days now there have been stubborn rumors coming into camp from the outside. They are somewhat confirmed by the guards' hints that the camp will be liquidated in March. Some of us are supposed to be released and some of us are to be transported elsewhere. The prisoners that up until now have been working on construction of an electrical plant in Żarnowiec are supposed to return to Strzebielinek.

In the afternoon, during a meeting with the cell representatives and the major, the latter told us that these rumors were untrue. Our stay here will be a long one, and only the seriously ill who require hospitalization will be released. None of the sick internees are eager to go to the prison hospital in Fordon near Bydgoszcz. Major Kaczmarek also announced that, as of two days ago, he is in complete control of the center and that Captain Maciuk, the spokesman for the police chief of the voivodeship, will come in twice a week to handle "his" business. Because of the laxity in camp discipline, as he put it, the Ping-Pong cell would be closed down and there would be no watching of television between the hours of 5 and 7:30. He was also limiting additional visits and returning to the regulation one visit per month, and so on. Of twelve internees who had violated regulations, he was pressing charges against four. It is possible to apply for transfer to another internment center, and at a later time, to apply for the permission to work at a halfway job outside the center. According to the major, our camp is the most "lax" and the hunger strikes still on in the two pavilions were not as widespread in other camps. He said that in the future, the prison personnel would use the five forms of regulation searches. As an example today, the guards did a classic *kipisz** in Cell 5, and turned up a diary kept from the very first day, various materials published by the Solidarity underground, radio equipment made from prison bugging devices, and commemorative stamps made in camp.

Another group of nine persons was brought in from Słupsk today, all of them from Sezamor,† including the director. They had been arrested for a fifteen-minute strike on February 13.

Camp body count for today: 137 internees.

THURSDAY, FEBRUARY 18

Nothing new, I am still sitting in prison at Strzebielinek. I am leading a pretty normal life-style and although I am making no moves, the radio and press report that someone is still engaged in anarchy, although thousands of Citizens' Committees have been formed and there are nothing but declarations of loyalty on television. It is difficult to understand this. I am worried because I see that the government is beginning to test its strength against the Church. For the time being only against the clergy low in the Church hierarchy, but that is always how it has begun. A propaganda campaign verges on the dangerous and delicate boundary beyond which the pos-

---

*Search in which everything is turned upside down and inside out.
†An industrial plant producing shipbuilding materials.

sibility of controlling the behavior of society vanishes. If WRON, as it advertises itself, uses syllogistic methods and a constant analysis of society's moods to tighten the screws accordingly, then it ought to feel the imminent threat. The figure of the Pope appears in the radio commentaries in ambivalent contexts, as a sign of what WRON can do with its propaganda to "protect socialism." It foregoes no underhanded trick.

After the major's announcement, sports activities, such as the hour of Ping-Pong allotted every two cells every two or three days, were eliminated from camp. That schedule allowed each person to play for ten to fifteen minutes. This is a way of resocializing the camp in retaliation for the singing and other forms of insubordination to superiors. Our routine is now getting closer to that of the regular prisoners although, apparently, ours is still far from it. The increasing confinement will inevitably breed conflicts, and that is how the system is set up: to create endless punishments and retaliations. It will be bad in here if things begin to move down this inclined plane.

Books: Right now I am reading a biography of Winston Churchill borrowed somewhere outside of camp. His life was so colorful, so rich and full of a sense of freedom, that it is no comfort to me at all in my present state. He was interned, too, as a war correspondent during the Boer War in Africa. So there are certain analogies. Except that he was treated with full courtesy and escaped after three or four weeks by jumping over a fence. He escaped into a country that was alien to him, though not as militarized as ours. The last Saturday-Sunday police action in Poland resulted in the detention of about 150,000 people and of those 3,500 remained under arrest. This operation was advertised as an attack on secret hideaways and stills, and mentioned in the same breath as news about the uncovering of new points of distribution and printing of Solidarity materials. The insidious practice of informing the public of the sentencing of common criminals along with Union activists was a little too transparent.

We reflect on the wave of terrorism, foreign to Polish society up to now, that has been unleashed by martial law. Breaking off all talks and avoiding dialogue while increasing accusations will only trigger actions such as the planting of a bomb at a gas station (Lublin), the blowing up of a man who was handling a grenade (Wrocław), the shooting of a policeman (Warsaw), or disarming a soldier (Warsaw).

Captain Maciuk's mysterious "own business," which he was supposed to take care of in camp after turning over the center to Major Kaczmarek, was shortly explained. Eugeniusz Maciuk, who bragged about having a law degree (completed by taking extramural courses), and who had been an altar boy, a boy scout, and was now an *ubek*, thought up little temptations in the form of declaration of loyalty forms for the sick internees. Maciuk would hand these forms to the internees practically on their way out the door. This was a real test of character, and a few of us, unfortunately, lost this round to that old, but rather primitive, fox.

SATURDAY, FEBRUARY 20

Yesterday Bolesław Hutyra was brought to camp and today Teodor Herra, both from the PLO.* Altogether, the PLO has nine representatives in Strzebielinek. Analyzing this case, we come to the conclusion that the dimensions of internment are decided by good or bad relations with the authorities in a given milieu. It is from the party committees of a given shop or factory, that is,

---

*Polish Oceanic Lines, Polish shipping line.

from trusted colleagues or informers of the SB, that certain recommendations emanate. In the case of the PLO, not without significance was the fact that during the period of the Union's activity, the wife of Colonel Ring, the spokesman for the police commander of the voivodeship and our acquaintance from that memorable meeting in Strzebielinek, was dismissed. Hutyra was badly beaten by police during that time that he was held in arrest in Gdynia. The prison doctor who examined Hutyra confirmed the beating. Herra was interned a few days after his return from a four-month business trip as a representative of the PLO in Hamburg, where he had been since November of last year. He is an older man, over sixty, who has serious health problems.

MONDAY, FEBRUARY 22

Today Cell 27 has been having a row with the guards. One of the internees had permission to keep an appointment at the Medical Academy where he and his wife were to have a mandatory blood test. His wife is in an advanced stage of pregnancy and there is the possibility of complications because of serological incompatibility. In spite of the gravity of the situation, no transportation arrangements had been made, and the entire cell was protesting this handling of the matter.

The growing conflict between the cell of singing internees and the neighboring ZOMO cell finally came to a head on Sunday over the matter of disagreement as to repertoire. During Sunday visits, the internees in the first pavilion sang their (by now traditional) song. One of the ZOMOs, a certain Romek Malinowski, apparently from Stargard Szczeciński, with whom the internees had long been having various problems, brought a tape recorder with a powerful amplifier and loudspeakers. They put the speakers in the windows and began to drown out the singing with discotheque music. In this way, they also drowned out the group singing at the gates outside. The warden reacted to the shouting that was beginning by going to those internees out on their walk and accusing them of organizing a demonstration. It was pointed out to him that the ZOMOs were acting even more like a demonstration than they were. The major sent a lieutenant in to speak to the ZOMOs and the discotheque was silenced. From then on, we handled Malinowski and his discotheque by putting a metal insert into the socket which caused an immediate short circuit.

Today we received word that Janek Samsonowicz, who was released from here on February 13, was transported to the camp in Iława. We thought that he was at home. It turned out that he had been transferred as punishment for organizing the hunger strike here. This is not the first time that the authorities' information is well off the mark. Our colleague, an altogether likeable fellow, tried to dissuade us from the strike. On the other hand, the truth is that earlier in the opposition movement he had taken part in hunger strikes. This is how the authorities project certain patterns of behavior. Knowing about how the authorities like to isolate leaders, we do not create any official organizational structures here in camp.

SUNDAY, FEBRUARY 28

Another month is already a closed chapter. A period of some kind of inner concentration has begun. The Church is helpful here because Ash Wednesday (on the 24th of this month) draws special attention to man's ephemerality. I have the feeling that the current rulers of Poland have forgotten about this. After all, their rule will also end one day. It seems likely that history will not be kind to them. Even when looking at it from a contemporary perspective one can see how the incessant taking away of a people's hope leads to the growth of anger on the one hand, and on the other, inner frustration. More and more social groups are "internally emigrating." The "emigration" of the younger generations is commonplace. These are generations born and raised in People's Poland. This whole falsified system of shaping attitudes and opinions fell apart in the sweltering days of June 1979 during the Pope's pilgrimage to Poland. It was then that the Polish nation, passed over in the power struggles of the elite, deprived of its dignity, divided into classes, strata, and into party and other "dialectic" categories, raised itself from its knees and showed its real countenance of youth and bravado. There, too, at those meetings attended by millions, it began to believe in itself. It reached the maturity to make decisions for itself about the future of Poland. It took only a year more for it to be capable of fighting for its own rights. The beginning was the work of the young. They not only could not remember Stalinist times (October 1956 was ancient history) but even December 1970 was only a vague memory.

It seems that on the occasion of the last Communist Party plenum, the fate of the interned, mainly young people (the average age among internees is barely 30), was decided. We still have a few long months ahead of us, unless the Holy Father comes this summer. In his last statements, the Pope talked about his concern for the interned and arrested. As if in confirmation of these distant words, the following personal message from the Pope reached Adam Kinaszewski via Kraków: "Dear Adam! I am writing to you after getting news from Andrzej. I want to tell you that I pray for you every day and for all of those who are sharing your ordeal. It is good that you were in Rome. February 8, 1982. Your Uncle."

Something has finally been done about the most seriously ill internees. At first, those who were undergoing treatment at the Medical Academy were supposed to be released. Instead of them, another two internees were released in the last few days. These were very serious cases: one of the internees had such constant high blood pressure that we feared for his life; the other had a liver ailment which required long-term treatment. This sudden interest in the sick seems to accompany news about the activities of the Red Cross in Poland. WRON wants to show the world their "humanitarian" method of internment. That is why, as the press says, it is possible to visit the internment camps, and to appeal for release of some internees for health reasons. Of course, in the case of our colleagues their health problems were too serious to wait for a delegation of the International Red Cross to appear in our camps. The International Red Cross has been in six internment camps since January 22. It had not been allowed into the remainder of the camps "for administrative reasons." Commentators from world news agencies drew attention to the fact that this was the first case in which the Red Cross was allowed to visit the camps or prisons in Eastern Europe.

At any rate, lots of activity in camp. Groups of prisoners are cleaning, shoveling away the rest of the snow, raking the lawns, painting the curbs, and are fixing up the volleyball court.

From the rumors originating with prison authorities, it seems that there will be a meeting of all internment camp wardens, probably to agree on a set of uniform regulations for the internees. In some of the camps, in Wierzchowo Pomorskie, for example, where most of the internees were from Szczecin, there had been a "truncheoning" of over half the inmates, while in other camps the cells are open. There are also no guidelines as to how to interpret the specific formulations regarding our required routine. In some camps the walks are done by individual cells or in groups, in others entire pavilions go out. The same with masses. In some camps there are masses for everyone at the same time, in others, only for individual groups at a time. The most important reason for this meeting of wardens, however, will probably be to exchange information having to do with the efficacy of our "resocialization." After all, the authorities want to divide and conquer people from Solidarity and to find those eager to cooperate with WRON. As of now, the results of this "resocialization" are meager. From what we know, the talks between *ubeks* and individuals from the National Commission have not yielded the expected results. Those who were able to avoid arrest and internment have also refused to cooperate with WRON.

An example of the real methods used by the authorities is today's interview with the Minister of Internal Affairs, General Czesław Kiszczak, who promises society an amelioration of martial law rigors if it is "good" and also says that further release of internees will depend on their individual behavior.

TUESDAY, MARCH 2

Piotr Rosa's marriage took place today at noon. For this solemn occasion, which took place in the camp visitation hall, the bridegroom could invite only his cell mates. By way of special permission, he also received an additional sixty minutes of visitation. For the entire ceremony, therefore, and for conversations with close family members, he had 120 minutes, except that his colleagues were led back to the cell after the marriage ceremony. The warden would not agree to leave the bride and groom alone. The bride's wedding bouquet decorated our chapel.

We have been having discussions about emigration for quite a while now. More and more people are reconsidering leaving Poland. They hope that they can remove the internment decree from themselves in this way. There seem to be two distinct positions on this issue: some, actually a good majority, simply cannot imagine their lives far from Poland; others, envisioning quite a stretch of time ahead for martial law, feel that by emigrating from Poland, the social pressure for the release of the interned is diminished, which will make it easier for the authorities to get out of this difficult (in terms of prestige) situation. Besides these basic considerations, there were also very prosaic reasons such as taking advantage of the opportunity to arrange a comfortable life for oneself, as those eager to emigrate think, abroad. This has been the main topic for many days. Some attempts to articulate positions on this issue in writing have also appeared, and often even people in the same cell are divided. Recently there have been appeals to colleagues having the intention to emigrate to consider the moral consequences of their decisions:

(a) We were not interned on the basis of individual responsibility for specific actions but rather for reasons of collective responsibility as representatives of an organization which is currently being repressed; and (b) hastily undertaken individual decisions remain in sharp violation of Union statutes in a situation when others are being sentenced because they tried to free us. That is why applying for emigration or even inquiring about the conditions necessary for emigration is wrong. This is an activity which is neither in the interest of those writing nor in the interest of our Union.
Konrad. February 12, 1982.

We seem to be doing a lot more reading. At first most of us borrowed books from the poor prison library collection, but now each of us tries to have more interesting books brought in. We read everything: belles-lettres, mysteries (these are prison favorites), popular philosophy, and history books. The last of these add to the historical arguments in our discussions. We are trying to organize self-improvement activities. Cut off from everything, we act just as the nation does. This is normal and understandable. In Professor Bogdan Suchodolski's last work, *Poland and the Poles,* is the note: "We have always reacted to our defeats with organic work. This is the natural reflex of every living organism, and of every social system, which is under attack and whose existence is threatened. The reflex comes from the desire to stay alive, to regain strength, and to return to more basic and complete conditions of existence." That is what Franciszek Bujak wrote at the dawn of freedom. Analogies with national insurrections immediately come to mind: for some with the year 1863, for others 1830/31. These are not, however, the discussions of professionals, but of people who, facing a situation that they have never had to face before, desire to understand it, in order to draw lessons from it for the future. They worry, too, that their opinions, formed in conditions of camp isolation, might not coincide with those of society at large. That is why we always refer to current affairs, discuss them, but without making them the basis for projections as to future trends in Poland. We talk about the future more in personal categories: when I get out I will do this and that. We realize that developing a society mature enough that it will fight for its lost rights is not easy. It would be nice if that period of fighting were going on now, but it is just now that social consciousness has begun to mature. This demands time and new people. They have already appeared and have occupied our vacant places. They, too, must have time to create structures which are appropriate to the demands. Solidarity's Committee of Resistance, constituted on January 13, is far from being capable of creating an Underground Poland, as some of the less patient would like to believe. The internal events of the years 1976–80, the Pope's visit, the activities of the Polish Church prepared the ground for the singular, massive explosion of Polish social and political activity that was Solidarity. On December 13, however, this period came to a close. It is also doubtful that it could be repeated once again in this form. One of our colleagues who picked up this theme in a message smuggled to the outside, indicated the need to maintain independent thought, which must be rescued from the lawlessness of WRON. He quoted Erich Fromm, who, in connection with the "madness of our times" wrote: "I hope that great charismatic individuals will appear . . . that they will appear, and as has been the case in the past, will tell the truth to people in a way so clear and indisputable, that it will have results. Truth, if it is the whole truth, strikes man like a thunderbolt."

Many different forms of literary creativity are appearing: poems, small prose pieces, facetious verse, jokes, and even memoirs and diaries. The last two of these have become so common that they pose a certain danger. This was proven when a volume of memoirs was confiscated during a cell search not too long ago. The honesty of the writing revealed the mutual and often even friendly relations between some of the guards and the internees, and indicated how the internees were allowed to go from cell to cell to exchange information, how the guards passed on information from prison authorities, and also how the guards mediated in making contact with the families of internees. After this unfortunate incident, Major Kaczmarek began a series of inquiries which were to gauge the degree of the guards' "demoralization." Those affected did not hide their feelings toward us and told us many times that our imprisonment destroyed something within them: they suddenly understood the hypocrisy of the entire system. When we were brought in, they were told that they would be dealing with dangerous criminals, who sought to murder all those in uniform together with their families. The same thing that Deputy Przymanowski said not long ago in the Sejm. They quickly saw, however, that we were normal people who were locked up because we wanted to change a few things in this country. The most open of the guards had sought contact with the Solidarity faction that was forming within the branch of the Ministry of Internal Affairs. They warned us about certain colleagues of theirs who remained faithful executors of each order. Moreover, these zealots would outdo each other in thinking up ways to cause the internees trouble: frisking, informing, causing confrontations at bath, walk, and roll-call times. Since they were used to strict discipline, it was incomprehensible to them that we did not rise for morning roll, that we did not have a cell mate chosen to report the number of internees in the cell, or that we would scold them if they referred to us in the impersonal or third person. We have to admit, however, that the authorities also demanded that they address us courteously and that they treat us as persons with a special status.

In the end, however, the guards that appeared in the confiscated journal were called in "on the carpet" and had to explain their relations with us. All of those involved in this incident or even suspected of favoring us in any way, were transferred from one pavilion to another. If that did not help, they were transferred to duty on the roosters, that is, the watchtowers. At any rate now only the most trusted guards or ZOMOs did duty at the gate on visitation days. In spite of the precautions, however, there were radios in both pavilions right after the first visitation day, not to mention the large transistor that somehow had made its way in past the guards. Now we are also receiving a steady stream of underground publications, even the kind that are made up of a few dozen printed pages. This is undoubtedly an interesting chapter in the story of our relations with the guards and of our ingenuity, but for obvious reasons, I cannot write about them.

SATURDAY, MARCH 6

We get some news at camp with a substantial delay. This especially pertains to activities which aim to secure our release. Sometimes we do not realize the incredible number of such initiatives. On the one hand, there are the bishops of both the Gdańsk and Chełm dioceses, factories, individuals (some of which even have the respect of the authorities, such as Lech Bądkowski); and, on the other hand, families, working for the release of individual internees. In two cases, lawyers demanded access to the charges in the name of the interned. As yet, however, none of these attempts to have us released have had any results.

The attempts to intervene on our behalf showed up the schematic ways of thinking of the masters of our fate. Each of us was accused of, if not membership in, then at least cooperation with KOR, KPN, or RMP. Or we were accused of organizing strikes. An authoritative confirmation of this fact was enough to prove our desire to overthrow "socialist Poland," which constituted proof of activity against "our system." The only way to be released from internment is to sign a declaration in which we cut ourselves off from all previous activity.

Within these last days we have been getting answers to our appeals for a withdrawal of the internment decisions. This is a very strange document. We wrote to the Minister of Internal Affairs, to complain about a decision of an organizational unit subordinate to him, and we get an answer from that very same unit in the minister's name. This paper was a xerox copy with no official stamp or even the name of the person that wrote it. Instead of a signature, someone had written "Police Chief of the Voivodeship of Gdańsk." This is probably a form commonly used in camps that are under the supervision of the Gdańsk security forces as there were blanks in the appropriate places: "Police Headquarters in the Voivodeship of

Gdańsk, date (place for the date) 1982. Center of Internment in (name written in)."

SUNDAY, MARCH 7

During mass today one of our colleagues fainted. The same thing had happened to him a week ago, but it was ignored by the camp doctor. Her behavior had angered others in the cell because she began to ask if he was a worker in the Ministry of Internal Affairs by any chance. The internee, who was semiconscious, began telling her about his activities in the opposition. After fainting during mass, he was suspected of having epilepsy and was sent to the hospital in Wejherowo for a checkup. The final decision in even such clear-cut matters belongs to the security police. I would not want to say anything bad about the doctors who took the place of the civilian teams that were there at the beginning. It sometimes turned out, however, that even those prison doctors that were known in the medical world for steering themselves by considerations not of ethics but Party hierarchy, often tried to help us in their own way. Of course, their "help" consisted of a referral of the seriously ill to outside specialists, but at that time and in those circumstances, even these referrals were not straightforward matters. The doctors could have just as easily ignored the symptoms of illness, and that is exactly what they did in many cases. The truth is, however, that the teams of prison doctors and nurses had acted routinely in a penal institution and were accustomed to dealing with criminals who used any means available to avoid punishment, including swallowing a variety of dangerous objects, slashing themselves with razor blades, and so on. These medical crews transferred their attitudes toward criminals to the internees, who found them unacceptable. The way in which the internees were addressed in the doctor's office was in itself the source of many conflicts.

A certain "popularity" was gained by a team made up of a woman doctor who held the rank of captain, an E.N.T. specialist who actually spoke Russian, but with a Polish accent. "The Russian," as even the guards called her, usually worked together with a young nurse (from the prison hospital in Kurkowo), the wife of the prison chauffeur. "Female-ZOMO" is perhaps too much, but both women treated patients very unceremoniously: let him come in, let him sit down, what is the problem, and so on. Having cast off what they considered to be dispensable amenities, they handled the patients in their own way, and were in no way inhibited in their conversations by our presence. The most important element of their conversations was the purchasing of such luxury items as automatic washers, carpets, furniture, sheepskin coats, and winter boots. Martial law proved to be a time which presented all kinds of possibilities for them in terms of obtaining rationed items.

This is how the generals' junta and security forces rewarded their faithful servants, who had been badly shaken during the period of Solidarity's control by the thought that their system of private stores and canteens at the police stations, of special coupons and quiet redistribution, could be ending. Regaining control of the situation and "reversing the tide of events" had a completely concrete and material dimension for that entire clientele of the political system created by martial law. A return to canteens full of goods, a return to a system of buying "at the old prices," allocations of goods "on sale" meant that the period of threats and social control was over. This is a time of great plundering, as is the case during war. Society is being plundered.

Both of the above-mentioned women were very irritated by one of our colleagues who, during a visit to their office, demanded that they refer to him in the accepted manner between doctor and patient, instead of talking to him in the third person. In a short time, a small incident grew into a major affair. It probably would have ended with a report about "the inappropriate behavior of an internee" but this time they hit upon a man who decided to treat the entire matter seriously. He showed that in his health records he had read that he was "unbalanced, excitable, and arrogant. During the examination, he demanded that he be addressed as Mr., slammed doors, etc. . . ." The medical files containing data about camp illnesses and applied treatments were not the place for settling personal accounts. Called in by Maciuk for a "lesson" about respect for a "superior," the man demanded, in the presence of Major Kaczmarek, the removal of those remarks from his health file and the instruction of prison medical personnel in the customary forms of address in a doctor-patient relationship. The matter ended with Major Kaczmarek's acknowledgement (in contradiction to Maciuk's position) that the internee was right, and Kaczmarek promised to remove the comments.

During the course of today's visits, the Major played one of his psychological tricks. He went through the guard booth into the visitation hall and told the waiting families that six internees were being released. Some were happy, others very sad. A natural reaction is to consider every possibility for release. It was with these thoughts that the families came to today's visits. And that was the main conversation topic. Of course, the number one issue was whether or not to sign, and that was the point.

The last unofficial surveys in some of the factories in Gdańsk confirmed our suspicions, that the workers are unequivocally convinced of the need to reactivate Solidarity in spite of the fact that it had not turned out to be everything that they had imagined. People foresee its reactivation by June of this year. We hope that the whole survey will reach us. People are saying that Rakowski met with Wałęsa. That this was apparently their second meeting since the declaration of martial law. And, rumor has it, Rakowski told journalists that it was a tough talk, but that he was satisfied with it. The question remains as to what that means. There is much speculation as to the possibility of releasing Wałęsa for the baptism of his youngest daughter, Maria Wiktoria, born just a few weeks ago. The baptism is to take place on March 21. Father Henryk Jankowski, who, until recently, was in touch with Wałęsa, worried that this church ceremony would change into an enormous manifestation during which the security police might try a provocation.

The camp was visited today by the Primate's representatives: Romuald Kukołowicz and Stanisław Czartoryski. They spent only a moment speaking with a few colleagues while presenting them with gifts brought from Warsaw (coffee, cakes, toothpaste, detergent, etc.). This is the kind of Church support that has been provided to the interned.

The disagreement between the camp authorities and ourselves on the subject of singing during walks on visitation days (Sundays and Thursdays), entered its final stage. As usual, we sang our songs, during the course of which the major came out and said that he is suspending all Sunday walks.

The English translation of a book about Wałęsa that was published here in Poland (only a fraction of the books reached the bookstores, the rest were shredded) has appeared in the West.

As for more mundane matters, the homemade stuffed cabbage rolls that I received during my family's visit were received with great enthusiasm (as was the cheesecake). For me this is very moving evidence of concern and a way of keeping in touch with the warmth of my table at home. It is also an extension of our short meeting . . . It takes three or four days to react to the monthly visit, which alters the rhythm and mood of life in the cell, and the vectors of my thoughts. I have given up chess, it began to bore us, and for the last few days we have been able to play ping-pong again. We have been reliving our youth at the ping-pong table. I have come upon a noteworthy book which has made the greatest impression on me since Julio Cortázar's *End of the Game*. It is Gabriel García Márquez's *One Hundred Years of Solitude*. It is a wise book, intimate with old age and the amplitude of human emotions, contradictions, and the entire dialectic of human bonds, family mechanisms, and social diagnoses. There is a miraculously penetrating description of the mechanism of power, revolution, and the swindle of propaganda: all of these actions are carried out like an operation on the body of a living society, which is so defenseless in the face of the mad, justified "superior right" of the authorities' excesses. How does it happen that the author, a Colombian so far away from our immediate experiences, can also write about our life so penetratingly? That is the miracle of great universal literature: the fate of a people in another hemisphere, in another culture, in a fictitious world that is a writer's creation, suddenly turns out to be a portrait of our own experiences and deepest concerns.

The flowers which we got during visits prompted us to wash the cell windows. The approaching spring causes a burst of longing for the outside world, for our loved ones. You can feel spring jitters in our behavior towards one another. Everyone becomes more "external," as if they had lost interest in one another. We begin studying foreign languages.

TUESDAY, MARCH 9

Yesterday five more of our colleagues were supposed to have left camp. They remained, however. They have to wait. We are all waiting. No one knows when and in what conditions we will meet with our closest kin. Each of us would like to be home as soon as possible. Each of us is homesick. Each of us would jump at the chance to leave but most of us know that it cannot be done at the price of humiliation, degradation, or the destruction of the man in us.

I know that we must survive this, that we must come out of this stronger than we were before. This is not the last time we will be cheated, this is not the last time that we will have to remind others of our rights. We cannot, however, reverse this process. We can only stop it, and not for long. In the end we will find ourselves back on our own road. Maybe it is a difficult one, but it is ours.

Camp censorship is going crazy. Not long ago, it deleted a dedication in a colleague's new copy of the Gospels: "So that Truth will always be victorious." Censorship has been cutting out fragments of letters and scratching out bits of information on postcards, so that only the greetings and signature are left. Some of us are thinking about repeating a joke from one of the camps. They made up a message which, in keeping with the plan, fell into the hands of a guard. The note contained the brief message that "Honorata is supposed to give birth."* For a few days the guards were on the alert. Then we passed another message with the information that "Honorata has not yet given birth" and that they should not come. It was only then that the camp authorities figured out that they had been had.

Yesterday's body count: 113 internees.

---

*Code for an operation that is about to get underway.

WEDNESDAY, MARCH 10

The continuation of Captain Maciuk's "own business": a conversation with everyone who intends to emigrate. Of the whole group of thirty internees, only eleven took applications, the rest had come to listen. Maciuk's information was exactly like that in the daily press. It is obvious that the authorities are not at all prepared for this matter of emigration. They are counting on the fact that the internees will be worn down by the indefinite term of confinement and the fear of a future without work.

Today in the morning news I watched a segment showing the release of internees from a camp near Bytom. Our comments are varied. We feel, however, that these releases were the result of pressure from miners and the need to show acts mitigating the rigors of martial law here and abroad. This is supposed to calm things down internally and to win the West over so that it would withdraw its economic sanctions against Poland. Only the workers are to be released, however, as they created the "good" Solidarity while the rest lent the Union its "antisocialist" character.

We notice a change in the meaning of the word *prominent* as used in official propaganda. Up to now it has been used to designate those representatives of the authorities who had abused their power and now it is beginning to be used in reference to Solidarity leaders. We have nothing against this word semantically or linguistically speaking, but we do feel the need to protest against it when it is used in its social and historical sense to refer to members of Solidarity. The word *prominent* has acquired a pejorative connotation within the last few months because of its association with crime. Using this term in reference to Union leaders is supposed to suggest to public opinion that the leaders of Solidarity had somehow acted against the law.

WRON's propaganda offensive is still going full steam

on a few internal fronts (Solidarity, society, the Church) and external fronts (attacking the United States, the Madrid Conference, and the matter of realizing human rights in Poland). It turns out that it is very difficult to govern society without society, which is what the government spokesman, Jerzy Urban, calls for in the last issue of *Polityka*. The collapse especially of the economy, brought about the necessity of engaging the army in all decision-making processes, even on the lowest rungs. The army left its barracks and wants to win by order what was unattainable by any other political means. The first months of martial law prove, however, that the army has gotten tangled up in various minor matters which it cannot handle. None of the basic political problems have been solved. Slowly society is developing a double life. On the one side there is the conviction that this entire state is temporary, and that one should not get involved. Society will feign acquiescence because of the brutality of the new order, but, it is, in fact, waiting. On the other side, the impatient (and impatience is the domain of youth) are preparing for action. Another, underground life is being organized which the authorities label "illegal" and whose activities include everything from publishing to full-scale political activity. This phenomenon will grow in response to the worsening political morass of the current government. Life does not tolerate a political vacuum. The only road left to the authorities is that of dialogue.

SATURDAY, MARCH 13

Tradition has been satisfied: just as last month, yesterday we marked the three-month anniversary of our detention. First there were lighted candles and torches placed between the bars of each cell. Then there was our "music," played on bars, bowls, stools, and doors. It lasted for fifteen minutes beginning at midnight. At that time all the guards left the pavilions. They had told us earlier in the evening that they expected our pounding and that is why they would leave the pavilions because the noise in the corridors is deafening. Yesterday Captain Biegaj went from cell to cell to persuade us to forego the "demonstration." He threatened that if we did not heed his appeal, "freedom" would be curtailed in camp. Today at 12 noon the groups of internees out on walks sang their usual songs, and in the evening we lit candles.

A minute ago, the *kolkhoznik* announced that walks on Sundays have been limited to a half hour. This is in retaliation for our singing during visitation times and yesterday's actions.

FRIDAY, MARCH 19

There has been a lot of nervous activity in the camp for the last few days. The prisoners are removing the rest of the dried grass, a volleyball court is being prepared, and the day before yesterday, there was a search in camp for stools which were in need of repair. Finally it all became clear: a two-man delegation from the International Red Cross in Switzerland appeared. First the authorities "worked over" the members of the delegation for a few hours, and later, they unexpectedly opened our cells and encouraged us to leave them. We decided that since we had been sitting locked up in our cells up to that time, we would not take advantage of the authorities' "benevolence" now either. We all knew that the Red Cross delegation was in the camp, and that the prison authorities were trying to implement one of our first demands: open cells. The warden even tried to convince us to go out into the corridors of the pavilion, where we were supposed to meet with the Red Cross delegation and the representatives of the Ministry of Justice and the Polish Red Cross. The tension was broken by the arrival of the Swiss.

One of them, a doctor who spoke fair Polish, said that he understood what was going on but that they would like to invite us to meet with them, nevertheless. Then they came into our cells together with their Polish companions and began noting the various problems and inadequacies. There were a lot. They noticed our threadbare, dirty blankets; the tattered floor coverings; the primitive furnishings; the mold on the walls and ceiling; and the water standing in the bathroom. They were interested in the number of people in each cell, and even in the layout of the beds. They also wrote detailed reports about the health of internees and about the sanitary conditions in a few of the cells. These were also the subjects discussed at meetings with cell delegates and during individual conversations with internees. One of the doctors became interested in the matter of drinking water, about which we complained and which was located next to the camp pigsties. In the front part of a small building was a one-car garage and in the back of it was a pigsty from which manure was tossed right next door. Major Kaczmarek wanted to cover up the whole matter, but after we mentioned possible contamination of the water supply, the doctor in the company of our colleague-translator went to take a look at the building. Straight out of the pigsty ran a nice-sized rat. In the pigsty and in the cracks of the cement gutters that passed right through the center of camp, the rats had found conditions in which they could thrive.

During our talks with the Swiss, we found out that the Red Cross considers us to be political prisoners, similar to those in seventy other countries in the world. Our status is rather strange, however, in that the Hague Convention, dating from the beginning of the twentieth century, stipulates the rights of the interned only for people interned on foreign soil and not as citizens of a given country. That is why the Red Cross must count on the goodwill of the Polish authorities in its contacts with internees. This limits what they can do. Their main goal is to visit the internees and to propose the release of the most gravely ill. They are also supposed to help establish decent conditions for us in prison and to help our families, who find themselves in extremely difficult circumstances. The Red Cross delegation that came to Poland also tried to gain access to those arrested and sentenced "for continuing Union activity." The Red Cross also considers those people to be political prisoners. Unfortunately, the Red Cross has been unsuccessful in its attempts to meet with this group. The authorities will simply not allow it. The Red Cross is also getting no help from the authorities in determining the number of internees. They have received no list of names, locations of internment camps, nor, of course, any list of those dismissed from work for Union activity. The Red Cross must get all of its information from private sources, or by individual questioning of families, internees, or Church representatives. As of now they have visited one-third of the twenty-four camps still functioning. The problems are similar in all of them, even though the living conditions may vary. They assured us that they will remain interested in our fate and promised to return to camp in a few weeks if we were not released. Each transfer would be noted in a special file, so that we would not disappear somewhere. They did not, however, want to say too much about the conditions in the other camps, nor did they want to talk about Lech—about whom we inquired on several occasions—because they received permission to visit the camps only on the condition that they would not pass on any of this kind of information, and that all of their notes, outside of their personal and medical nota-tions, could be checked. In spite of this, they were asked by internees in a few of the cells to mail letters and literary work to the West.

A few colleagues took advantage of the presence of representatives of the Ministry of Justice to get some legal advice regarding their detention and the ways of invalidating the internment decision. The only useful information we got out of these conversations was the representative's "private" statement that the way to invalidate the internment decision was to have the matter brought up by a lawyer, who must demand access to the charges. In that case the institution which interns someone must justify its decision. This reverses the method of action used up to now. It is not we who must then explain our innocence, but the police commander who is obligated to prove our "guilt." This is, however, the logic of a dreamer who believes in the fiction that the law is still functioning. So far, all the lawyers who have tried to apply this reasoning have had no luck, as they never gain access to charges. Only the phrase that the "reasons for internment have not been nullified" is being upheld.

During the Red Cross visit twenty-four persons expressed the desire to leave Poland permanently. Other information revealed that four people lost their jobs during internment, and that, in camp, there are two secondary-school students, five students from the Politechnic in Gdańsk, one student from the University of Gdańsk, as well as people from all professions excepting the medical.

A soon as the delegation left camp, yesterday and today, we were immediately locked up in our cells. The prison authorities would not allow the Swiss to spend the night in our cells.

SATURDAY, MARCH 20

Here is a poem by Nikos Chadzinikolau from the last issue of the weekly *Literatura* from "before the war":

Hold me by the hands.
Too many road signs,
Sharp turns, grades.
Hold me by the hands.
Steps hurrying between oblivion
And hope.
It is not enough to look.
So many obstructions.
Even Ariadne's thread
Will not lead out of this labyrinth.
Hold me by the hands.
Too many setbacks.
Frail hours,
Forked roads.
Hold me by the hands,
Like the earth holds an apple tree,
So that it will not split
To the core.

I got this poem during our walk today from a friend. It arouses certain personal associations. I would like to feel the touch of your hands, to hear your voice, to see your face up close, and to have a normal conversation . . . without guards, without the eternally overcrowded and smoke-filled visitation hall. Without the nervous looking at the watch and the question: how much time do we have? I have to toss out the sentence-watchwords which have accumulated in me for a month, and with which I want to communicate. Hurry, hurry. We cannot be silent, and cannot have our own quiet thoughts, holding each other's hands . . . Why? These questions keep returning when one goes through the camp routine day after day. I ask myself these questions as do most of us who have been touched by physical force. Why? What for? Why me? The question ought to be: For what? Simple answer: As an example.

Number of internees in camp: 107 (55 in the first pavilion, 52 in the second).

MONDAY, MARCH 22

The hundredth day. We have been thinking about how to commemorate this day for a long time. Most of us feel that commemorative stamps should be made. New and very interesting designs have been proposed, and we lack only envelopes and ink. Some of the internees have become specialists in making these stamps and have achieved technical perfection. One can only wonder that stamps and seals so intimately connected with our lives can be made with such primitive tools as a penknife, razor blade, or needle. Camp motifs dominate: watchtowers, barbed wire, and prison bars with the word Solidarity worked into the design.

Determining how we should commemorate this anniversary of 100 days was a real problem. At night some of us banged on the bars and doors of the cells, others did not participate. The ZOMOs were put on combat alert: there are reinforcements in the towers and armed patrols at the gates. This is probably their "swan song," as it is said that regular prison guards are supposed to replace them. One element of dual rule would be over in camp. Even Major Kaczmarek, who generally tried to maintain discretion in these matters, lets it be known that he himself has had enough of this arrangement.

SUNDAY, MARCH 28

Each Sunday we listen carefully to the mass broadcast on the radio. Even those of us who suffer from insomnia and fall asleep only around morning, a condition that is spreading, always asked to be wakened. Those out on walks also stop near the windows to listen to the homily. We notice that the Church is moving away from subjects that concern us directly. If there is some reference to these subjects, it is only through elaborate commentary on liturgical readings. This is the Church's way of avoiding speaking directly. We do not understand these tactics. Our chaplain surprised us the other day when, on the way to mass, he stopped some of the men and asked: "Do you want to emigrate, too?" He was dismayed by the list of internees who were willing to emigrate (the list was shown to him by the prison authorities). Of one hundred internees, thirty had applied to emigrate. He considered this a personal defeat. Earlier he had emphasized that the Church would abandon no one left without work. He was unable to keep himself from mentioning this during his sermon. And when, after mass, the men began to sing "God, Protector of Poland," he ostentatiously walked away from the altar, not joining the singing as he usually did. After the singing, he turned to those present and said that this hymn had been sung in moments of greatest danger when people were being exiled to Siberia, when everything was being sacrificed for the homeland. One should not sing that song if the homeland is being left in need. He told us about an older woman who came to him after morning mass in the barracks church in Gdańsk with a letter, in which she asks us not to emigrate, and says that our attitude takes hope away from those who are counting on us and on our being faithful to the ideals of August 1980.

While the second mass was going on, one of our younger colleagues went to the prison authorities and withdrew his application for emigration. He tore it up in front of the astounded Captain Maciuk and Captain Biegaj. Other internees say that they do not treat the applications seriously, that they only wanted to be "covered" in case they could not get work or to see if they could not be released from camp sooner. Once on the "outside," they would refuse to emigrate. Now they realized that their attempt to outsmart the authorities had turned against them. They found themselves among people from whom society demands a great deal and from whom it does not accept such explanations. They found themselves under the ban of public opinion. During today's visits, someone brought the news from other camps that nowhere had the problem of emigration taken on the proportions that it had here. Everyone knows that only certain individuals apply to emigrate. This is confirmed by the official statements of government representatives who at first mentioned only ten and then later a few dozen applications for emigration. Compared with us, where thirty percent of the camp population is considering this move, the news is rather depressing.

This was the number one topic all day in the cell today. The cell representatives decided to take a position in this matter. We understand that we must put up a unified front, often against the colleagues in our cells. It turned out that among those willing to emigrate were two signers of the Gdańsk Accords. The rest of the internees have a history of collaboration with the older opposition groups. There are also a few activists from the factory levels.

SUNDAY, MONDAY, MARCH 28, 29

I don't know how many days have passed during which I am constantly thinking about you. Too much of this probably, but how can I prevent myself from running in your direction away from this inert world, in which I am stuck, nourished only by strength of will and deprived of all life-giving dramaturgy? The days are beginning to pass more and more slowly, the more light outside the window, the more sun. Time is stretching on like rubber, like a coagulating brown mass, which someone has poured out under our feet. Everything sticks in it, changes proportion, stiffens, like an insect in cooling sap . . .

WEDNESDAY, MARCH 31

In the late afternoon, we received a transport of long-awaited colleagues from Potulice. Our cells which, since the ZOMOs left camp, had been open, were immediately locked. At any rate, forty-five persons were brought in and there are to be more transports from other camps within a few days. People are saying that our camp is preparing to be a central "isolation center" in the Pomerania region and is to include all of northern Poland. Of those people that we know, Jan Bartczak, Regional Chairman from Lublin, is supposedly here along with Antoni Stawikowski, Regional Chairman from Toruń, a leading figure from the horizontal structures of the Party, Zbigniew Iwanów from Toruń. Most of the presidium from both Toruń and Bydgoszcz are also here. They promise to provide us with a description of how martial law was implementedinToruń, which now has the most internees.

Yesterday, too, a very popular camp personality, Maciek Jankowski, was released. Weighing about 300 pounds and over six feet tall, Maciek was also a judo champion. His presence during our walks, in spite of his gentle disposition, impressed the ZOMOs. He would jog around in an old, tattered, hand-me-down sweat suit and a funny ski cap. During the Solidarity Congress he was chosen to be a member of the National Commission as a representative of the University of Warsaw, where he played the role of a "jack of all trades" because he could solder anything together. A solderer from the University of Warsaw, was how he introduced himself at the Congress. That was pretty good. We said our good-byes with a harmonica, guitar, and songs (the instruments we have had since last Sunday).

SATURDAY, APRIL 3

The two-day recollection led by Father Edmund Piszcz, professor at the seminar in Pelplin, has ended. His deeply thought-out teachings help us pull ourselves together internally. Many internees went to confession. Together with Father Piszcz, who wanted to spend the night with us, came other priests from the diocese of Chełm: the chancellor of the curia, Father Andrzej Sliwi ń ski, the pastor of the parish church in Wejherowo, and our chaplain.

After recollection, each of the cells tried to detain its guests in order to get the latest news about Church-State relations as well as about the latest speculations in world politics. The Pope, beginning with the first day of martial law, has taken the position of clear opposition to Jaruzelski and the activities of WRON. First there was John Paul II's personal letter to Jaruzelski, directed to him as a Pole, citizen and soldier, and later his public appearances, his prayers for the intention of Poland, the arrested and interned; and now he emphasizes his lack of acknowledgement of the junta through the fact that up to now he has not notified the Polish authorities of the candidate to replace Glemp in the diocese left vacant by his appointment of Glemp as Primate. He does not want the authorities to interpret this information as the Vatican's acknowledgement of WRON. The authorities are courting the Episcopate in a variety of small ways, which draw it away from a staunch commitment to the reactivation of the trade unions, Solidarity included, and draw it away from making demands for the release of the interned (with Wałęsa at the top of the list), and from pressuring the government to begin talks with Solidarity. Not long ago, Czesław Kiszczak, head of the Department of Internal Affairs, officially declared that there was no need for the Church to remove crosses from workplaces, schools or public institutions. Yet there is great pressure put on the lower clergy to cut itself off from supporting the activities of the Solidarity underground, and to occupy itself only with matters of charity.

A supplement to our discussion on emigration is the news of the last episcopal conference that was supplied by Bishop Szczepan Wesoły, representative of the Primate in affairs of emigration in Rome. Job prospects in Western Europe and North America are far from cheerful. The governments of Western countries, that is, the United States, Canada, and even Australia, have closed their borders to immigrants. The conditions in the transit camps set up for Polish refugees, on the other hand, are very bad. Even now, those who want to emigrate are encountering a lack of enthusiasm and a lot of caution in the attitudes of Western embassies. Besides wanting to protect their job markets, these countries fear the infiltration of agents who could later play a serious political role. This fear has been confirmed by our colleagues and their families who have applied to emigrate.

The Church is still counting on Wałęsa, although the authorities are trying to undermine his importance. The Secretariat of the Episcopate got an appraisal of Wałęsa from the authorities: "We had to intern him, as he is politically immature and the situation which developed before martial law got too big for him to handle." In spite of this, the Church feels that he can calm the situation, which the authorities really fear.

The sharpening conflicts between the State and Church are causing the Pope to refrain from giving the date of his pilgrimage to Poland. He does not want to give WRON cause for arguments which could be used against the people of Solidarity. He does not exclude the possibility that the visit may not take place for another year, after the suspension of martial law. In spite of the difficulties, or perhaps because of them, the Church is gaining strength. It is getting involved in the lives of people who are persecuted, who have lost jobs, and who have been interned or arrested. Bishop Bronisław Dąbrowski has been delegated to handle the affairs of the interned on behalf of the Episcopate. He, next to Father Alojzy Orszulik, press spokesman for the Episcopate, visits Wałęsa most often. Individual bishops also work in their regions on behalf of all those touched by martial law. Today, during the mass preceding the recollection services, we were read the pastoral letter for Easter Sunday written by the bishop of Chełm. The following is from the passage devoted to the arrested and interned: "In spite of a certain lack of harmony in the lives of Poles, Easter morning, with its victory of good over evil, introduces a great hope and hope goes together with optimism." Concluding with Easter wishes, Bishop Przykucki writes: "I would like these words to reach each family; all the internment camps and prisons; and all people of good will who work for the good of our country. Let these words act to join all of us in unified action for the common good. Let them be an augury of internal peace in our country."

We have received no word on the course of yesterday's meeting of Common Committee, just as there is a lack of details about the arrangements made during Cardinal Macharski's visit in Rome. The Primate appeared as an observer at the main trial of Szczecin activists in Bydgoszcz.

The prosecutor's office has gone mad again. Recently, after a meeting of the Political Biuro, the attorney general demanded a review of forty cases for which sentences have already been determined. The highest sentences have been meted out by the naval military tribunal in Gdynia. The government obviously intends to intimidate and paralyze the coastal area which was Solidarity's base.

From the Toruń internees we got a description of what happened there after the declaration of martial law.

. . .

Arrests in Toruń, as in the entire country, began on the evening of December 12th and went on into the 13th of December. The first and strongest wave of arrests washed over Toruń apartments before midnight. At the beginning, the *ubeks* "worked" calmly: they summoned people for sudden questionings, raided basements, and broke into factory offices. After midnight, the operation really got underway. We were gathered in three Toruń police stations: on Wały Sikorskiego, on Grunwaldzka and Słowacki Street. Some of us were shown arrest warrants at home before being taken away. The majority, however, did not find out that they were interned until they got to the police station. Before they were locked up, they were frisked; the police took away scarves, belts, and penknives. Around 5 A.M., they pack us into transport vans. We drive along dark streets handcuffed together in pairs. We do not know where were are going. After a few minutes, we stop at the airport. Bizarre scenes. Along the runway are patrol cars driving in circles, flashing signal lights. A helicopter circles overhead. A string of ZOMOs with machine guns. Your spine tingles. Someone sees ditches: fear has big eyes. It is cold. More cars. A column forms. We are transferred to a larger ZOMO van. That is a little better: there are windows, we can see what is happening all around us. Ambulances drive up. At 6 A.M., the anthem is played over the loudspeaker. Jaruzelski speaks. We already know what has happened. The cars move. There are several, maybe a dozen. We cannot count them. We drive in the direction of the city. Dawn. Empty streets, it is Sunday. No public transportation. No people. We pass the city center, turn on the bridge in the direction of Bydgoszcz. We figure out that they are taking us to Potulice. On the outskirts of the city, there are people in front of the buildings. We raise our handcuffed hands to the windows of the van for them to see. Let them see what is happening.

We are first greeted in Potulice by barking dogs somewhere in a dark tunnel under the administration building of the prison. They pull us out in pairs. They take off the handcuffs. Under the walls, there are people in camouflage jackets with enormous German shepherds. They quickly form groups: we in the middle, and along the sides, the guards with the dogs. There are about a dozen of them. They lead us along the buildings. We pass fences of barbed wire, and towers with floodlights. Someone shouts from a window: Long live Solidarity! Those are the prisoners. There are about 2,000 here. We raise our hands and nod to them. We feel better already. They lead us into pavilion VII. They push us into our cells. They must have vacated them just a few minutes before we got there. They left books and some food behind. The action also took the prison staff by surprise. Tiny cells. Eight people to fifteen square meters, bunk beds, a table, the toilet not separated from the living quarters, broken windows, dirt. We wonder how long we will have to bear this. Will we be able to stand this and not break down?

After a few hours, they give us smelly blankets, dishes, spoons, one knife to a cell. They take away our money, and fill out a file card on each person. The guards are very obviously afraid of us (later we found out that they had been briefed and told that they would be dealing with extremely dangerous, ruthless assassins).

Bustle outside the walls. Our men are next door. We knock a hole in the wall next to the central heating pipes. First we pass messages, then we put together a list of the interned. There are 170 of us, about 100 from Toruń, the rest from Bydgoszcz. We exchange information. By evening we have organized a communication system on our level and between the various levels and the ground floor. We settle the details of a prison postal system. Before going to sleep, we pray together near the open windows and sing a hymn. And that is how it was throughout our stay. We were together although we did not know what the next day would bring.

The singing together drove the prison authorities to blind fury. They worried about the effect we would have on the regular inmates. They looked for the instigators, and watched the cells. Especially determined was the camp warden, Captain Wysocki, a psychopath devoid of all scruples. For a while the punishment for singing the hymn was the dark isolation cell. We responded to this by making a racket. After a while they stopped the repression but we did not stop our singing.

The first conversations with our "guardians" from the SB began before the holidays. They came regularly on all days of the week, with the exception of Mondays and Saturdays. After a while, we recognized them. The older internees, who were very dignified, were from Bydgoszcz while the younger boys, who were poorly prepared for this, were from Toruń. A good many of our colleagues refused to talk with the SB, others signed declarations and were not released, and the remainder of the internees lectured the SB about why the Union was right and pointed out the weaknesses in the government's arguments. The voivodeship police commander in Toruń interned so many people that he tried to have the number lowered in keeping with the country's average. They released the first twenty internees before Christmas. Among those released are people from the university; a few people from factory committees; the Second Communist Party Secretary, Masłowski; the Secretary of the University Committee (University of Nicolaus Copernicus in Toruń), Witkowski, all from so-called "horizontal structures." The next group left for home before New Year's. Up until then we had 204 names on our list.

On January 13, we had our first head-on confrontation. From the kitchen, next to which we walked, came terrible odors, which were unbearable. Our colleagues decided to change the direction of their walks. They wanted to get to the walk areas designated for the regular prisoners. They were attacked by a few dozen police functionaries, at whose head was Colonel Józef Brauzg, assistant to the prison warden. Dogs and more police were brought in. Brauzg directed the operation, cursing all the while. We watched this clash from our windows, not being able to help our colleagues in any way. Maybe that is better. Those walking did not respond to the blows, they acted very calmly. None of the internees allowed himself to be provoked. Three were subsequently put in isolation cells. Immediate banging on the walls: the next day we begin a hunger strike. Two return. The third one sits out a week in the isolation cell. A half-victory. On February 13, the next hunger strike. We protest against the Draconian sentences issued by summary courts against Union members in all of Poland. In the Toruń region, six people got three and a half years apiece for lighting candles on the anniversary of the December 1970 strikes. We cannot do anything else for them, our helplessness hurts. We were able to stand five days of the hunger strike. Almost all of us held out with the exception of the sick. Our hunger strike triggered a reaction in the office of the police commander of the voivodeship. The head of the SB, Colonel Grochowski, came to see us personally. They tried to dissuade people from striking and sought the leaders. They even promised to release those who would capitulate. News of the hunger strike soon got to Toruń, in spite of the fact that no one was allowed to see us; even the priest was denied entry on Sunday. At the same time there was a trial going on in the voivodeship court against people from Regional Headquarters. This was not a summary trial and the sentence was suspended. The public in the courtroom stood up and applauded, and handed red and white carnations to our colleagues. We felt that, in our own way, we had also participated in this trial.

They would regularly release five to six people per week. The released internees refused to sign loyalty oaths. From time to time, however, they tried to convince us to collaborate with the SB, but later they gave this up. The police functionaries from Bydgoszcz wanted to be apolitical, at least that is what they said in conversations with our colleagues. There is also a certain loosening up of camp routine. One day the cells were opened for a few hours. We could move around freely. We were in no hurry, however, to make these little excursions, certainly not then when they wanted us to make them.

They even offered to let us watch a film after the television news. At the beginning there were no takers. The guards began to change their attitude toward us. After three months, they understood that we had nothing in common with the label "dangerous assassins." A thin thread of understanding is being woven between us. The visits of Bishops Przykucki and Czerniak contribute a great deal, as do the Sunday masses and the books which we request from home.

There are fifteen-minute strikes in Toruń and Bydgoszcz on March 19. People are locked up. Our "guardians" try to blackmail us: you will be released when there is an end to Union activities, when the leaflets disappear. In spite of this, people are being released. Something begins to happen around us. The prisoners notice a sudden tightening up of camp routine. They tell us that this is a sign that changes are underway. On March 31, the guards tell us to pack up because we are leaving. Some of us do not want to move until we know where we are going. Others feel that this type of resistance is senseless, especially since our pavilion is suddenly flooded with blue uniforms. Under the circumstances, the rest of us admit that it is senseless to resist. Trying to soften the situation, the warden promises that as soon as he finds out where we are to be, he will inform our families. All forty-five internees are piled into three waiting vans. At first we drive to voivodeship police headquarters in Bydgoszcz, where we get gas and where the drivers probably get their instructions. We know that we are supposed to go north, in the direction of Gdańsk. After a few hours of being on the road and losing our way, the convoy drives up to Strzebielinek. The prison warden, as it turns out later, Major Franciszek Kaczmarek, greets us as does the singing of our interned colleagues. There are shouts and greetings. Now we find out that only people from Gdańsk are here. The two cells which housed the best singers were vacated for our arrival. We found out quickly that we had to preserve that fine Strzebielinek tradition. The prison authorities were mistaken to think that the singing would end, and at 10:45 we said the "Our Father" and had singing as usual. On April 12 two more of our colleagues from Toruń, from the textile firm Merinotex, were brought to camp.

MONDAY, APRIL 5

The last visitors brought a lot of new information about camps in all of Poland. Some of our colleagues are in camps that enforce a very strict prison regimen, not differing much from the one imposed upon regular inmates. In others there are incidents of beatings: the most drastic example of this took place in Iława and that barely a few days ago. The matter is still unresolved. The Church became interested in this by accident, as did the deputies and the western press agencies.

On Sunday, in his conversations with women waiting for their visits, the major confirmed the rumors that many internees were about to be released before the holidays. He was supposed to have said that about thirty people were going to be released. We assume that those will be released first who have applied to emigrate or those who are ill and appear on the Red Cross lists. Except that the list of those who want to emigrate has suddenly shrunk. Many internees decided to rethink the issue and decided that the earlier decision was too sudden. As a result of the releases, which are supposed to affect all the camps, some of the camps will be closed down altogether. The guards say that our colleagues from Mielecin will be brought here. Among the ill, there are many whose health would invalidate the internment so they could undergo treatment. But the doctors do not decide who will be released, the security police do.

Our colleagues from Potulice are in the first and second pavilions. They have already been absorbed into our life here and they fight hard to regain the rights that they had won in the other camp. They encounter the major's resistance and he defends himself by saying that he is acting on the orders of the district police office in Toruń, which desires that our group be isolated from the one from Potulice. This is not even technically possible as, except for two cells in the second pavilion, they are all located in the first pavilion. The warden tries to maintain this division at least superficially, but it is easy to see that this will break down any day now and we will be able to meet together even if only within the pavilions.

Our colleague, Janek Samsonowicz, sent us, through normal, censored channels, a description of his new "home." He was taken from Strzebielinek to an unknown destination by way of Gdańsk. He ended up in Iława:

> This is a regular pen, with all the usual "comforts," including a toilet that is not separated from the rest of the cell. The windows are covered with "blinds," from which you can see only a piece of the street (ten square meters of it), one 100-watt light bulb, small cell. The prison library is well stocked with rare books that are hard to find even in the Polish Academy of Sciences. The people, as everywhere, are cheerful and uppity. We live in a several-storied building where we occupy two of the stories. There are internees here from Elbląg, Olsztyn, Gdańsk, Ostroda, and other smaller towns. An additional "attraction" are the prisoners (from seventeen to twenty-five years old). The internees cannot attend the inmates' carpentry school. There is, however, an hour's walk, a reading room, television, and a bathroom where you can get fungus. As in the rest of the camps, so here, too, the menu is dominated by "a liter of soup that is impossible to identify."

They are visited by strange people who claim that they are there privately or on goodwill missions. The bishop of Płock came to see them (the letter was sent before the last "truncheoning" on March 25). Antoni Macierewicz is also among them and he claims that, thanks to internment, he will finally be able to complete work toward his chronically neglected doctorate. He is doing a study of some ancient civilization.

Today there are 144 internees in camp plus seven of us in the hospital in Wejherowo. Two hundred eighty-four internees, counting ourselves, have passed through our camp. According to official statistics, there are currently 3,147 internees in Poland.

THURSDAY, APRIL 8

Today we inaugurated lectures at our camp "university." Jasiu Bartczak, a theologian, began classes with a talk on the social teachings of the Church. Already we see how enormous the subject is and how little known it was in the Union. Actually, Solidarity not only took its inspiration from these teachings, but also concrete formulations of its own program. The first lecture had an incredible attendance in our camp chapel. It was decided that there would be more of these kinds of lectures from all disciplines. We will be adding sessions on the history of art, the development of culture, political thought, as well as on astrophysics. We will not exclude new subjects if we have the people to conduct the classes. There are already three language classes on two levels: German, English, and French. All of this is the result of the arrival of the internees from Potulice, who helped allay the authorities' fears that this kind of activity did not go on in other camps. This certainly was not the case.

After almost a week of discussion, we decided that the subject of emigration must end in some kind of general declaration that must be signed by members of the National Commission and Regional Headquarters who find themselves here in camp. For the last few days, this text has circulated in camp. A definite majority is against the suggestion of some of our colleagues that those should emigrate who have the trust of Union leaders, so that they could finally introduce a little order into the organizational activity of those who found themselves abroad when martial law was declared. We feel, however, that sending "special" people would bring the Union more harm than good. It would give the authorities a good reason to show that Solidarity "plays dirty." At any rate, this declaration is undergoing animated discussion. It is worthwhile, therefore, to include it here:

Colleagues! In connection with the emigration operation carried on by the SB in our camp in Strzebielinek, we feel obliged to state the following: (1) We feel that everybody who emigrates and holds a Union office by election should resign from that office before leaving the country; (2) When going abroad, Union members or those performing various Union functions should go abroad as *private individuals.* In no case should they consider themselves representatives of our Union abroad, nor should they be viewed as people acting abroad with the permission of the Union; (3) In normal conditions, permanent emigration would be the private matter of the émigré. In the current situation in which our country and Union find themselves, and which finds us hostages in the camp in Strzebielinek, we do not consider anyone's leaving the country exclusively his own private matter.

For the members of the National Commission
and Gdańsk Regional Headquarters,
Konrad   April 2, 1982

Yesterday a special team from district police headquarters in Toruń arrived in camp. That team consisted of the police chief, Colonel Zenon Marcinowski, and the chief of the SB, Colonel Grochowski. They came now, as they said, because there had not been enough time in Potulice.

Now they wanted to find out what conditions their wards found themselves in, and "to have a little talk": There were not too many internees eager to have a conversation with them, but those who did decide to see them later emphasized their unusual kindness and courtesy. As a result of their visit, one man from Toruń was released, and two received seven-day passes. These were the first passes ever issued in our camp.

From monitoring radio broadcasts, we know that purges are taking place at higher institutions of learning of rectors chosen democratically during the Solidarity period. Professor Henryk Samsonowicz, the rector of the University of Warsaw, is no longer fulfilling his duties. People say that the government is preparing its next moves, and that the rector of Gdańsk University, Professor Robert Głębocki, will be the next to lose his job. In spite of these threats, others do not seem intimidated. Irena Sankiewicz, the deputy rector of Gdańsk Polytechnic, has already visited a group of students here twice and she let them know that the Polytechnic was trying to get them released.

GOOD FRIDAY, APRIL 9

I went to the chapel a few minutes before three today. No one was there and I sat alone for fifteen minutes under the window from which I could see, between the neighboring pavilion and the garages, a small stretch of forest. I opened the Gospel According to St. Mark and then that of St. Luke, which described the Passion of Our Lord. Of course I know these words well, but I have never tried to delve as deeply into the words of that description as I did today in camp. It is true that man is incapable of completely understanding someone else's tragedy until he himself has experienced something similar. The attitude of the Sanhedrin, Pilate's actions, the manner in which Barabbas was released: today all of these seemed to be a part of a universal description of the workings of a specific mechanism, made up of political obstinancy, someone's cowardice, another's laziness, which cause one not to think through certain moral principles out of fear of complications or simply out of fear. That is how the people reacted when they were asked: whom do you want me to free? And the crowd, infiltrated by bribed agents, shouted: We want Barabbas!

Then suddenly others appeared in the chapel and we began to sing Lenten hymns.

HOLY SATURDAY, APRIL 10

Today we have an unexpected visitor, one of the bishops from the diocese of Gniezno, Jan Nowak, who came in the company of the prison chaplain from Potulice, Józef Kutermak. This works out well because we have just put up a six-foot, rough wooden cross with barbed wire wrapped around its arms and a white piece of cloth speared to the wood and hanging from it, creating something like a figure. Tadeusz Szczudłowski and Jan Koziatek designed this moving arrangement. The cross was made in camp with the help of the rest of the internees and regular prisoners and we asked the bishop to bless it. This solemn occasion was attended by practically everyone in camp and the ceremony ended with everyone signing the cross. The priests accompanying the bishops brought packages from farmers who had belonged to the local rural Solidarity union. The pastor from the church in Gniew also gave us eggs along with Easter wishes from local farmers.

Because of this we almost forgot that we were spending the Easter holidays in prison. We looked forward to Easter Sunday with as much excitement as usual.

Taking advantage of the presence of the priests, we asked about how much truth there was in the rumors about internment of disobedient priests. In the voivodeship of Gdańsk, the names of twenty-five priests were included in the lists of potential internees, among them: Henryk Jankowski, the pastor of the shipyard parish; Stanisław Bogdanowicz, pastor of the Marian Basilica; Hilary Jastak, pastor of the Most Blessed Heart of Jesus parish in Gdynia; and two priests from the Gdańsk Curia, Stanisław Dułak and Zbigniew Bryk. Yesterday, probably in order to allay people's fears on this subject, fragments of a press conference with Minister Kuberski were shown on television.

MONDAY, APRIL 12

The Church wants to make up for our having to spend another set of holidays far from our families. Another gala today: the Gdańsk bishop who has been anticipated for so long, Lech Kaczmarek, has finally come to Strzebielinek. Before mass, we had a chance to meet with him as a group in one of the cells.

The bishop told us about the results of the various attempts at intervention with the government on our behalf. Apparently the way in which the refusals are made by the army spokesman, Colonel Zenon Molczyk, is significant. He dismissed some of the appeals with a short refusal, at other times the refusal was accompanied by the short comment "Release is impossible at this time." We asked the bishop about his meeting with the new Gdańsk *wojewoda*, General Mieczyslaw Cygan. The brutal repressions used against us do not exclude courteous treatment of the Church hierarchy. In answer to the bishop's words about the universal imperatives that issue from the Gospels, the General eagerly conceded that he agreed with them, and that they were the same as the ideas of Communism. So it seems that all differences of opinion are reconcilable in his office, but we gain nothing by it.

The last traces of bitterness vanished during the extraordinarily interesting homily improvised by the bishop. Our cross deeply impressed him and his sermon was dedicated to the symbolism of the cross. He talked about the two tendencies that dominate the life of a man: the one that draws him toward what is higher, toward God, and the other which draws him on his own level, the horizontal, to that which is the human community.

From our visitors we get information about the trial of a group of shipyard workers including Alojzy Szablewski. Members of the Shipyard and general Polish December Strike Committee were charged with violating Article 46 of the decree: organizing a strike during martial law. The testimony of witnesses is very interesting, especially that of Klemens Gniech, the former director of the Gdańsk Shipyard. He was asked to describe the damage done to the shipyard by the strikes. He answered that greater damage was done by the tanks that broke down the gates and by the forces of law and order that smashed offices and destroyed things. He also added that if it had not been for martial law, the shipyard would have been able to meet its production quota by the end of the year. Director Gniech will remain in the memories of the shipyard workers as a man who was able to maintain his dignity at one of the most difficult moments for dockworkers and for himself. That is probably why he was removed from his job.

Another incident, an article that appeared at the beginning of April in *Gazeta Współczesna*, will go down in the annals of infamous journalism. The article was called "A Day Among the Interned," and described the women's internment camp in Gołdapia. The author's name is worth remembering: Dionizy Sidorski. The article reeks of revulsion towards the women locked up in camp. He writes of women growing fat in luxury who have gone a little crazy from being locked up and so attack the young and elegant soldiers indiscriminately. The soldiers turn away from these solicitations with repugnance. In their free moments, between stuffing themselves and soliciting the soldiers, the women spend their time composing vicious songs, in which they threaten that avengers will come. Sidorski suggests that no one will come to help these women as none of them could possibly find anyone willing to do so. These words were written by a Polish journalist about women deprived of even the opportunity to defend themselves. The nauseating hatred permeating that whole publication is even more incomprehensible when one takes into account the fact that this journalist's own daughter by a previous marriage is among the women in Gołdapia. Together with the article came the news that Sidorski's daughter considers her father's article reason enough to finally break off all relations with him.

THURSDAY, APRIL 15

Today they gave "passes" to freedom! Usually for a few days, but in some cases up to the maximum, one week, after "consideration" of a particular case. These passes were immediately taken by some of our colleagues, who had either serious family problems or matters that needed attention, i.e., health problems. Others took advantage of the passes to get away from here for a few days.

The news that such possibilities exist was told to us by Major Kaczmarek two days ago. Not too many people know about it, however, because some of us disagree as to what the request for a pass means. One has to write a request for a pass in order to get one.

The passes were issued by the acting commander of the voivodeship. People say that this man, Colonel Paszkiewicz, will become the next commander in the near future. Paszkiewicz received people in a room where a psychologist had been installed not too long ago. The psychologist was accompanied by a dark, intelligent *ubek*, who during his talks (done individually) with internees, would shuffle through dossiers and hand his boss the more important material. Both of them were very nice and emphasized that they were not treating the internee simply as a camp number. They took into account the internee's background, his education, and professional status before internment and they did not avoid the courteous forms of address such as "Mr. Engineer" and the like. Real courtesy . . . they were interested in camp conditions and fretted over the mistakes made during the mass arrests on December 12/13, assuring us that if they had to repeat this operation on such a massive scale, which they hoped, for our sake and theirs, would not happen, then they would try to carry it out even more efficiently and without those little mistakes. They emphasized that there was not a single life lost that night on the Coast in spite of the scale of the operation, and that they personally were very happy about that. They warned the internees who had gotten passes that, contrary to the practice in camp, no one was allowed to wear Solidarity or any other union pins outside the camp gates, and that commemorative ceremonies marking anniversaries of the workers' strikes were also banned, or one "could have trouble," including a sentence and prison term.

We said good-bye to our colleagues who left with passes. Some of us feel that this type of contact with representatives of the organs of repression are a manifestation of weakness and an indirect acceptance of martial law. Others feel that freedom is freedom and that there is always more to do outside of the walls than there is sitting here. What the *ubeks* think about the matter is unimportant.

I personally feel that perhaps it would be best if we demurred on the passes, but each man carries within himself the consciousness of his own limits which he cannot overstep, so that personal motives may justify applying for a pass.

SUNDAY, APRIL 18

As if in answer to the question bothering us about what society is feeling and thinking, a questionnaire has appeared in camp. This is a survey that was done at the end of March and beginning of April of this year in Gdańsk.

The survey covered about 108 people most of which are technicians, doctors, and teachers. We judge that the small number of participants in the survey was determined by practical difficulties: this kind of activity would certainly interest the SB. The first question pertained to the duration of martial law. Thirty-nine persons answered that it would last two to three years. The characteristic remarks of those who believed that martial law was short-lived were "It won't last long because people will rebel," "One or two years, otherwise there will be a revolution," and "It will only last a short time—one year, but the ban on strikes and censorship of letters will last longer." Others said: "until there is a revolution in the USSR," "until the Russians attain their goal, complete control of Europe," "as long as the USSR and the Communist system exists," "when the authorities decide that they are safe" and "until civil war breaks out."

In answer to the next question over fifty percent of the persons participating in the survey felt that trade unions would resume activity this year. But there are doubts as to the authenticity of the "reinstated unions."

The next question was: Will any of the Solidarity leaders work with the "reinstated" trade unions? Forty-seven persons were convinced that they would, fifty-nine said no. Some of the answers were: "No, I do not believe at all that they will be released," "Yes, they will try to be active somewhere, in order to salvage what they can," "Perhaps individuals," "They will not, until the unions are truly free," "A very few, if any, who will justify their move by saying that they must save the Union, but, in fact, they will be adjusting to the system for the sake of their careers," and "It depends on the unions and Wałęsa's behavior."

In answer to the question: will you join the trade unions when they are reactivated, twenty-three persons said yes, twenty said no, adding "certainly not those which will be dependent on the Party and the government," "to independent and real unions—yes," "only if Solidarity will be around," and "I don't know—perhaps they will make me, but I will not be active."

The last two questions of the survey pertained to general problems in Poland connected with elections to the Sejm and to national councils and an evaluation of the media. The survey participants were asked whether they would have a greater or lesser influence on the outcome of the elections compared with the last elections before August 1980. Results: Greater, 15 persons; No change, 34; Lesser, 48. A characteristic comment for those who said they would have a greater influence was that "people will not be voting." Those who said "no change would result," also added "no change, that is, I have no effect on the outcome." One more answer was: "This socialism acknowledges no choices." In the matter of the media, the majority expected only a further deterioration of the media's credibility.

After reading the survey we saw clearly that people on the other side of the prison wall were thinking, as we were, that there was no future in Poland. I do not know how we will live with the consciousness of this fact.

FRIDAY, APRIL 23

Those returning to camp from leaves have to tell us about everything that they saw and heard on the outside. Today I think that there is no sense in looking at what others do, if I get a chance I will try to get a pass. It is not right to cut ourselves off from the life which is going on around us. I have to see how life looks now, I have to boost my family's spirits.

It seems that the workers are maintaining quite a radical position. Some are of the opinion that only a general strike will get rid of martial law. Certain signs indicate this. Those not interned count on our working out a plan of "what to do." The problem is that there is probably no one in Poland who knows what should be done. Nor is there an answer from the groups that were not subjected to pogroms. There are strange proposals of help from organizations and individuals activated by WRON. These people who want to save face offer to help get some of the internees released. They are treated by the internees in the manner they deserve.

A sad realization for us was the observation that "life does not tolerate a vacuum," it goes forward, new people take our places. On the other hand, however, the attitude of large sectors of society toward the internees and their families is very moving. There is much evidence of help, thoughtfulness, and recognition of our struggle and the expectation "that we will survive." That is all true, but at the same time, we see that we are on the sidelines, that those that are out there count first. Quite a few bitter thoughts.

SATURDAY, APRIL 24

It was not until the arrival of the internees from the camp in Potulice that we realize how different the two camps were, shaped by the varying conditions of internment. The group from Potulice arrived with its rank and file intact, organized according to Union organizational models established during the period when Solidarity functioned normally. Their structures, union hierarchy, their unified actions in specific matters, the ability to work out a definite position on various issues, and also the institutionalization of certain habits and camp liturgy. Compared to them we appear to be quite a loose collectivity, made up of many individualists and I cannot say whether that is good or bad . . . In Potulice, the internees made up a separate group, occupying a separate section of a prison that housed 2,000 inmates, and it was necessary for them, in these circumstances, to emphasize their otherness and to demonstrate their belonging to Solidarity. In Strzebielinek, meanwhile, we were a group "for ourselves" and we did not abide by Union structures and organizational hierarchy. We formed, instead, informal bonds of affection and respect, that were based on the behavior of that individual in camp. During the few months that we were together, there was no lack of opportunity to observe and evaluate our colleagues. We were a collectivity that reacted very sensitively to that which went on around us, and now we know quite a bit about each other. This kind of evaluation is based not only on one's belonging to this group or another, when the dockworkers had it good and could decide their views in an open forum, but also, and perhaps even first of all, on an internee's behavior during a hunger strike, his skill in arguing with the representatives of the prison warden, a boldness in voicing an unpopular analysis of his own mistakes and the unmasking of demagoguery, little needed in our circumstances.

But that is probably how it is. One set of characteristics is demanded during a period of fighting, others at a "dark hour," still others during a time of summing up experiences and planning for the future.

Now it is easy to see that a relatively strong spirit of self-government was characteristic of Gdańsk as a whole. The actions here were not as coordinated as in other regions, where often the whole organization acted on one word from Union headquarters. That is probably why there were relatively fewer mistakes during the period of Solidarity's existence and that is why Gdańsk was treated by the authorities as the most dangerous "source of the plague."

MONDAY, APRIL 26

There is a great offensive on to get internees to sign the declaration of loyalty forms. This is Captain Maciuk's last great effort before the anticipated release of a large group of internees. That is why he admitted that letting people know about this without attaching a list of those to be released, creates a situation in which people "soften up," especially when some have been counting on being released for a month now.

The release of internees is connected, of course, with

May 1 and will be accompanied by a lot of hullabaloo—that is, the participation of press, television, and radio reporters. The authorities are frantically searching for someone willing to say a few words to the camera in the name of the released internees. This time the text of the declaration of loyalty forms sounds like this: "I declare to the undersigned, and I confirm with my own signature, that I vow to strictly abide by the existing legal order, and, specifically, not to undertake any kind of activity harmful to the Polish People's Republic." We assume that WRON must have a present for public opinion in the form of releases and that this business with the signature is only its swan song. We inform our colleagues, who are called in for talks, of this.

Expecting a television show to accompany our release, we organized a meeting in the reading room, during which our more experienced colleagues inform everyone that they still have a right to their own faces and that television will be acting illegally if it tries to film us without our knowledge. We discuss how to get reporters sent to us by the UB off our backs.

FRIDAY, APRIL 30

Yesterday, a few minutes after eight, a whole *ubek* television crew showed up. The internees who were out on a walk interrupted it so as not to lend themselves to any special shots. Certain internees were called into the visitation hall right away. It was decided that since they had missed their freedom, they would gladly agree to appear on camera at the moment when a police representative solemnly presents them with release papers. They were shocked that the internees preferred to return to their cells. Those who remained in their cells refused to meet with these people. Suddenly there was a running around and many attempts to convince us to attend the "ceremony." The determined resistance of the internees finally convinced them to remove the television crew from the camp grounds, but, even so, the majority refused to go get their release papers. They felt that since they had been taken from their homes at night, there was no need to celebrate leaving. In the first pavilion, there was a television editor from a Gdańsk station, a bald, blond type who kept spouting something about "the truth of this moment" which he wanted to capture. We asked him where he was when we were being arrested and why the sudden longing for truth? He was a real turnip, completely devoid of dignity and pride in his importunity. His name is Dziedzic. Captain Biegaj walked around in the company of Alexandra Chomicka, a woman journalist from *Wieczór Wybrzeża* who was suddenly advanced to reporter during "the war." Earlier she was in charge of writing trivia for the city desk. She, too, pestered us to say at least a few words. She was also asked why she got interested in the problems of the internees so late. Yesterday, during visitation time, we also find out that one of the editors from the radio, Lidia Dąbrowska, is trying to get the students who are leaving Strzebielinek to talk with her. There was something strange in this. All of these people, who were our age and working in the media, were utterly without tact and a feeling for the situation in which we found ourselves. There is an abyss of moral judgment between us, between what we are living through and what for them is only the fulfillment of a police order given to their superiors.

Yesterday people were released and today a few more internees were released from the hospital in Wejherowo. Forty-seven persons were released (altogether, 102 are left). The television editor who was flushed out of camp, reported in a local television program that sixty-eight persons remained. He ignored the group of internees from Potulice. Among the released were two secondary school students, one student from Gdańsk Polytechnic, a few chairmen from Solidarity factory committees from the Tri-City area and the voivodeship of Gdańsk, two members of the presidium of Regional Headquarters, and three Union workers from the region. Teodor Herra was released from the hospital and was supposed to have been transferred to Darłówek, but the sharp opposition of the doctors fearing more heart problems protected him from that transfer. This was one of the many examples of a personal settling of accounts. Mr. Herra was a serious candidate of the team that belonged to Solidarity for director of the shipping warehouse in Gdynia, and, in addition, was a well-known and highly valued professional in the shipping branch of the industry. He had great prestige in professional circles. Dr. Włodzimier Misiewicz, or "the lawyer" as we called him in camp, was also released. He was the author of many legal documents concerning the functioning of the Union. He was already interned when he received a government award for one of his publications. In his time he was the chief justice of the county court in nearby Lębork, where, apparently, he did not subordinate himself to police suggestions zealously enough. Most recently he was the chairman of the workers' union in the Maritime Institute.

Analyzing the releases, except for the releases of the ill, we noticed a clear trend in the direction of releasing workers, and even regional Union leaders if they were workers. Captain Maciuk once told someone in conversation that he prefers to release a worker who will return to his job rather than an intellectual, who will begin to write, muddle the waters and do more harm than good on the outside. For this reason, Zbyszek Lis, a man already well known at the time of the shipyard strike, and Henryk Łapiński, a member of the shipyard commission of Solidarity, are released.

There have been 800 internees released in all of Poland

and 200 are "on leave." Jan Kułaj also found himself among the released internees and after watching an interview with him on television, we do not know what to think. It looks as if the rumors about his lack of psychological resilience and political experience are true. Kułaj, who became a symbol of farmers organizing themselves, is now nothing.

While some of us are being released, the SB is attacking the young people who have committed themselves to defend Solidarity. A sentence of three years in prison was given to seventeen-year-old Anna Stawicka, a fourth-year lyceum student.

Our students from the Independent Student Union were prepared to leave us for the umpteenth time. This time their deputy rector, Irena Sankiewicz, came to pick them up. It turned out that she had been given the wrong information. Maciuk claimed that he was not satisfied with the progress of their resocialization: they participate in camp demonstrations, they put candles in cell windows, and show no remorse.

MONDAY, MAY 3

We have May 1, the working class holiday, and the anniversary of the Constitution of May 3 behind us. On May 1, a symbolic ceremony was organized by the internees. A column of fours with Leon Stobiecki, who carried red tulips, at its head, read the roll of the dead with Konrad Maruszcyk leading the invocations:

> I invoke you, workers, who died in the first demonstration in Chicago for freedom, dignity, and the right to form unions and better living conditions— May they rest in peace!

I invoke you, workers of Poznań, who died in June 1956, while fighting for bread and freedom—May they rest in peace!

I invoke you, workers of the Baltic Coast from Gdańsk, Gdynia, Elbląg and Szczecin, who gave your lives in 1970 while fighting for better living conditions and for new trade unions—May they rest in peace!

I invoke you, miners of Katowice, who in December 1981 died at the hands of the police while defending our organization, the independent, self-governing trade union, Solidarity, and our inviolable rights, in the defense of freedom and democracy—May they rest in peace!

In invoke all of you, who gave your lives so that we could live in freedom and dignity—May they rest in peace!

The text of the roll of the dead was repeated from behind the bars by our colleagues from pavilions I and II who were not allowed to take their constitutionals. A 100-voice chorus repeating the invocation "May they rest in peace!" moved those of us who were participating as well as the prison guards, who seemed to shrink when confronted with the power of the idea which we were expressing. The reading of the roll was followed by a moment of silence. We concluded with the singing of the national anthem and returned quietly to our cells.

Today, on the anniversary of the May 3 Constitution, a special mass was said and in the afternoon, we all sang the national anthem and religio-patriotic songs. In the afternoon in the chapel, Antek Wręga lectured on the history and significance of May 3.

In the morning hours, the first groups to go out on walks painted a "V" sign and The Fighting Poland sign (a P with an anchor) on the guard booth between pavilions I and II. In all of the cell windows were small commemorative posters depicting a crowned eagle holding a May 3 Constitution scroll and red and white flags in its claws. Some of the cells hung out masts (some were quite a few yards long) with flags that were visible from beyond the prison compound. Competition was a factor: which cell would erect the highest mast. In the III pavilion one of the "builders" shot a mast eight yards into the air. It was made of slats from the paneling in the reading room, tied together. The guards panicked because the symbols of the resistance movement were painted practically on their very backs, and they ordered the internees to remove them. Neither paint thinner nor soap did the job, however, and the guards ordered the internees to plaster over the area. After the plaster dried, the signs "miraculously" floated up from below. The secret was a special mixture of shoe polish, oil, and soot, concocted by colleagues who were experienced in this sort of thing.

Just as yesterday the warden had to do battle with the flag that was displayed high above the prison wall over pavilion I (he had to order the guards to climb onto the roof and break the flagstaff), so today Captain Maciuk had his share of camp warfare. He tore a flag with a white eagle off of one of the cell walls and a colleague tore it out of his hand. At first Maciuk was struck dumb but then he began to shout that this constitutes an attack on a prison functionary and that he would have everyone sent to a camp with more severe regulations. The boys in the cell looked at each other and asked: Did anyone see anything? Maciuk had committed one of the classic violations of regulations: he was alone. He had to satisfy himself with slamming the doors. The prison authorities are visibly tense. The Commemorations had exceeded their expectations. The major threatens to have those who participated in these "confrontations" shipped to other, stricter camps.

While thinking about the significance of the May 3 Constitution, I flip through the last issues of weeklies that were published before martial law. In *Życie Literackie* (early December 1981) a fragment of an interview with Professor Henryk Samsonowicz, who has been removed from his post as rector at the University of Warsaw, is reprinted:

> The May 3 Constitution functioned for exactly one year and two months. It was defeated but, first of all, let us consider what an enormous role it played not in the course of that year, because not much could be changed then, but in the course of the next decades, when it gave faith and strength, when it shaped the national psyche and allowed us to survive 150 years of bondage. Secondly, the May 3 Constitution, which changed a very bad system and was not really timely, was able, despite the fact that it was overthrown by force, to formulate certain issues in such a way that the new Grodno constitutions had to accept some of the ideas of that Constitution even though they were its negation. In short, there is no going back from certain phenomena and certain achievements . . .

Will this be true for Solidarity?

A moment ago I returned from watching the second edition of the evening television news. Our national "unity" looks pretty pathetic. On the one hand, there are numerous demonstrations in many cities, especially in Warsaw and Gdańsk, which are an expression of the feelings of the people; and, on the other hand, the session of the Sejm, which is labeled historical. Comparisons are made with the May 3, 1791 session, during which the most famous of our constitutions was ratified. The whole propaganda concept is contained in the following contradiction: the Sejm currently in session, "the representative" of the national will, lent its full support to the government, which appears in the role of martyr to "unity." This "unity" was undermined by society, which gave in to the rabble and did not listen to the government which was doing so much for the people. The authorities, therefore, have no choice but to eliminate all opponents of national "unity." On the one hand there are blackmail and threats, and on the other, especially after Rakowski's address to the Sejm, there are attempts to win the young people and the scholarly and cultural community. He appealed for action and discouraged "internal emigration." Except that the field of action must be delineated not by those interested, but by the authorities themselves!

We received another transport of internees (two re-internees from Słupsk and four students from the first and second year of study at the Higher Naval Academy in Gdynia). Preparations are underway in camp to receive another transport. We assume that this time these will be people who participated in the May 1 and May 3 demonstrations and we hope to get a first-hand description of what went on.

TUESDAY, MAY 4

We are getting more and more information about the actions in the Tri-City area. We get accounts of the May 1 ceremonies in Gdańsk. "You want a parade, you will get a parade!" was the battle cry of the demonstrators. Even when we had no information, we were sure that something would be planned in Gdańsk and that the people would not let us down. In Gdańsk people marched past government buildings in independent groups and took down the flags on display as if to show that these colors were their property, not the government's The crowds got as far as Lech's apartment house on Zaspa. So we were not alone in Strzebielinek that day during the reading of the roll for the dead.

There were rather dramatic occurrences in the Marian Basilica in Gdańsk during a solemn mass celebrated on the anniversary of the ratification of the May 3 Constitution. As early as 4 P.M. ZOMO patrols were breaking up people that were calmly heading for the Basilica. The patrols would not allow them to get near the church. In spite of these obstacles, and the use of tear gas and petards, the Basilica was full before 6 P.M. and, as there was no more room in the church, several thousand people gathered at the gates. These people became the targets of police attacks. After the sermon, the police began firing petards directly at the crowds gathered at the gates of the Basilica. The church square was full of thick smoke. Through the two open doors of the Basilica, the police fired two petards which went right over the head of the priest (Wiesław Lauer, Chancellor of the Bishops' Curia in Gdańsk) celebrating mass. The petard landed in the chapel of Our Lady of Częstochowa and tore through a national banner. Panic broke out in the Basilica. The pastor, Stanisław Bogdanowicz, managed to calm the people down. Flames appeared in the choir loft, next to the rebuilt organ. The fire was put out with the help of fire extinguishers. In the meantime, people began carrying the wounded into the sacristy. A teenage boy had two fingers blown off of one hand and another person was suspected of having had a heart attack. Over a dozen people received medical treatment.

After mass, the people leaving were showered with tear gas and petards and sprayed with water. The crowd was in disarray and threw itself into the narrow streets of the Old Town, where it was pursued by ZOMOs and often got caught in ZOMO crossfire. People hid in whatever homes or apartments were nearby, but even there they were pursued by shots aimed at the windows of the buildings. The police detained several hundred people.

Today's sensation at the hospital in Wejherowo was the visit paid to our colleagues by Danuta Wałęsa and Anna Kowalczykowa, Lech Wałęsa's secretary. A few of our internees happened to be at the hospital for examinations. They brought a lot of news back with them. Each of us wants to find out as many details as possible, someone is always asking about something.

WEDNESDAY, MAY 5

We are anticipating about fifteen lectures in May under the auspices of our camp university. They will be given in the chapel on Mondays, Tuesdays, Thursdays, and Fridays, at 5:30, two hours before evening roll. Subjects: Workers' Rights (Dr. L. Kaczyński), The Social Teachings of Catholicism (J. Bartczak, M.A.), The Development of Polish Political Thought in the Nineteenth and Twentieth Centuries (A. Jarmakowski, M.A.), The Holy Father, John Paul II (Dr. A. Drzycimski), The Primate of the Millennium, Stefan Cardinal Wyszyński (J. Bartczak, M.A.), Sacral Art (A. Szymkowski, M.A.), and Astrophysics (Dr. A. Stawikowski). Some of these subjects were prepared as topics presented in the context of a larger cycle of lectures, others are connected with sad occasions, such as the attempt to assassinate the Holy Father and the anniversary of the death of the Primate. At the same time we will continue a cycle of discussions during which we analyze Solidarity and its specific political currents.

Another four people from the Tri-City area: a student from the Higher Naval Academy in Gdynia, a docent from the Gdańsk Polytechnic, an artist, a sea captain, and five re-internees from Toruń. These are not yet the people from the May demonstrations, because these internees were detained in late April. All of the internees from the Tri-City area, just as the four students brought in the day before yesterday, have a clause ("participates in activity that supports the illegal actions of criminal groups in the conspiracy") inserted into their bills of internment. Our new colleagues had not been on the initial internment lists. In camp there are already 117 internees.

THURSDAY, MAY 6

From Ryszard Kapuściński's book, *Shah of Shahs:*

The Shah's reflex was typical of all despots: first strike and suppress, then consider your next move. First show muscle, show force, then prove that you also have a head. It is important to despots that you admire their strength. It is less important to admire their wisdom. After all, what to a despot's thinking, is wisdom? It is skill in applying force. Wise is he who knows when and how to strike. A constant demonstration of force is necessary because the pillars of dictatorship are the lowest instincts of the masses, which the dictatorship liberates in its subjects: fear, aggressiveness toward other men, and servility. These instincts are most efficiently aroused by fear, and the source of fear is the fear of force.

. . .

We are getting more details about the ideological pacifications of various sectors in Gdańsk. In addition to doing direct battle on one front with dockworkers, who have been "verified" several times beginning with the historical act in the hall, "Olivia," the government is also taking stronger measures with writers, and radio and television personnel.

From the actions of the police it would seem that WRON wanted, first of all, to destroy all symbols of Solidarity as brutally as possible. The hall in which the first National Congress of Solidarity was held was used by the government to issue work permits, to "break the spell" of the various places which were so full of meaning for the people of the Tri-City area. The moderate and increasingly popular Gdańsk weekly, *Czas*, suffered most, along with the Party daily, *Głos Wybrzeża* and the local television station. There were somewhat fewer workers dismissed in the local Polish Radio station.

The WRON representative in charge of journalists in the Gdańsk area was a certain Commodore Franciszek Czerski, whose wife was the director of personnel in a Kraków publishing firm in the 1950s. I don't need to remind anyone of what this meant at that time. She is still in journalism and now works in the offices of *Dziennik Bałtycki*. It seems that people are chosen according to the old *ubek* models, the most efficient ones in times of great change. Commodore Czerski vel Krawiec, as he was called in the 1950s, was a jurist who took part in the bloody trial of high-ranking naval officers, which ended with death sentences and prison sentences so brutal that only a few people survived to be rehabilitated in the post-October upheavals. It was this Commodore Krawiec-Czerski who received full power over journalists. He took advantage of it without embarrassment and let the world know that he was going to destroy everyone who had taken any part in the post-August changes. And not just people who had been for Solidarity but also those activists from the Association of Polish Journalists who wanted to create self-governing organizations which would protect journalists from the manipulations of any political decisionmakers.

As a result of the verification process (carried out by people unknown to anyone) undergone by the editorial board of *Czas*, that weekly closed down. Altogether about ninety Gdańsk journalists were dismissed from the publishing house RSW Press, the Party press, and from radio and television. Television and radio operators and technicians were also included in that number. In proportion to the whole country, where it is said that about 500 journalists lost their jobs, this was the highest percentage because, of the 300 journalists working in the Gdańsk area, one-third had lost their jobs. During the verification process, there were a few very curious incidents and arguments. An example of this could be the verification procedure for Gdańsk television workers, where the editor Bielecki, from Warsaw Television, tried to convince the technicians who prepared films with journalists belonging to Solidarity that they took part in a criminal act, which reminded him personally of the building of crematoria by Nazi criminals in Auschwitz! This is how the Party and WRON settled accounts with the profession that promised the workers in August of 1980 that it would try to present events and the workers' views objectively. An action reminiscent of the cultural revolution in China was the shredding of all Union publications. We were told that, in Łódź, the entire edition of an illustrated album of the August strike was ordered destroyed.

The vacancies that resulted from the dismissal of journalists were filled by the junta with editors professing strict obedience to the new regime or with self-declared *ubeks*. As is always the case in times of trouble, new people show up: unknown publicists; young people ready to buy a career at any price or deceived by the thought of "organic work"; the legions of those who think that they can do their job and still maintain their own opinions; or those who have no such notions.

SATURDAY, MAY 8

We have received information from those close to the Episcopate and the Sejm that indicates the government is wavering and that it lacks a long-term plan for dealing with the internal political tensions in the country. During the night of the first day of war, the authorities wanted to talk to Primate Glemp through the mediation of Kazimierz Barcikowski from the Politburo. The Primate was told about the declaration of martial law and that talks would be held with Wałęsa. It was true that they wanted to talk to him and that is why he was taken from his home. The entire communiqué was kept in this tone. The idea broke down when only minor officials were sent to the talks. This stage of the talks ended with the pacification of the mines in Silesia. The next attempt to ease tensions was made during the implementation of price increases (February). The government proposed that the Church create Christian trade unions, which would function side by side with the unions remaining under the control of the Party. This division was referred to as the division into "yellows" and "reds." The Church staunchly refused, interpreting this as a move to undermine Solidarity. The third stage began recently with talks at the highest level: Glemp, Jaruzelski. We still have no word on what went on at these meetings just as we have none on the talks with the Vatican. We can only assume that the Primate is upholding the position of the Episcopate in matters pertaining to the internees, and that he is fighting for the reactivation of Solidarity while WRON tries to deceive him with promises of relaxing martial law rigors and promises to release some of the internees. In this way, WRON tries to keep the Pope from further involvement in Polish affairs. The government is also probably trying to get new loans and extensions on its old debts through the mediation of the Vatican.

The incessantly repeated information about the relaxing of martial law rigors introduced on May 2 is supposed to mollify world opinion and calm things down at home. It is worth noting this report from *Polityka* (No. 12, May 8, 1982):

A communiqué from the Ministry of Internal Affairs reports the release of 800 internees and the conditional leave of 200 others; the decision to abolish curfew in the whole country; the lifting of the ban on organizing and attending meetings, conferences, training and group excursions without the permission of the authorities; the lifting of the ban on limited travel in areas of Pietrowice, Głuchołazy, Łysa Polana and Piwniczna. On May 10, automatic telephone communications between voivodeships will be restored. *Życie Warszawy* reported the first releases of internees. Included are 351 workers, 24 farmers, 367 intellectuals (31 researchers, 1 actress, 2 writers, 35 students), 64 women (one-third of all the women interned), 154 paid workers of Solidarity. Also released were actress Halina Mikolajska, Dr. Roman Zimand from the Institute of Literary Research (PAN), Ryszard Rubinsztejn and Marian Srebrny from the Institute of Mathematics (PAN), Dr. Jerzy Holzer from the Department of History at the University of Warsaw, Lothar Herbst from the Wrocław branch of the Polish Writers' Union, publicist Alexander Małachowski, Dr. Halina Suwała from the University of Warsaw and historian Władysław Bartoszewski. Wiktor Woroszylski and Adam Macedoński were released on temporary leaves. Also released was the chairman of Rural Solidarity, Jan Kułaj, who after his meeting with the chairman of the Chief Committee of the United Peasants' Party, Vice-Premier Roman Malinowski, appeared on television and expressed his intention to actively participate in the work of the United Peasants' Party.

       .   .   .

From Ryszard Kapuściński's book, *Shah of Shahs:*

Even though the dictatorship despises the people, it curries the people's favor. Even though it is illegal, it cares about maintaining a semblance of legality. It is extremely sensitive on this point, pathologically oversensitive. The dictatorship also suffers from a feeling (deeply hidden) of insecurity. It expends every effort to prove to itself and to others that it has the support and approval of the people. Even if these are just pretense, the dictatorship derives great satisfaction from it. So what if it is all a sham, the entire world of a dictatorship is one great sham.

       .   .   .

People are still being "conscripted" into the camps. At the same time, the guards tell us, on the basis of information from "a certain source," that ten more internees will soon be released. They were talking about this even before May 1 and 3; the authorities thought that the people were pacified and that they would not demand their rights. The communiqué about further releases was supposed to ease tensions. Now the government will want to show how tough it can be and will not go through with the releases.

SUNDAY, MAY 9

From Ryszard Kapuściński's *Shah of Shahs:*

A people oppressed by a despot, reduced to the role of an object and degraded, seeks refuge for itself, seeks a place in which it can entrench itself, shield itself and be itself. This is indispensable for a people to maintain its separateness, its identity, and, simply, its ordinariness. But the entire nation cannot emigrate and that is why it travels not in space but in time. It returns to the past which, in the face of its daily concerns and threats, seems like Paradise Lost. And it finds its refuge in old customs, so old and because of that so sacred, that the ruler fears to attack them. That is why, under the cover of every dictatorship, and in spite of it, there is a gradual rebirth of ancient customs, beliefs, and symbols. They take on new meaning, new challenging meanings. At first this is a timid process and often a clandestine one, but its power and range grow in proportion to the excesses and increasing burdens of the dictatorship.

. . .

Bishop-elect Edmund Piszcz paid us a visit late this afternoon. This time there was an amusing incident connected with his arrival. Maciuk customarily drives the chaplain to camp and this time he wanted to bring the bishop, but the bishop did not wait for him and came on his own. Maciuk arrived after the bishop, livid with rage, because he always emphasizes that no priest can come here without his permission. Captain Maciuk would not earn his keep as an *ubek* if he did not try to make trouble. In his conversation with the bishop, Maciuk said that two masses have to be said, one for each pavilion. This was a strange decision because only one mass had customarily been said for each pavilion. The special intervention of our colleagues allowed us to return to our earlier arrangement. It was important to us to be all together because Bishop Piszcz was supposed to bless the painting of the Madonna of Strzebielinek (done by Antek Szymkowski from Toruń) during that mass. The picture was quite a good copy of the painting of Our Lady of Częstochowa, and Szymkowski intended the Madonna for the Marian Church in Toruń. The painting was framed with large, rough-hewn slats into which were written words that represented the struggles of many generations of Poles. At the top were the words "Faith, Hope and Love," and at the bottom were "Truth, Dignity and Equality." On the sides of the frame were small strips of barbed wire into which were fixed tiny red and white flags. In addition to the painting, the internees from Toruń gave the bishop a message for the people of Toruń. They asked that the words be read in the city's churches. The painting, however, remained in our chapel, because the bishop felt that as long as we were here, it was a very apt symbol which, like the cross, grew out of our faith. He also felt that there would be undue problems with Maciuk, who had already had doubts about the picture made in camp and dedicated to Lech Kaczmarek.

After mass, we talked to our guests as usual. We could see that they were anticipating a worsening of the situation. Even the clergy was expecting repressive measures. Apparently the government has made up lists of priests who are to be interned. People say that some of the May 3 demonstrations were provocations. This would confirm the thoughts we had after watching a short television program on Gdańsk TV. The camera was focusing its attention on a hot-headed fellow who seemed very suspicious-looking to us. A policeman walked up to him, in the presence of a very large crowd, and led him away. Of course this caused some consternation in the crowd that was gathered near the Sobieski monument. It also seems true that the government is looking for someone to guarantee their loans and has turned to the Vatican. But these are secondary matters, because the most important thing is whether or not the Holy Father will come to Poland this year. In his last statements he said clearly that he wants to visit Poland in August of this year on the 600th anniversary of the presence of the painting of The Black Madonna, Our Lady of Częstochowa, on Jasna Góra. The authorities, however, are reluctant to answer, suggesting that the visit should be made in "a more positive political context." Only for whom will it be more positive? The current actions of the government indicate a victory for the confrontational line of thinking. The Solidarity underground has also announced a short strike. People say that mass pressure on the underground leadership of Solidarity is so strong that uncoordinated actions, easy to stifle, could result.

THURSDAY, MAY 13

Yesterday evening we got another group of "new" internees. After a period of quarantine beginning with their detentions of May 1 and 3 at the police stations, they finally got to camp yesterday. They were brought from Grudziądz, Toruń, Gdynia, and Gdańsk. We greeted them solemnly with the song, "So that Poland could be Poland," which we played on the record player. People say that this is not the end and that cells are being prepared for the next shipment of people. Some of the confusion, which is intentional, as usual, is caused by the fact that many of the newcomers are people from the so-called "peripheries" and we are never sure exactly how to treat them. We are obliged to help on principle, but without initiating them into our affairs.

Today at night we reminded everyone that another

month of internment had passed by banging on the doors.

Today's camp count: 156 internees.

MONDAY, MAY 17

Two lectures that had been announced earlier were given today: an official one in the chapel; and then another in pavilion I, in the cell of the internees from Toruń. Krzysztof Wyszkowski, one of the founders of the Free Trade Unions in Gdańsk, talked about their founding and activity.

Of the four new internees brought in today, two of them are here because they were photographing the demonstrations. They were identified by use of the same instrument: the police took pictures of them with their cameras. There is a contest on: who will photograph whom. For the time being, only the people photographed by the plainclothesmen have been punished. Perhaps one of these days, we will balance this account of mutual recognition in photographs.

In cell 17, the major accidentally mentioned something about the mass release of internees in June. Unfortunately, we get confirmation of the rearrest, this time from the camp in Iława, of our "minor," Artur Pisarski. He was accused of taking part in the demonstrations of May 1 and 3, while, in fact, his mother had kept him at home, fearing that he might be arrested again. He was taken from the courtyard of his home, where he had been playing ball with his friends.

THURSDAY, MAY 20

A visit by a delegation of the International Red Cross, accompanied by representatives of the Polish Red Cross and the Ministry of Justice, lasted two days. This was a new group, while we had been expecting the people whom we already knew from the March visit. Both of the representatives of the International Red Cross, two Swiss, were far more tense than their predecessors. It turned out that the others had had problems: they had been accused of too much interference in camp administrative matters, and of acting outside of their areas of competence as established in the agreements between the International Red Cross and WRON. That is why these representatives (who had a great deal of experience and were quite competent—one had just returned from El Salvador) constantly emphasized the limits of their competence as being restricted to matters of health and social welfare. The delicacy of the agreement was, as they put it, based on the fact that they had the regime's permission to do their work, but could simultaneously look into the dirtiest corners of that new order. We understood this and limited ourselves to the issues they indicated.

They asked us to put together a complete list of internees: first and last names, date of birth, place of birth, date and place of internment, address, the first names of both parents. They explained to us that this information would help them set up (in Geneva) one central, world file of political prisoners, and that this file would be useful as evidence allowing them to keep track of us in the case of an eventual deportation into the "unknown," in the footsteps of our forefathers. The world, it seems, has not forgotten that experience. At the same time, we were able to figure out that the average age of an internee in Strzebielinek is 31.5 years. A similar visit was paid to the hospital in Wejherowo, where they thoroughly familiarized themselves with the files of the internees undergoing treatment.

At then end of April, beginning of May, we had a camp branch in Wejherowo. The sick internees who were hospitalized by doctors' orders formed a separate section in the hospital and were watched by a special guard, who wore no uniform and carried a pistol under his jacket. In spite of this official guard, the life of hospitalized internees was pretty close to that in a regular hospital, as there was no way to isolate the Strzebielinek internees from the regular wards. This was one of the brighter sides of internment. Although the doctors had various attitudes toward Solidarity (many of them, especially the ones in high administrative positions, were Party members), they took tender care of our sick internees. Many sick internees regained their strength there and overcame the illnesses they had contracted in camp during the winter months.

The most important thing was that the sick internees could be visited without any limitations except for those governing hospital visiting hours. Because of the steady camp clientele in Wejherowo, Strzebielinek began getting an abundant stream of underground publications, needed books, radios, medicine, and information. Internees were allowed this permanent access to hospital treatment as a result of the International Red Cross visit. Even though we never got a copy of the reports, they were important. The relaxation of prison regimen, which could be seen in the dispatching of the ZOMOs, was also reflected in the treatment of sick internees, who now had access to hospitals other than prison hospitals. Earlier, the sick internees were placed in the prison hospital on Karkowa in Gdańsk, while others were "offered" treatment in the prison hospital in Fordon near Bydgoszcz, where no one wanted to go because of the serious difficulties created for visiting families and because of the strictness of the regulations.

The appearance of the Strzebielinek internees caused a

few small problems for the hospital in Wejherowo. The young boys who worked as help in the hospital told the internees that the UB wanted them to watch and listen to what the internees said, who visited them, and so on. When they refused, they were threatened with complications at work. Some of the patients attached Solidarity pins to their bathrobes, which caused immediate spasms of fear among the hospital zealots, including the hospital personnel officer. After a while, so as not to cause additional problems for the doctors, the Union pins were replaced with an "Internee" pin designed by a visitor who also happened to be an artist.

Because of the visits, a stay in the hospital was almost like being free. One could even take walks off the hospital grounds, in a nearby forest. A few patients could even see their children in relatively normal surroundings after not being with them for a long period of time. Visits from work colleagues, a group of Gdańsk actors involved in charitable aid, and students became a regular custom. The students would often come to one of the interned lecturers of the University of Gdańsk for a preliminary exam before the end of the semester.

Lech Wałęsa's wife, Danuta, also found time, in spite of her own difficult situation and family obligations, to visit the sick internees several times. It meant a lot to us in camp, when, together with news about Lech, we found out about her visits. Wejherowo was like a place of pilgrimage for colleagues that had been released. They considered it their duty to be concerned about the well-being of those who still remained on duty. Among the guests were Dr. Jan Strzelecki (released from Strzebielinek in December) and Alojzy Szablewski, who was released after being given a suspended sentence. Nor did the priests from the diocese of Chełm forget about their pastoral duties. The newly named bishop, Edmund Piszcz, and Father Henryk Jankowski from St. Bridget's in Gdańsk also visit the sick internees, while the hospital chaplain,

Father Władysław Fidurski, looks after the patients during the weekdays and on Sunday.

SATURDAY, MAY 22

Today Wyszkowski led the second part of the discussion on the Free Trade Unions. He began with a critical and very interesting lecture on the subject.

From my notes: In his opinion, the merging of the Free Trade Unions with KOR arrested the development of the very conception of a trade union and its organization. KOR was afraid that the Free Trade Unions would create a third power center, outside of the government and the opposition. KOR wanted to steer this movement politically. This did, in fact, happen fairly quickly, but this also eliminated the possibility of pluralistic influences (other than KOR's) on the Unions. This hurt Solidarity later on when, as a great mass movement, it took over all the weak characteristics of a small opposition. The opposition was pushing its way into the Union too violently, and dominated the agendas, created tensions at the meetings, and did not always take into account the general good but sought to realize only its own interests. In critical situations, like that created by August 1980, one should have respected the principle that one must be humble in the face of spontaneously crystallizing tendencies toward independence in society. Society should have been allowed to create its own organizations and representatives, and they should not have pushed their own people into all the responsible positions and public information jobs. In his opinion, the opposition should have stepped to the sidelines right after the August strike, after setting a pace for the Union's struggle. Actually, such decisions had been made. The political opposition, however, wanted to take over control of the Union. It was this opposition that led to the formation of one union on September 17, 1980, and did not allow for the natural growth of the movement from various sectors.

This fragment of the lecture seems too one-sided. It is obvious that a multiplicity of small union organizations, unbound to one another and incapable of coordinated actions, would have been incapable of bringing about the changes that the nation awaited. This is very clear from today's perspective. A large Solidarity did not manage to change one single corrupt *wojewoda* or secretary, so what then could a little regional or factory organization have done? Not to mention attempting to modernize a political system, significantly limiting the general monopoly of political power, liquidating the system of *nomenklatura*, resisting division of society into two categories of citizens, eliminating discrimination against believers, and so on.

My notes, continued: The attack made on Wałęsa underscored his weaknesses: his funny way of acting, a certain buffoonery, and his lack of a precise program of action down to the very last day. But people forget about the most important thing: he never put his interests, or the interests of his social group, above the interests of society as a whole. And in that lies his greatness, in spite of all the critics. It is characteristic that he was criticized for this by both the government and the opposition. It is clear that he was a threat to both groups, but for different reasons. He understood the need to work "at the grass roots level," to create groups of people there that in the long run would undertake more widely coordinated action. This was giving the Union a chance to have a longer life span than those short sixteen months. Many things that the Union did not have the time to do, such as introducing a new curriculum of humanities and education for the younger generation, would have become facts and would have allowed society to prepare the next stage. The same with self-government, which got stuck halfway there.

Krzysztof's lecture had an indisputable value, even though it was irritating in some of its categorical judgments: it extracted the real weaknesses and shallowness of the activity in that period of time, even if from the position of a devil's advocate. In the discussion which exploded after his lecture, we talked about the enormous problems in the first phase of organizing the Union. Society, which was still uncertain of real changes and still intimidated, was not eager to take up Union work. There were no people. People who were qualified were afraid, that was human enough, experience had taught them a lesson: not to involve themselves, even though in their hearts they were behind the Union. Under these circumstances there was plenty of room for those who could surmount their fears. It was enough to overcome fear to become a Union activist. The fears bred into society for the last thirty-five years were, however, substantiated. The government did not allow the experiment, and showed once again that it knows how to punish the arrogant. The Union's lesson in democracy remained incomplete. Now again, when the time comes, extraordinary inner strength will be required to conquer that bigger-than-ever barrier of fear. Therefore, the "fault" of the KOR people, or that of other opposition groups, is more problematic than it seemed during the lecture. A far greater responsibility for the failure of that great Polish hope belongs to the government. We should have demanded that the government, if it really wanted to play a historical role, create a "protective umbrella" for the changes that were taking place, that it undertake a real dialogue, that it indicate the dangers and compulsory political limits. Similar expectations were voiced by people from the lower Party levels, so that this aspect of Polish consciousness transcended political divisions and was an objective need of the Polish people. It took blindness and a total lack of good will to ruin these expectations. Perhaps it was as some people say, simply a cynical game, and not people trying to act in the best interests of the nation.

These discussions allowed us to relax camp regulations during this time. All the cells were open and passage from one pavilion to another could be taken care of by way of talking to the guard on duty. This destroyed stereotypes, broke up the ghetto atmosphere, introduced a variety of viewpoints and resulted in a greater independence and responsibility of thought.

In spite of the many difficulties with defining the various ideological orientations contained in our community, there were a few issues that elicited such sharply delineated positions that they allowed us to indirectly define the views of the speakers. Some of the issues which were such a "litmus paper" were the attitude toward the political legacy of the interwar period in Poland, and, of contemporary issues, the views on the subject of organizations like the Free Trade Unions, KOR, the Young Poland Movement and an assessment of their roles and influence on the post-August changes. Many of us discovered—and this happened only in the course of the discussion—the real political pluralism that was the contribution of the interwar period and, practically speaking, was eliminated from social consciousness by the postwar programs of teaching history, which juggled the terms "base" and "superstructure" to the point of nausea and divided everything into "backwards," that is, prewar, and "progressive," that is, associated with the People's Republic. In the sixteen months that Solidarity existed, it tore the veil from the eyes of millions of Poles and reminded us of our political origins. We have to admit that our knowledge of these subjects is neither complete nor thorough, but we feel our way intuitively into the subtleties of the personalities, convictions, and views. The common, unquestionable level of our understanding is a program that resulted from the development of social thought within the Church, a program contained in the Church's great encyclicals, and in some peculiar way, formed by the confrontations and experiences of living "in a society that builds socialism." Only by looking at ourselves and listening to one another do we see the influences of schools of political thought that had once existed. The group drawing on the program of the Polish National Democrats and its leader, Roman Dmowski, is obvious; and there are even a few legionnaires that seem to be taken straight out of an album containing old photographs of Commander Piłsudski. Unfortunately, there are those in the new military regime that also feel that unruly citizens should be "grabbed by the snouts" and brought to order. There is quite a numerous group that approaches the views, and not just the romantic posture, of the prewar Polish Social Democrats. We also have one "real" Communist, who claims that Communism in Poland has nothing in common with true communist ideals, and that is has been reduced to an ideology serving to justify the superiority of the power-elite. The political views of these colleagues seem inadequate to the Polish situation, although some political background is always helpful in analyzing reality.

Much livelier discussions are triggered by assessments of contemporary phenomena such as the short period of activity of the Free Trade Unions, KOR, or, specific to the Coast, the Young Poland Movement. Each of these organizations had its part in breaking through the network of political taboos constructed in postwar Poland.

The Free Trade Unions contributed their share in the form of a raised consciousness regarding the existence of various types of agreements and contracts between employers and employees in the free world, and about the existence of MOP* conventions, about which the authorities had kept silent. The government had presented all worker gains as "socialist achievements" and did not mention that the western world had elaborated a system of contracts that effectively protect workers, and which were ratified by Poland itself. These conventions bind Poland not just formally.

Even in camp the dispute surrounding KOR revolved around the familiar division that had appeared even in Solidarity's heyday: some recognize this movement as having contributed a significant service by creating certain embryonic forms of organizing society, which, up until KOR's formulation of a program, was defenseless against government manipulations. Others say that the Polish Church and the moral impulse of renewal resulting from John Paul II's visit-pilgrimage were incomparably more influential in preparing August. From this range of viewpoints, one can see how the various contents and experiences worked together to prepare the idea of an independent society, not just one that can be pushed around and ignored by an increasingly rotten, ideologically speaking, power-structure. The Young Poland Movement lent a certain romanticism to the actions of the younger generation on the Coast, and worked to increase political awareness among the young. They formulated and implemented their own, often risky, attempts at sociopolitical activity for their own purposes.

A very small percentage of colleagues admit to ties with the KPN,† and these ties, it is clear, are inspired more by that organization's symbols of patriotism than by a real knowledge of its program or confidence in its proposed political solutions. Generally speaking, the great majority

---

*The ILO, International Labor Organization.
†*Konfederacja Polski Niepodległej*, Confederation of Independent Poland.

of us is of the opinion that seeking a political gear for Solidarity in the form of a political party that derives from the Union in some way, would be a repetition of familiar historical solutions. The source of the new hope about which Czesław Miłosz spoke, the source of the fascination of the working world in many countries on almost all the continents was a certain untested construction: Solidarity was a mass social movement, above politics, that steered itself in the direction of humanistic solutions beyond the classic political struggles, strove for the self-organization of various sectors, and sought a form of cooperation between itself and the government. It was this that was called the "third road" in the world and which was brutally halted in its initial phase by dogmatic "Communists" terrified by the scale of potential changes.

TUESDAY, MAY 25

The spring air, sun, and nature have a greater influence on camp routine than the most serious memorial ceremonies. Awakening nature causes the authorities themselves to see camp regulations as something surrealistic. The walks inevitably grow longer. We stay outside longer and longer, most often gathering on the patch of lawn between pavilion I and III. We carry blankets and chairs outside, and settle down with our books and chessboard. The space between pavilions at times looks like a field hospital. Someone puts a rheumatic shoulder up to the sun, someone else limps along on a crutch: one of our colleagues has a leg cast molded up to his thigh. We help him to get out for the walks, to take a bath, and get him to the visitation hall. . . .

We also take advantage of the time outside to read some of the more interesting letters. One of them got to us from

France without being censored and is another comment on the ever-present issue of emigration. I think that it is sad, as is the fate of an émigré, and as it will always be: the quiet drama that incessantly returns in our history.

THE LETTER FROM FRANCE
(FRAGMENTS):

Things are not the greatest here in the West as far as an understanding of Polish affairs goes. Economic trends and sensationalism that can be turned into business are what dominate the news here. Poles who are in the West and are organizing aid for Poland complain of the indifference. It is difficult to organize anything, and a lot of energy must be spent getting important people interested in our affairs. The only problem is that these contacts vacillate between those with people of the extreme Left, of the Marxist-Revolutionary League type, and those of the extreme Right, for example, the parliamentarians of the opposition party in Canada (the conservatives). Along the way there are dissidents from the CGT,* offshoots of the Christian Democratic Party, and Socialists, Austrian and Japanese liberals. Of course, all of these groups put their own interests above our problems, which, objectively speaking, have no meaning for the rest of the world. Europe has no concrete plan of action, it is divided. There are, however, people who are very involved, usually younger people. There are definitely more of them on the Left than on the Right. It is paradoxical that we have

*Confédération Générale du Travail.

more in common here with representatives of the Left, but that in order to help our country, we must work together with personages from the ultra-Right, with whom we often have absolutely nothing in common. In political circles in Europe, the same problems are discussed over and over again: mainly what attitude to have toward the Soviet Union, and then, somewhere within this context but remotely so, comes the issue of Poland. Europe seems to be more and more dependent on the Soviet Union because of its financial and business involvements. The Committee for Aid to Poland is most active in Paris. The 1968 emigration plays a large role in the Committee, and still reflects heavy KOR influence in its thinking and actions. This Committee publishes an informational bulletin. They do not, however, have enough people, as the old emigration is exhausted and it is not clear whether or not it will be replaced by the young KOR people. Chojecki is publishing the monthly *Kontakt*. The Historico-Literary Society and the Polish Library in Paris have shown a certain amount of initiative, especially with help in procuring stipends for doctoral studies. The president of the French Polonia participates in similar activities, especially in Lille.

Our "reading" of letters has a rather exclusive character by necessity. The last wave of internees is quite a strange mixture of people. Perhaps this is accidental or part of a certain plan, we do not know. There are hard-currency vendors, ex-criminals, owners of private businesses, and very often people who show absolutely no interest in Union matters. They are obviously interested only in their own private affairs. They consider the possibility of bribing the prison warden, and they demand to talk to the *ubeks*. The most important thing for them is to get out. They found themselves here, as they say, quite accidentally, caught in the crowds or photographed in cars passing through places where there were confrontations. There is a problem with arranging our lives in such conditions, as these people intrude upon our former intimacy, the atmosphere of trust, and the familial character of our living together. We made up a cell chart so that we could get together in the free, prearranged cells according to common interests and affinities.

In the local paper, *Dziennik Bałtycki*, an article entitled "Destroy this Wall" appeared. The article was written by someone whom no one knew: Bolesław Jaks. Andrzej Brodziński had written about Strzebielinek earlier in the newspaper *Gromada Rolnik Polski*. During Brodziński's "230 minutes among the internees" he cast doubt on the authenticity of our hunger strike in February in addition to writing other falsehoods. Major Franciszek Kaczmarek, the prison warden, was the chief source of Brodziński's information and it was with reason that someone called him "the false black major" right at the very beginning of our internment. Despite his appearance of friendliness, the major could not refrain from giving inaccurate information about us to a second-rate writer who wanted to further his career by writing this way about an important political issue. The major could not be honest enough to confirm that our hunger strike was real and that it had been bought at the price of genuine personal sacrifice and regarded by us as something that we owed ourselves and others. That is how these people are.

So in this next article, "Destroy This Wall," in *Dziennik Bałtycki*, the author claims that the internees cast off the hand that is extended to them in peace and that we ourselves built the prison wall waiting all the while for the liberation which tanks are supposed to bring us. It doesn't say whose tanks nor does it say whose hand is extended. Perhaps it is the hand of the UB that is extended and we do not want to touch it because earlier it was around the throat of a society that was struggling for freedom.

What should we do? What next? Strange leaks from government sources say that Jaruzelski is not so bad, that his star in the Warsaw Pact is on the decline, that he himself is provoking attacks from other representatives of socialist countries. They claim that he did not intend to implement this type of martial law, that the general's road is too liberal. The leaks are supposed to let us know that a far worse cabinet of phantoms is forming and waiting in the wings. A group stemming from the UB and ruthlessly committed to the repression of all democratic impulses. These theses were "bought" by our Primate (proof of this is Glemp's statement after May 3). He threw his still rather frail authority into the balance, and supported Jaruzelski, in a way, by telling young people that disputes are not settled by throwing rocks in the streets. In the opinion of people close to the Episcopate these words were dictated by the fear that the developing situation could cause Soviet intervention. I think that the Primate believed in the reality of the supposed division in government circles, the myth of "cement" and liberal tendencies. Our Primate forgets about one thing, that this division is illusory, and that it is used to deceive the naive. The imaginary division constitutes a psychological ploy "if not me, then someone worse than me," so sit quietly and be satisfied. Whenever the cards are laid out on the table, they always turn out to represent the same homogeneous package of people ready to act in the defense of their own interests and in an absolutely coordinated way. First come the *ubeks* who have the last word about everything, independently of the various political shades in the civilian circles of the government. Having declared war on society, the UB also prepares a new type of prison: camps for the interned. It is true that the camps were thought up by the English eighty years ago during the Boer War. The isolation centers were called concentration camps then. But the idea of locking up a country's own citizens was contributed by Nazi Germany. In our camps, despite the relatively mild conditions (for the Polish penal system), three aspects of concentration camps were retained: strict isolation from society, random distribution of internees in the cells, and total dependence on the good will of the warden or guards. The authorities consider our internment to be a normal component of life in our country, and let us know that they could have applied more ruthless methods.

TUESDAY, JUNE 1

Church-State relations are worsening. During the ceremony in Rywałd (May 20), the first place where Primate Wyszyński was interned, Glemp said that it may not be long before he follows in the footsteps of his predecessor. The priests who are involved in organizing help for internees, for those sentenced and their families, are once again threatened with internment. There are currently no talks being conducted between the Episcopate and any government coterie. The last statement of the Katowice bishop, Bednorz, on the subject of the Pope's trip to Poland in August of this year, may break through the impasse. Some of us feel that the Pope's trip may sanction martial law; others, that this is John Paul II's usual way of seeking solutions to various problems (his visit to England during the British-Argentine hostilities over the Falkland Islands is another example). His coming to Poland would once gain raise Poles to their feet, and would give them many new incentives, whose long-term effects might have a more important meaning in current conditions.

Yesterday's camp count: 164 plus 12 in the hospital equals 176 internees.

WEDNESDAY, JUNE 2

Some of the guards are becoming more open with us. They speak about their family troubles and share gossip and information from the warden's office. They keep saying that two months before the declaration of martial law, some sort of special commission showed up in Strzebielinek and examined the number of buildings and their security. On December 12/13 of last year, the prisoners here were told that a war had begun and that they might be shot. They were told that to speed up the evacuation to Wejherowo. Now we understand why we had to wait so long that night to get accommodated in cells.

Somewhere in my head, scraps of criminology theories having to do with the relations of the persecutor-the persecuted, victim-executioner, and other related juxtapositions from books and films are floating around. There is something to them. After a few months of being interned here, a very strange bond has been formed between us and the guards. It varies, depending on the experiences which we have shared with them. Earlier we treated their attempts to get close to us as a kind of game, but receiving Communion together in the camp chapel creates a certain bond that cannot be ignored, especially when incidents like the following took place.

Many of the guards have pseudonyms, sometimes amazingly accurate. One is called "Helmut" because his *idée fixe* is emigration to West Germany. Often he would bring us a letter in German and ask us to translate it for him. One of us tutored him in German in his guard booth, to which he brought a tape recorder and tapes with German lessons. Shortly thereafter, he was transferred to the gate. It was only after a few incidents that we understood the guards' true attitude towards the entire internment business. Once when we were passing around Stefan Bratkowski's letter which contained an analysis of the junta's crimes and was an account of society's enormous losses, including the biological ones, that this state had brought about, one of our less nimble colleagues was surprised by a guard who grabbed the copy of the letter sticking out of his pocket. We expected to pay the consequences for distributing this document, but the letter vanished and we never heard anything about it. I suspect that it began to circulate among the guards.

One of the guards in charge of internees in the hospital in Wejherowo had a rather strange habit. Because guard duty in the hospital lasted for an entire twelve-hour shift, and because it was already quite hot, the pistol protruded from under the guard's light jacket and the internees noticed it. The guard, who wanted to take advantage of duty time to have a little social life (lots of young nurses worked in the hospital), did not want to strut around with a "piece." The best solution seemed to be to leave the pistol with the internees.

Knucklehead, Morocco, Beerbottle, Belladonna, Mademoiselle, Flex, Bacon, Bishop, Ox, Somoza—there were many of them and after a while we knew which of them to watch out for and which ones were capable of turning an internee's cell inside out right before a visit. We also knew which ones would turn their backs no matter what was happening.

Familiar with the mechanism of osmosis, we fear for Lech, who has been alone except for the carefully chosen *ubeks* with whom he must spend his time.

Our major is also undergoing a certain noticeable evolution, especially since the doctor confirmed that his three-year-old daughter has a brain tumor. It was during one of those conversations that, depressed, he told us about his daughter. One of the internees offered to help locate the child, who was rapidly losing her vision, at the Children's Health Center in Warsaw. Later, after this plan was to have been carried out, the child was going to be treated by a priest-homeopathist. Only accidents of fate, such ordinary human misfortunes, revealed the normal attitudes of people on both sides of the front.

This front had a rather irregular line. The structure of camp authority was certainly not monolithic and under the cover of identical uniforms seethed struggles for careers, pensions, awards, and promotions. This was confirmed by the following: one day one of the internees had the opportunity to go through the pockets of the assistant warden's jacket. In one of the outer pockets, he found the minutes from a Party meeting in prison. From his quick reading of the minutes it was clear that the Party was doing "ideological" evaluations of some of the prison officials. One of the department heads was being discussed at the meeting and it was said that his leaving the Party indicated a certain "wavering" on his part and that this fact should be taken into account as far as his advancement was concerned. They voted to remove him from his position. The Party wanted only its own people in administrative posts.

It was the same in the courts, propaganda bureaus, police, administration, army, and economy. That is, everywhere outside of the Church, although the Party would surely have liked to take over the Church as well. Strange information has appeared on television regarding the meetings of the Ecumenical Council. The program was prepared in such a way as to show the Catholic Church as just one of the many churches functioning in Poland. People from PAX,* CHSS† and PZKS‡ were presented and shown as activists attempting to repeat the PAX model of economic promotion at the side of the consenting Party, and at the price of supporting and forti-

---

*A government-launched (1947), pseudo-religious organization meant to undermine the Church.
†Christian Social Association.
‡Polish Catholic Social Union.

fying the Party's moves. These groups, their positions and appearance greatly confuse people, who cannot differentiate between the labels. It's strange that the Episcopate does not articulate clearly who, in its opinion, expresses the opinion of the Church in this game. Rumor has it that Stefan Kisielewski has proposed a collective name for this new attempt by the government to mount a front of Catholic activists who support WRON: The Christian Union of Unity, whose acronym is obscene, Kisiel [Kisielewski] style.*

We call the *ubeks* that have been showing up in camp to hold talks "peddlers." This name accurately describes their function. Today the "peddlers" came from Gdańsk and Toruń: as usual, they wanted signatures, but they also tried to intimidate us, this time using our wives and children: "Something might happen to them . . ." Zbyszek Iwanów was told outright that they would lock up his wife if he did not quit organizing aid to the interned and arrested. We have also found out that some of the taxi drivers from Toruń, who have been driving families of internees to Strzebielinek, have lost their licenses.

During the talks, after exhausting all "ideological" arguments, the "peddlers" threaten us with long internment and even, if necessary, exile to Siberia "where there is a lot of room for people like you." They seem to have a complex, however, a feeling of doing the dirty work, as most of them introduce themselves as officials dealing with economic matters. They say: "We were told to have a talk with you. But what should I really write in my report? Perhaps I will write down that you have been acquainted with the rigors of martial law?" They also suggested that the best solution would be emigration. When the conversation turned to an assessment of the police, they gladly admitted that the ZOMOs were the

*The acronym in Polish is ChUJ or "cocksucker."

worst. "You know, that is where the worst people go, it is different with people in other areas of police work. Only highly trained people work in those areas and they often have a higher education. No one can say that they are thugs. Those are people that police forces in many other countries would pride themselves on having." We told them openly that the police will not regain their authority until they concern themselves only with what belongs to them.

THURSDAY, JUNE 3

We get news that a group of twelve members of the Young Poland Movement has come out of hiding. This entire group went into hiding right from the beginning of martial law, and some of them were playing a very important role in the underground. This sensational news is the number one subject of all of today's discussions. The internees here from the Young Poland Movement avoid commenting, saying that they lack any real details outside of the information that the group includes: Bożena Rybicka, Lech's secretary; Maciej Grzywaczewski, office director of Solidarity's National Committee; Magdalena Modzelewska, known for leading prayers for the intention of arrested colleagues after May 3, 1980, in the Marian Basilica in Gdańsk; and Ireneusz and Zofia Gust. They also know that the person who encouraged them to come out of hiding was Wiesław Chrzanowski, the coauthor of the Solidarity statutes, who had obtained assurances from Minister Kiszczak through the vice-marshal of the Sejm, Halina Skibniewska, that the bills of internment waiting for the group since December 12 would be annulled the minute the group surfaced. In spite of the fact that the decision in this matter was made by the Minister

Exercising at the camp: walking, weightlifting, and volleyball. A "spartakiad" was organized by the internees.

A poster of Lech Wałęsa, November 1982.

A mock ID of the Association of Internees of the Polish People's Republic.

Camp bulletins put out by internees on Christmas Eve. RIGHT: *A takeoff on a carol, titled "In the Silence of the Camp."* BELOW: *The anthem of the internees.*

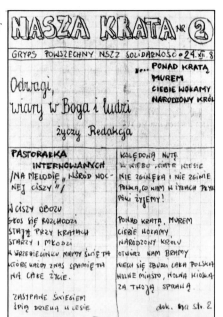

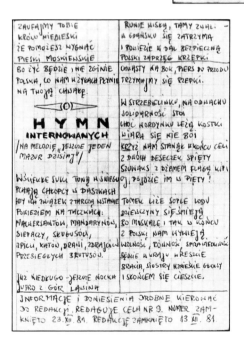

A protest by the internees against martial law.

PROTEST

13 GRUDNIA 1981R. WŁADZE GWAŁCĄC PRAWO I LEKCEWAŻĄC INTERESY NARODU I PAŃSTWA, WPROWADZIŁY STAN WOJENNY. ZAPROWADZONO RZĄDY TERRORU MAJĄCE ZŁAMAĆ SPOŁECZNĄ WOLĘ DEMOKRACJI, WOLNOŚCI I PRAWDY. NASZ ZWIĄZEK NSZZ „SOLIDARNOŚĆ" KTÓRY WYRAŻAŁ TĘ WOLĘ NAJPEŁNIEJ, ZOSTAŁ PRAKTYCZNIE ZDELEGALIZOWANY. CZŁONKÓW NAJWIĘKSZEJ W HISTORII POLSKI ORGANIZACJI SPOŁECZNEJ PODDANO REPRESJOM I SZYKANOM. TYCH SPOŚRÓD NAS, KTÓRZY NADAL STARALI SIĘ WYPEŁNIĆ SWE STATUTOWE OBOWIĄZKI, SKAZANO NA WIELOLETNIE WIĘZIENIE, INNYCH ZMUSZA SIĘ DO PODPISYWANIA NIEZGODNYCH Z ICH SUMIENIEM DEKLARACJI LOJALNOŚCI.

PROTESTUJEMY PRZECIWKO ŁAMANIU PRZEZ WŁADZE PRAW CZŁOWIEKA I OBYWATELA. ŻĄDAMY UWOLNIENIA OSÓB SKAZANYCH I ARESZTOWANYCH ZA DZIAŁALNOŚĆ ZWIĄZKOWĄ.

ŻĄDAMY ZNIESIENIA STANU WOJENNEGO.

ŻĄDAMY NATYCHMIASTOWEGO PODJĘCIA PRZEZ WŁADZE ROZMÓW Z NSZZ „SOLIDARNOŚĆ" NA TEMAT PRZYSZŁOŚCI KRAJU.

WYRAŻAJĄC SWĄ SOLIDARNOŚĆ Z PRZEŻYWAJĄCYM TRAGEDIĘ SPOŁECZEŃSTWEM MY, INTERNOWANI W OBOZIE W STRZEBIELINKU, PODEJMUJEMY PROTEST GŁODOWY.

STRZEBIELINEK
2 LUTY 1982 R.

BELOW AND OPPOSITE PAGE: *Examples of messages and reports smuggled in and out of camp.*

ZABRANIA SIĘ:
1. WYSTAWIANIA KOSTEK NA VORHTARZ.
2. USTAWIANIA SIĘ DO APELU.

PODPISANO:
OŚRODEK DYWERSJI WEWNĘTRZNEJ
17.12.81 R.

Zabrania się
1. Wystawianie Kostek
2. Ustawianie się do apeli
Ośrodek dywersji wewnętrznej
Strzebielinek 17.12.81

Bardzo prosimy o podawanie składu osobowego wszystkich cel: imię, nazwisko, stanowisko oraz adres zamieszkania. Dostarczyć koniecznie do celi 33

BIPS podaje:

Podobno wczoraj strajkowały Stocznie im. Komuny Paryskiej w Gdyni i Stocznie Lenina oraz porty.

Podobno w nocy wojsko czołgami weszło siłą na ich teren. Nie wiadomo, czy są ofiary, nie wiadomo, czy strzelano.

Opór społeczeństwa, jak widać, jest duży.

Podobno załogi ~~zostają~~ zajętych zakładów ~~zostały~~ zmobilizowano.

~~[skreślone linie]~~

W wyniku brutalnego oderwania od Rodzin, od załóg zakładów pracy, od Polski - internowani członkowie NSZZ "Solidarność" podejmują:

"AKCJE ŚCISŁEGO POSTU

w okresie Świąt Bożego Narodzenia począwszy od Wigilii.

Masowe aresztowania w całym kraju zwane internowaniem, pustka przy świątecznych stołach w naszych Rodzin, ranni i zabici - są symbolem stanu wojennego w naszym kraju.

Nasz protest głodowy stanowi odpowiedź na atak na naszą godność. Takie święta zgotowano tym, dla których "SIERPIEŃ 80" był nadzieją, że:

... można postępować naprzód tylko za cenę prawdziwej przemiany umysłów, woli i serc ...

(Jan Paweł II w "Redemptor hominis")

BELOW AND TOP OPPOSITE PAGE: Release from Strzebielinek.

Camp art. "Don't worry, I'll visit your wives!"

Release form of one of the internees at Strzebielinek.

Ośrodek Odosobnienia
w ~~Strzebielinku~~   ~~Strzebielinek~~ dnia ██████ 19 8̶2̶ r.

ŚWIADECTWO ZWOLNIENIA INTERNOWANEGO

Ob. ██
Urodz. ████████████ w ████████████
Ostatnio zamieszkały w Gdańsk ul. ████████████
Legitymujący się dowodem osobistym nr ████████████ Prezydent Miasta Gdańsk
Osadzony w Ośrodku Odosobnienia w Strzebielinku
dnia 13.12.1981 na mocy decyzji nr ████ /81 z dnia 12.12.1981
Komendanta Wojewódzkiego Milicji Obywatelskiej w Gdańsku
został zwolniony w dniu ████████ 1982

W/w obowiązany jest zameldować się w Komendzie Wojewódzkiej MO
w Gdańsku najpóźniej do dnia ████████ 1982 r. 8⁰⁰

Komendant Ośrodka Odosobnienia
w Strzebielinku

Przy zwolnieniu z ośrodka odosobnienia
a/ wypłacono z depozytu zł. ████ słownie zł. ████████ 500/100 ——

b/ Udzielono pomocy _____
/podać rodzaj udzielonej pomocy/
na zł. _____ słownie zł. _____

nazwa organu udzielającego pomocy _____

of Internal Affairs himself, the UB in Gdańsk did not want to admit defeat so easily. Yesterday, the whole group finally returned to their homes.

There is a decided split in opinion in camp: some of the internees feel that it would have been senseless for the Young Poland people to have remained in hiding. Sooner or later they would have been caught, thereby only lengthening the list of arrested and later the list of those sentenced. In addition, their activity in the underground was rather minimal because as people who had been under surveillance for many years, they had little room for maneuver. By coming out of hiding, they not only wanted to solve their individual problems, but also to stop the exodus of younger "conspirators" into the underground. Some of our colleagues feel that by coming out of hiding now, the group has dealt the conspiracy an underhanded blow. This weakens the underground and undermines confidence in the people who are still there. Now no one knows whether they, too, might not take it into their heads to suddenly give up the battle, and society will remain without any representation. Shortly thereafter, the group visited the sick internees at the hospital in Wejherowo. They were accompanied by a few rather suspicious-looking people. It was not surprising that the group which came out of hiding would now find itself under the discreet observation of special security police.

SATURDAY, JUNE 5

We compare our experiences after returning from our leaves. The general assessment of the situation seems to be the following: society is probably willing to fight, even on the barricades, but it has to be soon. No one is ready for a long-term effort to regain what has been lost. Even we, the internees, are overrated. People overestimate the effect of our future actions and our capacity for turning the tide of events. It seems to us, rather, that the centrifuge of history has thrown us out into the peripheries of that process. The period that was earmarked for us ended on December 13. The new internees that come to Strzebielinek are dismayed that we have not worked out a complete plan of action for the future. They demand alternate solutions from us. The "old activists" feel that such solutions can be worked out only on the other side of the prison wall, that those that stayed behind must take the baton and run with it. We are expected, and we agree, not to do two things: sign loyalty oaths and emigrate.

The divisions within the underground are a fact. There are two currents. One is The Nationwide Committee for the Defense of Solidarity (OKO), and the second derives from the old Solidarity structures and includes people such as Bogdan Lis in Gdańsk, Zbigniew Bujak in Warsaw, and Władysław Frasyniuk in Wrocław. OKO wanted to act as a great, centrally controlled underground organization. This proved unrealistic under the circumstances. More traps and arrests. The activity of loosely bound groups acting within their own individual sectors has a greater chance at efficacy. This activity consists of mainly two things: distribution of publications and material aid to the families of those persons that have been interned, imprisoned, or deprived of work. Unfortunately, there is less and less money, but oddly enough, more and more people ready to actively participate in the conspiracy regardless of the risks involved. Underground activists seem tired, but they have no intention of capitulating. They want to broaden their sphere of activity with quickly distributed publications. People are talking about setting up a Solidarity radio station, including one for northern Poland. Two notions of doing battle are crystallizing: a general strike, to take place soon on June 16 to show the power of the Union, or waiting until society is clearly fed up with the burdens of everyday life in Poland. For the time being, people are chasing after additional income, after consumer goods, which are still (if not readily) available. When this is no longer the case, then the people will be ready to act. This state of affairs is recognized and taken advantage of by the government, which is clearly concentrating on further dividing the well-situated workers from the big factories and mines (with the government's system of coupons and discounts), from the less threatening intelligentsia and cadres of workers in small factories and plants. The differences in material well-being between the various social strata are augmented in keeping with the maxim "divide and conquer." While the mining community is being fortified, the Coast is submitted to more and more terror, surveillance and the show trials of various "rabble-rousers."

JUNE 10, CORPUS CHRISTI

This is martial law, Polish style. Captain Maciuk drove from parish to parish today with our chaplain in search of a monstrance for the camp Corpus Christi procession. They drove around for over an hour.

After mass we held the traditional procession. The procession route led around the walkway by four altar stations. The stations were prepared by Antek Szymkowski from Toruń. They stood, one after another, at the entrance to pavilion IV, by the water tanks, at the camp entrance gate, and next to pavilion II. Not all of us participated in the solemnities, because Maciuk, feeling that such a gathering was dangerous, had the passages between pavilions blocked off, which made it impossible for about forty people to go to the chapel. This was probably the first and only time in Poland that this solemn procession took place with four stations in the "pen."

FRIDAY, JUNE 11

Fifteen people are being released and of that number, ten have been here from the very beginning, that is, for an even six months.

SATURDAY, JUNE 12

"Rota," "God Protector of Poland," and our hymn, as well as lighted candles, remind us today that six months of internment have passed.

After midnight, after finishing our singing, the "banging" began. This time our major prepared a small surprise for us in the form of an intervention squad armed to the teeth. The squad indicated its readiness to act. Two photographers also joined in and tried to photograph the internees who were pounding near the bars. They were rather timid, however, and scurried away at the sight of a broom handle poked through the bars.

Today I had in my hands a copy of the apparently authentic May 13 memo from the Cabinet to the Committee to Trade Union Affairs. In the memo, which has been circulating in camp, are guidelines for army officers. The main points are that the final determination of Solidarity's right to exist, along with the decision regarding formation of other unions, will be made by September. That is the deadline for taking care of matters having to do with the emigration of some of the internees. On the propaganda front, there is to be a confrontation with the Church.

The radio broadcast information about the release of 257 internees.

SUNDAY, JUNE 13

WRON has incredible luck. After the winter floods, the people will be distracted by the world championship soccer matches. We are suspending all lectures and classes during the matches.

During mass the chaplain read the statement of the Episcopate made after its June 8 Conference. This is the official invitation extended to the Holy Father to visit his homeland in August. The radio broadcast some details of the conditions which the government is setting for the Pope's visit.

SUNDAY, JUNE 20

Here are the results of a camp survey, prepared beginning a month ago:

Average age: 33.6 years old
Social origin: Working Class, 72 persons
                Intelligentsia, 73 persons
                Peasant, 12 persons
Total number of internees: 157

SATURDAY, JUNE 26

Today Rysiek Olkiewicz, called "Gypsy" or "Little Sun of Freedom," was taken to the hospital. He has pneumonia and other ailments as well as a speedily deteriorating asthma condition. I should have written about him long ago, but I just got to know him better recently. He is a 42-year-old stevedore from Gdynia, of genuine working class background, the same working class on whose hides the Party and WRON had carved their whole interpretation of the theory of proletarian dictatorship. "Gypsy" was a popular figure in Port Administration in Gdynia and was well known for his outstanding composure during the August 1980 strike. Later, during the endless negotiations, he somehow lost his way, stepped aside, and it was not until a bill of internment was written for him that he was found in the ranks of those who were accorded special attention by the UB. They thought that since he was one of the strike leaders from a year and a half ago, he could still rally the people to protest. "Gypsy" was guided in his judgments by a well-functioning instinct which Marxists call a "class" instinct. This purely class instinct led him to camp. We worried about him a lot: he was very ill even though he looked strong and athletic and had a manly bearing. From the very beginning, he was racked by a severe cough, so much so that he reminded me of a fragment of a grade school poem, which sounded quite differently in this context, "Elegy on the Death of Ludwik Waryński": "Lungs already spat out give no pain . . ." There was no way to convince him that he should try to get out of here and into a hospital. He said: "That's the doctor's job, if he doesn't want to do it, that's his choice. I won't ask WRON for a single thing." It was true that the doctors often responded to pressure put on them by the parties concerned, and Rysiek never asked . . . Sometimes he would get up in the morning with that awful cough, look out the window and say: "Look, today the sun of freedom is shining." He was an honorable man, without a shade of duplicity. When right before May 1 (when he was scheduled to be released) he ran into Maciuk and the latter asked him what he would do when released, "Gypsy" answered: "I will fight for Solidarity to the bitter end." He was not released.

MONDAY, JUNE 28

We commemorated the anniversary of the Poznań riots of June 1956, and two days ago was the anniversary of the events in Radom in 1976. We prayed in the chapel for those who had lost their lives then. In the afternoon there was a roll read for the dead, and then a lecture by Dr. Jerzy Keiling from the University of Gdańsk (he was brought here at the end of May).

The internees from Toruń got the following message from someone on the outside:

The terrible atmosphere created by the trials of our colleagues, by arrests, internments, and questionings, is not conducive to writing letters to internees. I would not want you to think, however, that we have forgotten about you. So I am writing this letter even though it will probably paint a very pessimistic and dark picture.

In your letter you asked about our attitude toward the position of the Episcopate. Actually we have none, or perhaps our attitude is one of indifference because no one really believes in the junta's desire to carry on any kind of talks. If it gives the impression of carrying on talks, it is only to cover up its real intentions. It has always been the case, anyway, that the government agrees to talk only when it feels threatened, when it is backed into a corner. Even then nothing ever came of the talks. The entire post-war history of Polish communism shows clearly that the government made agreements only then, when a given partner was necessary to give it the semblance of sincerity in the eyes of society. The minute, however, that the government feels strong enough on its own, its gets even. That is how it was with the PPS* and the PSL† even though each of these parties was purged in a different way. The purges were quite effective nevertheless. Now Solidarity is to be added to the collection of annihilated "partners." As an answer to your question about my attitude toward the position of the Church, I am sending you Anka Kowalska's letter: I agree with it and emphasize its claim that this is not a political position. This letter is, of course, an evasion on my part, because my opinion about the Church's arguments is as above, that is, they interest me purely theoretically, and I do not believe that the government is really interested in them, either. The junta does not desire to be given an answer, and I do not think that it intends to negotiate with society, judging by the leaks from the closed Party meeting with the High Comrades. Pacifying us to the end, that is the only aim of the junta at this time. This is officially called "normalization." The trials that have been going on and that are going on now in Toruń are part of that normalization. Luckily the Rockefellers have stopped sending us money and that will make

*Polish Socialist Party.
†Polish Peasants' Party.

the junta think about the eventual loosening of our fetters.

Recently a French correspondent published a four-point project which was allegedly made up by PZPR comrades in order to get dollars from the West. Unfortunately, I can remember only three of them: (1) the end of martial law, but the Sejm will ratify special powers for the government (so that, as someone said, we will have a change of scenery without a change in the scenario); (2) the release of the internees (I do not remember what was said about those sentenced for violating the decree); and (3) the renewal of trade union as well as Solidarity activity exclusively in the workplace, so more cheating, because there would be thousands of small, unrelated unions that, left to themselves, would have no chance of surviving even if the old union activists would remain members (and the question is, will they want to). What's more, within an organization like this they could handle only the small social services for the work force. And let's not kid ourselves, we don't need trade unions like that. Poland needs Solidarity, just as it was, as a social movement. Why am I writing this, these are all truisms, and you have probably discussed and examined them many times.

Jurek went on trial on June 6, and it turned out that he is quite a hooligan! It is not enough that he takes part in illegal demonstrations, he also shouts out certain provocative and forbidden onomatopoeias (he yelled out caw-caw-caw, which might seem downright silly to the uninitiated, but for proponents of our progressive system this is slanderous, offensive, and degrading to the highest, if illegal, state organs). He also did not go home when representatives of the government ordered him to do so, and there was something else, but I don't remember what. Luckily, our government is understanding and sentenced him to only six weeks in jail. He has served some of it and is out now on a two-month leave (his sentence has been delayed). On July 25, he will grab his knapsack, toothbrush, and other personal belongings and will appear at the prison in Grudziądz to serve out the remaining sixteen days. That's good because by then he should be thoroughly resocialized and his inclinations to hooliganism will have been rooted out. Although, who knows? Can you imagine that when he was leaving prison for his furlough, he stole a cap from prison! He said that it was just for show, of course.

I was chastised for sending a May 1 card! I was told that it was a careless and unwise card and that it could result in unpleasantness. It was not said who would be caused unpleasantness, the sender or the recipient, and I would feel badly if it would be you. I simply had not thought about it when I mailed the card. It was only recently that I read the decree of December 12(?), 1981 and I now know why most of the contents of the card were crossed out: its contents must have "threatened the security or defense of the State"! And so out here in so-called "freedom," one idiotic thing outdoes another.

From current gossip: apparently the person chosen for the First Secretary of the Town Committee is that outstanding Party activist in the pre-August period, dug up by Party members at first opportunity, Comrade Józef Szymański.

I will close with a joke that circulated in Toruń after the May 1 and 3 "truncheonings": Two people who miraculously escape the ZOMOs run into the same house and, gasping for breath, tell each other what is happening out on the streets. An old woman who is in the house is hard of hearing and asks anxiously: "Children, what are you saying? Beatings? Call the police!" Exactly.

See you soon!

"H"

WEDNESDAY, JUNE 30

I have been here for 200 days. As if to celebrate this occasion, ten *ubeks* from Gdańsk and Toruń have been working in the pavilions since morning. Some of the internees have been vouched for by their employers, according to what they say. During his talk with the *ubeks*, Antek Szymkowski, an art historian and a man with a very ascetic look and a rather shocking way of behaving, who has the habit of expressing himself in the language of the Gospels, addressed an *ubek* as "My Brother." "What will you do, Brother," he said, "when you have to stand before the Lord? Are your hands clean?" he asked rhetorically until the *ubek* could not stand it any longer, gave up his questioning and asked Szymkowski to leave.

Twelve persons were released today, 133 remain; of those, 14 are in the hospital in Wejherowo.

SUNDAY, JULY 4

During the visit of Bishop Kazimierz Kluz and the priests from Gdańsk, we return to the subject of the

Pope's visit. Some light is shed on this matter by a document sent to the last Episcopal Conference on June 21:

Notes on possible dangers if the Pope should visit Poland in August of this year.

1. One of the most important elements of John Paul II's visit is assuring him absolute personal safety, which in the present circumstances is impossible:

a. The present state of Poland's security is different from what it was in 1979, and we cannot afford to have as large a concentration of law enforcement personnel as last time because this would cause other regions of Poland to remain without defense.

b. We cannot exclude the possibility of persons taking advantage of the crowds to create serious street excesses, examples of which were noted recently in Kraków, Gdańsk, and Wrocław where we had to deal with smaller groups of people.

c. Law enforcement officials also must contend with transportation and gas problems which make it impossible for them to make immediate transfers of personnel as need dictates.

d. Recent experiences indicate that the number of illegally possessed firearms is considerable. Within a few months this year, we have confiscated almost 1,000 firearms, 40,000 pieces of ammunition and over 300 pounds of explosives. Therefore we cannot ignore the significant number of explosives which are found in private hands. This was confirmed recently by attempts to blow up various buildings and monuments. Thefts of TNT and dynamite as well as other explosives from mines and quarries are reported daily.

Because of the alertness of the authorities, many of these actions have been prevented.

There have been groups in Kraków and other places that were ready to blow up monuments and gravestones of well-known people who had done much for Polish culture and science. They intended to do this in such a way as to cast the blame on the Security Forces. Such ideas still exist among some people.

e. In light of the attempts on the Pope's life, most recently in Portugal, such an attempt here in Poland cannot be excluded, especially as such an act could be used to compromise the current government.

f. During the last six months we have uncovered more than 350 various groups and youth organizations of which a good part had a terrorist character. Many of them were based on fascist ideologies and used Nazi emblems. Carrying out a terrorist act in a crowd would be a simple matter for this type of group and prior detection and prevention in current circumstances is practically impossible.

g. We cannot ignore the possibility of an attack on the Pope by some type of psychopath or person in a state of extreme emotional excitement.

2. In contrast to 1979, we currently have enormous difficulties with transportation. There is a lack of train and passenger cars that could transport people along the Pope's route and a lack of liquid fuel, which makes it impossible to transport people to places where the Pope will be. In the event that the visit should take place, many persons would not refrain from stealing gasoline, or illegally using state vehicles, and there could be serious disturbances in train and auto transportation.

This document, of which we had a xerox copy, bore no stamp nor signature.

The Pope has his own conditions for WRON to meet: the lifting of martial law, and the release of the interned and arrested. The government is even inclined to release a segment of the interned, but, according to our sources, it intends to keep around 120 people interned: people from the National Commission and Union experts. A partial amnesty will be granted to those sentenced as a result of violating martial law decrees.

Government talks with the Episcopate within the context of the Common Commission lead nowhere. The Church takes part in them so as not to give the impression that it is breaking off this one official line of communication.

During our conversation with the bishop, we also brought up the matter of transferring Lech to one of the internment camps, and that the Church should extend its aid to women sentenced for Union activity and those women dismissed from work (on the basis of "verification" proceedings in the various professions).

Just as the spell on shipyard workers was broken by "verifications" done in the Olivia auditorium, so, too, must activists be shown on television. Henryk Tarasiewicz of Port Administration in Gdynia received such a proposition twice. The subject of the show was to have been Solidarity's blockade of the ports in July and August of 1980, which consisted of stopping exports of foodstuffs until the facts concerning the food industry were made known by the government. When he demanded to be shown a script, the matter was drawn out until it fell through altogether. Another such proposal was made to Andrzej Kozicki via his wife. He was supposed to appear in a television program dedicated to Solidarity. To the "real" Solidarity.

Through a Gdańsk bishop we began efforts to have our chapel cross removed to the Marian Basilica in Gdańsk.

In spite of the initial go-ahead, probably a tactical move, we could not get this matter taken care of. The authorities were probably afraid of the impression this very expressive cross with our signatures would make on the people. The government fears another Union relic.

WEDNESDAY, JULY 7

Today's sensation was Konrad Marusczyk's release from camp. The government's decision to release him was preceded by two visits from the police (a colonel and lieutenant). Konrad's release is significant for those outside the wall, too. He was the vice-chairman of Regional Solidarity and Lech Wałęsa's right-hand man.

This may just be a signal that the government feels safer. Konrad did not have an easy time in camp. He had to conform to the narrow formula dictated by camp regulations, where there was no mention of any kind of representation for internees. Any attempt to break out of this, the most important of camp regulations, which was supposed to destroy the existing Union structures, would have resulted in a transfer of possible organizers to another camp and exchanging internment for arrest. Yet people did expect him to show leadership. In our opinion, Konrad was successful in getting out of this dilemma and his position was, in a certain sense, a continuation of a line that had been extremely popular: Lech Wałęsa's. It was also characteristic of Konrad that he accepted the style that was imposed on him by martial law, and turned it into a weapon. During our meeting with Colonel Ring in December, when the colonel began shouting and treating the delegates with obvious contempt (it was mutual), Konrad cut through this hostile atmosphere by demanding respect for himself as an officer, a lieutenant in the

Polish army. It was then that Ring reciprocated by introducing himself as a colonel. From this time on, Konrad
operated in this style, accepted by the majority in spite of
certain reservations. Especially from the time of the arrival of the internees from Potulice, who treated Konrad
as Wałęsa's man and clearly submitted themselves to him
organizationally. Konrad's authority was also enhanced
by his being related to the highly respected lawyer,
Siła-Nowicki, and certainly by the fact that his wife,
Maria, was the godmother of little Maria-Wiktoria Wałęsa. We gave him a proper send-off at the gate with three
hip-hip-hoorays.

THURSDAY, JULY 8

We have to admit that our camp "counterintelligence"
works pretty well: today we got information about why
Konrad was released. He was released on the personal
intervention of Minister Kiszczak, who again let everybody know that he is "human." Each satrap who wields
great power derives pleasure from it only when he can
indulge in a theatrical, highly visible gesture. Earlier
Kiszczak had entertained one of the writers on leave from
an internment camp, and complimented him by saying
that he knew his work. During coffee, he bestowed a little
patriotic speech on him to the effect that "the homeland
needs such artists!" He was saying that at a time when all
artists' unions were suspended, censorship was on a ram-
page, and all independent thought was being extinguished by his people in the voivodeships. But what a
gesture!
The so-called "talks" which are an obligatory ritual
before ending internment (the decision to release the internee contains a clause about going to voivodeship police

headquarters) consist of proving to the offender that martial law was a necessity, and that this is how the military government saved Poland's statehood, which was in decline after the bankruptcy of the Party. In addition the conversation was supposed to sound out the internee's attitude toward the new reality. It was not a matter of the internee's liking it, but whether or not he would actively participate in opposing it. Depending on the outcome of the talk, the released internee might remain under surveillance, his home might be searched, or they just might leave him alone.

MONDAY, JULY 12

Outside of camp matters and our constant bickering, outside of big politics and events on the other side of the prison wall of which we hear only echoes, life beats its complex paths. Jarek Pirowski, twenty-four years old, is getting married. There have been a lot of problems with arranging this marriage. He received a six-day pass to take care of the formalities at the City Registry in Gdańsk, but the prison authorities would not give him his i.d. When he turned to police headquarters in Gdańsk, they told him to go back to the registry, and that "they would take care of everything." It turned out that even being an *ubek* during martial law could not help cut through all the bureaucracy. Jarek returned empty-handed.

Another colleague of ours got permission to take care of the civil ceremony in the closest registry, that is, in Wejherowo. Two of our colleagues' families, on the other hand, cancelled divorce proceedings initiated before December. Internment has favored forgiveness, returning, and, in spite of everything, lent some hope to putting an end to personal defeats, which should be put aside at a time like this. There were, however, other incidents where an obliging colleague took advantage of the absence of the man of the house. The atmosphere of unity and conspiracy probably also helped to bring people closer together. On one of the visits, it would turn out that the wife was acting odd, rather stiffly, that she did not react nor return the signals sent to her by her impatiently waiting husband.

Twelve internees were released today.

THURSDAY, JULY 15

Summer dog days break down the camp machine. What should we think about? Our releases are, unfortunately, the subject. It is difficult to avoid speculating on how things will be on July 22. This is one thing the government has pounded into our heads: that during this national holiday, this most official holiday, when amnesty is always announced, there were always certain gestures and steps taken just for show. The same will probably happen now. Today three more internees were released.

We get bits of information from which we are able to construct a picture of how society is acting, how the neighbors react to the internees that have gone home, and how the conspiracy and underground activity look. We get this information from the outside, through the hospital, and from internees returning from leaves. One of our colleagues was in the former Solidarity building on Grunwaldzka Street during his leave.

There are only strangers wandering in the empty corridors and within the walls that are deprived of all life: no posters, announcements or satirical cartoons. The people working here now are part of the *wojewoda*'s staff which is to administer what is left, and the *wojewoda* himself has an office in one of the rooms. The surrealism of the scene is underscored by that which has taken the place of those old posters and announcements that were so full of the passion of the times. Now there are lists of payroll dates posted for workers still on the union payroll, advertisements of financial aid available to children going to camp, and other similar matters. Our colleague forced the grating that was blocking off the part of the corridor where Wałęsa's office had been. In the first room, where Lech's secretaries worked and where Pan Henio usually sat; where telephone lines crossed in midair and a mass of people with various problems would come to have them taken care of; in this room there were now only two tables and a wardrobe and, in the corner behind a door, a red and white flag. Amid the papers spilled all over the floor and stepped on by dozens of feet, there were telegrams sent to Lech in March 1981, expressing support for what he was doing by calling off the general strike. There were telegrams from the time of the Congress and less formal telegrams with namesday wishes. The saddest sight was that of Lech's room: torn curtains, a hole remaining where a telephone had been torn out of the wall, an overturned table, the torn couch on which he had caught his "second wind" in the most heated moments of deliberations. In the corner was a plaster model of some kind of monument, a figure with outstretched hands. All of this was covered with a thick layer of dust and sentenced to oblivion. . . .

THURSDAY, JULY 22

From deputy Romuald Bukowski's appeal to the Sejm: "I move for a gesture of largesse. Let this unity be begun with a general amnesty, with the activating of suspended social structures and organization, the restoration of citizens' rights, and the lifting of martial law or replacing it with something less drastic."

Such were our hopes, too. But it ended with the release of a few dozen internees in July. There is nothing said about those sentenced for violating the decree and nothing is changed in matters of dismissal from work for one's convictions. WRON announced the impending release of 913 internees, including all interned women, and 314 internees will receive so-called "furloughs."

In my cell, I write down Solidarity's Litany:

Mother of the deceived
Mother of the betrayed
Mother of those seized at night
Mother of the interned
Mother of those kept in the cold
Mother of the beaten
Mother of the terrified
Mother of the shot;
    Mother of the miners
    Mother of the dock workers
    Mother of the workers
    Mother of the farmers
    Mother of the students
Mother of the unjustly condemned
Mother of the truthful
Mother of the unbribed
Mother of the unbroken
Mother of the desperate
Mother of the orphaned
    Queen of suffering Poland
    Queen of fighting Poland
    Queen of independent Poland
Through the prayers of John Paul II
Through the imprisonment of your servant, Lech

Through the degradation of scholars and writers
Through the loneliness of the old
Through the hope of millions
    Grant us a life in freedom and truth

Amen

TUESDAY, JULY 27

The little birch forest surrounding the hospital in Wejherowo inspired our sick internees to make a starkly beautiful wooden cross with a kneeler. They offered the
cross as a gift to the shipyard parish of St. Bridget's in
Gdańsk. It is to stand next to the cross made by the
striking dockworkers in August of 1980 as a symbol of the
fate of the workers' union.

SATURDAY, JULY 31

Our end of July count of internees is as follows: seven-
ty-eight released, fifty-four remain. The average age of
the internees has gone up to 35.5 years. Nine persons are
on leave (seven from Gdańsk and two from Toruń), three
people refused to go on leave, and demanded instead to
be released without further conditions. The matter of
releasing Andrzej Zarębski from Solidarity's Bureau of
Press and Information has been dragging on since Easter.
His wife gave birth to a daughter during his internment
and he himself has been on the International Red Cross
release list because of his poor state of health. It looked as
if he would find himself on the list of internees to be

released on July 22. At the last moment a phone call from police headquarters in Gdańsk prevented his leaving the camp. The people from Solidarity's Bureau of Press and Information had been under special police surveillance. The regime was obviously rankled by their attempt to break the state's monopoly on information and now it was taking revenge. The transgressions of strike leaders and members of opposition groups could be forgiven, but the proponents of an independent system of information had to be burned out with a hot iron. The boys from BIPS are a very specific phenomenon in camp. Almost all of them have college educations and participated in creating a new wave of humanism on the Coast. Many of them have done a lot of writing and are undoubtedly talented.

Andrzej remains in camp.

TUESDAY, AUGUST 3

Yesterday evening a new transport of internees was brought from Szczecin. This caused the usual animation in the guard booth. We got news from the prisoners that there are thirty-four people from Szczecin, that is, thirty-four boarders from the camp in Wierzchowo. Among them is Marian Jurczyk, Regional Chairman of Solidarity; Stanisław Kocjan, member of the National Commission; and Przemysław Fenrych, Regional press spokesman and a member of the Primate's Council for Social Affairs.

This time our cells remain shut after evening roll. Our new colleagues are located in cells in pavilion II in haphazard groups of three or four people. The guards ignored the "special requests" made during the assigning of cells to the new internees, and said that all the changes could be made tomorrow.

Late in the evening, after the new internees had settled themselves, they began to tell us their stories and we exchanged information. They were exhausted. They had made their trip in police vans that are also called "refrigerators"—an inappropriate name this time, however, as the ride from Wierzchowo lasted the entire day in the scorching sun. Many of them got carsick (they looked ill), and some of them fainted. The convoy would stop for nothing.

WEDNESDAY, AUGUST 4

After two days of talks with the Wierzchowo group, we have an outline of what happened in Szczecin:

On the night of December 12/13, according to the martial law plan, Solidarity activists were detained in the voivodeship of Szczecin. The detentions took place at night, and in some cases doors were broken down to get at the desired individuals. We were taken to police headquarters and after a while we were transported in prison vehicles to the prison in Goleniów, one of the worst prisons. In this group were three women, who, after a few days, were taken to an internment camp for women in Kamień Pomorski. People from outside of Szczecin were automatically brought to the prison in Goleniów. Within a few days, the number of internees grew to eighty-six. Among them were Marian Jurczyk, Regional Chairman, and Stanisław Kocjan, Regional Secretary, who were arrested on their way home to Szczecin after the National Committee deliberations in Gdańsk. The vice-chairman of the Regional Union in Western Pomerania, Aleksandr Krystosiak, and the whole presidium of the Regional Union were locked up. At the beginning of January, the vice-chairman of the National Committee, Stanisław Wądołowski from the Szczecin shipyard, was brought from Strzebielinek. There were also people from Rural Solidarity, a few independent activists, and five members of the Police Trade Union, who were on a hunger strike until they were detained in the shipyard.

The internees were put in one of the multistoried wings of the prison. The four-person cells left the internees less than a square meter of living space, not counting the beds. There was no toilet and no running water. There were only metal pots which we called "wojteks."* After a few days we were able to use a regular bathroom during the day that had cold running water. This enabled contact and short meetings at the door to the bathroom, and one day there was even a meeting of the presidium of the Regional Union in this room. Earlier we had to resort to shouting from the windows.

At first our intention was to spend our time any old way, and just to wait things out, make time go fast. It seemed to us that this thing would have to end soon. We expected sudden solutions. Emotions ran high. Fear, shock, and disbelief mixed with the desire to act against this evil. We felt a complete lack of information. We were able to get bits and pieces from the news broadcasts that came over the speakers in all the cells. The leaks about strikes were the subject of endless discussions. Some of us said that we should have hope, that this is the last breath given off by that hated government. Others said that this might mean the end of the Union, that only severe repressions and terror would follow. Everyone was more and more convinced that we would not be released tomorrow and that we should fill this time and make good use of it. We read

---

*Diminutive formed from Jaruzelski's first name, Wojciech (Wojtek).

books. We could use the library every once in a while. Later many people began learning foreign languages. In the evening we held discussions, reminisced, and told jokes. After a week, we could visit other cells sporadically, if we asked the guards for permission. Later we did this regularly without any obstacles whatsoever. This made it possible for us to organize small meetings and get-togethers in one of the cells. There were meetings in the cells of Edward Bałuka, Z. Zdanowicz, and M. Jurczyk. One of the meetings had to do with the strike as an active defense of the workplace. Opinions were divided. The period just past was analyzed and attempts were made to introduce a prognosis of the development of the situation. The dates given for lifting martial law were now a few months away. The first smuggled messages, the first leaflets appearing under martial law were a real event. There were animated discussions about the contents, and the publications themselves raised emotions and spirits. The massacre in the Wujek mine struck us with horror.

The walks allowed us to have contact with one another in groups, but we were carefully watched. The attitude towards the guards was tolerant, and we often talked to them. Most of them were decent people and they acted decently toward us. We did not increase the tensions between us, and so the ZOMOs were moved out of the building. The ZOMOs had been garrisoned on the third floor in the reading room "just in case." The first family visits were conducted through glass and earphones, but after that, they took place in reasonable conditions at a table. Shortly thereafter we were able to drink our first cup of coffee, and eat food brought to us by our families. The prison meals were very bad at first, later they improved. Dinners were strictly one course. They were tasteless and did not satisfy our hunger. Medical aid was poor, at first we had only a medical assistant. This situation was alleviated somewhat by the presence of one of the internees, Dr. Zdanowicz, a member of the Regional Union.

Christmas Eve was a very moving time for us. Everyone gathered in the corridors and sang Christmas carols. We shared bread and the Christmas wafer at supper, and we talked about the past and the future. We talked about the uncommon and unexpected situation in which we found ourselves. Each internee thought about his family, about his loved ones, and Solidarity. Equally moving was the first mass, which took place on January 3.

We also shared the Christmas wafer with the prisoners who worked in our pavilion. They were very good to us and taught us how to manage in prison conditions.

On January 11 we were transferred to the prison in Wierzchowo (in the voivodeship of Koszalin in Pomerania). We had expected something better: better conditions and laxer discipline. Instead, we encountered a lot of hostility from the guards and prison administrators in Wierzchowo. The guards were gruff and pedantic about doing their duties. We saw pure hatred toward Solidarity. One of the lieutenants told us that he considered us common criminals and that is how we would be treated. This created a bitter atmosphere. The only opportunities for contact with other internees were the walks, talking through the windows or using the prisoner-workers, who distributed the meals. In addition to us, there were over a dozen Solidarity activists from the voivodeship of Koszalin. There were frequent cell searches and even frisking before the internees could go out on walks. Bishop Ignacy Jeż from Koszalin soon came to visit us. The bishops' visits were real events for us. Beginning with the following Sunday, bishops from Szczecin would come to visit. Bishop Kazimierz Majdański came to visit us, among others. The mass was solemn, patriotic and very moving. The hymn,

Rota, "God, Protector of Poland," "The Song of the Confederacy," and others.

Sometimes our emotions quieted down. Fewer discussions, less animated talks, except for when something interesting happened. More underground press was reaching us, and we read it from "cover to cover." There was a lot of joking around as an attempt, I think, to cover up impatience and uneasiness. Most of the time was spent in study, reading books, and playing cards and chess. We tried to make some sense of all that had happened since December 13. We waited daily for some sign that would give us hope, that would in some way mark the end of our internment and a resolution of the situation in the country. The SB questioned people. We tried to discourage internees from going to these sessions, but we tried to be understanding to those who went. We had a negative attitude toward those who signed "loyalty oaths," but no one condemned those who had signed them.

The prison guards began to apply force against some of the internees. A few colleagues were beaten in Koszalin. After finding bugging devices in a few of the cells, the guards began to act very aggressively. For three days there were cell searches to find the bugging devices that the internees had hidden. On February 13, the majority of internees was brutally beaten. Prison guards came into the cells armed with long clubs, gas, shields, and helmets. We were forced to stand for roll. The internees were dragged out of their cells and forced to "run the gauntlet." Some internees were chased through the snow barefoot. Everyone was beaten and the cells were gassed. The next day the internees went on a hunger strike. We tried this form of protest earlier. The hunger strikers demanded to see the International Red Cross, the authorities responsible for the behavior of the guards, and also demanded that charges be brought against them. The day after that,

Bishop Gałecki of Szczecin arrived. News of the beating spread. People from Central Prison Administration came to investigate and the military prosecutor began an independent inquiry into the matter, which is still going on.

In March we could have contact with one another officially, and could make more use of the reading room. The situation of the internees began to look more the way it had in Goleniów. The atmosphere became more relaxed. The doctor saw patients every day, and we could go to the dentist once a week. Some of the guards and prison workers were replaced. We could have a bath twice a week. Representatives from the International Red Cross and the Polish Red Cross finally appeared. We even received packages from the International Red Cross. The cell searches were rarer now. They were done only before anniversaries, holidays, and the 13th of every month.

The cells in Wierzchowo were opened on March 29. The atmosphere got better. A series of endless discussions, polemics, and meetings began. This was the beginning of a surrogate cultural life. We began to issue a prison daily called the *Wierzchowo News*. Sixty-four issues of this paper appeared. The production of various prison stamps began to get underway. We organized lectures, talks, and courses. Professor Łuczko's history lectures were the most popular. Lectures in sociology, the history of art, religious studies, and so on, also organized. Medical care was practically all in the hands of a single internee, Dr. Z. Zdanowicz. A choir was organized and directed by Zygmunt Dziechciowski, one of the internees, who was well versed in music. In addition, we had an electric organ that was a gift from one of the Szczecin bishops. The masses were always very solemn and accompanied by much singing. Z. Dziechciowski played the organ. The masses always ended with long conversations on subjects pertaining to religion and Poland.

We spent the Easter holidays rather quietly. The visits on April 11 and 12 were allowed to last much longer than usual. We had Easter eggs and a lamb made of sugar. There was a nice family atmosphere during the holidays and on both the eleventh and twelfth, Bishops Gałecki and Stefanek paid us a visit.

All of the anniversaries were prepared in advance and solemnly commemorated. On the thirteenth of every month at 9 P.M., we all gathered in the main reading room for an evening of reminiscing. The ping-pong table was covered with candles, we prayed for Poland, and sang hymns. The mood was solemn. We commemorated the miners that had been killed in the Wujek mine with a moment of silence. The evening's activities were led by Przemysław Fenrych.

Much emotion and discussion was aroused by the Primate's Council for Social Affairs, which issued a statement on the subject of national unity. We could not work out a single position on this statement. Some of the internees were released during this time. By May there were only sixty of us left. The events of May 1, 3, and 13 cheered us up and let us hope that society would not be divided and destroyed. After these events, our camp began to fill up again, and in a few days, there were already 130 of us. Emotions grew heated. Again a lot of talks, consultations, and lectures. Discussions of the situation developing in the country and the possibility of resolving the existent impasse.

In the camp in Wierzchowo, there was a real din from all the discussions and activities. There were league championships in table tennis, chess, and bridge, and one of the internees, Sławiński, prepared a cabaret. *Wierzchowo News* contained feuilletons and satirical cartoons as well as news from Poland and around the world. We joked about "the family," that is, the internees from the regional Solidarity leadership from Szczecin who were our informal representatives. Candidates were nominated to the group closest to the "family." Satirical cartoons and jokes on this subject abounded. There was a survey taken of political views, and a certain number of internees answered that they had no specific political viewpoint. The majority answered that it had social-democratic leanings, after that were Christian-democratic and liberal ones. The results of the survey were published in *News*. Cultural and social life blossomed. In June and July, Jerzy Zimowski conducted discussions on the subject of "struggle without force." The subject of the Primate's Council and its statement returned, and this time the statement was deemed worthy of attention and support. We still spent a lot of time reading and learning foreign languages, but now we spent even more time in relaxing outdoors because of the longer walks and the warm summer temperatures. T. Demko organized a course in Polish grammar.

The internees' attitude toward the guards and prisoner-workers was not hostile. Beginning in May, the internees organized almost daily masses. In June another camp publication called "Solidarity of the Interned" appeared. We had easy access to underground publications.

The gradual releasing of internees began in June. After July 22, most of the internees were released. Thirty-four internees remained. We felt that the government's actions on July 22 were for the sake of appearances and that the government had missed its opportunity. We were beginning to feel disillusioned. The releases caused a slowdown in the pace of camp activity. A quieter and slower period began. The day was measured by a steady, uniform rhythm. We devoted a great deal of time to cultivating a small vegetable plot. We had time to reflect, to analyze everything that had happened once again, even if it was just one's own part in everything that was going on in the country.

On August 2 we were transferred to Strzebielinek. This time we were searched for almost six hours and they tore apart even the laundry detergent. A long trip in stuffy police vans awaited us. The sun beat down on the vans mercilessly.

TUESDAY, AUGUST 10

Today I was at the beach in Sopot! This has been one of my obsessions for many months: to see the Baltic, to see the mountains, with my own eyes.

I am really at the seaside. I have been "free" for several days now. The term "free" was thought up long before martial law. I do not feel free. I have behind me another session with an *ubek* at police headquarters. The result seems to be that my generation will be hard put to find work, and will have a hard life. The generation of the Polish August will still have to wage a battle for its place in life. Will it have the same problems as the AK?* Is our place in the prisons? On the peripheries of societal life? Society will surely not forget about us, it will surely not allow itself to be intimidated in this way.

The beginning was splendid: visits, visits, from acquaintances, colleagues, neighbors. Flowers, help. But what about my job? Will I have a chance to work normally in my profession? In a union? I know only one thing, that I am a part of my nation, my fate is bound up

---

Armia Krajowa, Home Army.

with the fate of my country. If we are successful, I will be successful.

SUNDAY, AUGUST 29

The camp school of conspiracy has resulted in the fact that I can still continue this diary, even while remaining on this, or rather that, side of the prison wall. In a relatively short time we have established a few channels of mutual contact. A package containing the following notes reach me in this way:

August 24

The case of Marian Jurczyk. Most recently the camp has been living Marian Jurczyk's terrible tragedy. You probably know about the double suicide of his son and daughter-in-law. All of this hit him and us on Friday, August 6, quite unexpectedly. I remember how he was called from the walkway. There, in a very cold and impersonal manner, he was told about the suicide. It went something like this:

"Do you have a son named Adam?" "Yes."

"And your daughter-in-law's name is _____ ?" "Yes."

"I have been instructed to give you some very sad news: both are dead. They committed suicide. A moment ago I received a call from police headquarters in Szczecin with this news and with instructions to inform you. I know nothing more."

That is how much Jurczyk found out from Lieutenant Szafrański. The news about Jurczyk's tragedy went from pavilion to pavilion, from cell to cell. I don't know what Jurczyk thought at the time, but our reaction was the hideous suspicion of political revenge against Marian. I did not see him for a few hours after he got the news. He stayed in his cell.

Yesterday evening the Camp Council met. They decided to do everything possible to get as much information as possible about what happened and to help Marian contact his family. We spoke very seriously about the possibility of a revolt in camp, and even of burning this shack to the ground, if Marian did not receive complete and accurate information about the suicides.

The next day, though, was a free Saturday. Jurczyk and Jacek Merkel got permission to place a call to Szczecin. They could not accomplish a thing. They never got through to Szczecin, nor could they get a hold of the camp warden, he had already left for the weekend. Nothing. Madness. He had to keep all this pent up inside himself until Monday.

Przemysław Fenrych from Szczecin was to go on leave at noon on Saturday. We all chipped in to pay for a taxi so that he could get to Szczecin as quickly as possible and get some specific information. On Monday, the same problem with calling Szczecin as on Saturday.

During the night preceding the funeral, a few *ubeks* came from Szczecin and took Marian. Twenty-four hours later, he returned. He was exhausted and it seemed to me that he had gone gray. We did not ask him about anything. From what he did say, though, we found out that he was "in custody" during the entire time and was not allowed to visit his home or to be alone with his family. After the funeral, at the police station, he was told that he and his family could have an apartment rented just for them for three days if he would appear on television and appeal for quiet in the streets. He refused.

We don't even know how to help him. His closest friends are attending to him and we are not imposing our sympathy on him. He is holding up very well.

August 26: The 600th Anniversary of Our Lady of Częstochowa

10 A.M.: Mass. Instead of a homily, fragments of Primate Wyszyński's sermons and the Pope's prayers are read.

5 P.M.: Marian conference, at which Jasiu Bartczak talks about the social teachings of the Church.

10 P.M.: Jasna Góra roll for the dead (prayers and singing in the chapel). Posters hung in the cell windows all day.

August 27

Eighteen people were brought from Białołęka from the Mazowsze region. Among them are Dr. Gabriel Jankowski, vice-chairman of Rural Solidarity.

In the afternoon we received gifts from Father Jankowski's parish in Gdańsk. Anna Kowalczykowa and Dr. Budny brought them. There was margarine, ham, canned meats, cheese, coffee, tea, cocoa, candy, and toilet paper. Jacek Merkel found out that his wife has given birth to a daughter.

August 29

Dear _____ ,

We did not know that you were out already. You will get the next news regularly. Szczecin is here. Szczecin has a decidedly Union character. They lack certain political tendencies. Marian Jurczyk has an enormous amount of authority, and his position or statement unites people behind him. In speech and thought they show a consistent respect for the truth. They tell it as it happened. They do not try, in their letters to the Episcopate or to the Pope, for example, to say things in such a way as to gain something by it in the future. In Strzebielinek they are shocked by the political groups, the freedom of movement, the relatively relaxed organization of daily life, and the level of health care (dentist, hospital). They are very careful in expressing their opinions about the current situation and especially in expressing them on paper, in the underground press. That is a result of the warden's treatment of them in Wierzchowo (the beating in February) and the tactics of the police commander in Szczecin as well as the rather poorly organized underground in that part of the country. The entire Szczecin group attends mass, even the nonbelievers. They organize themselves around the weekly masses said by one of the bishops or around the masses and religious conferences organized by members of the Catholic Club in Szczecin (which, incidentally, was not suspended as WRON overlooked it). This is the most numerous group among them, and there is very nice cooperation between them in terms of ideas and organization. Przemysław Fenrych, a member of the Primate's Council and the only one in that council that is interned, is also among them (he is currently on leave).

This group has lent the people from Szczecin a specific political coloring. Around August 8, two members of the Communist Party club "Odrodzenie" were brought here from Szczecin. One is the press spokesman for that club. They keep to themselves, saying that they are here by mistake, and that they will not take part in any political discussions. That is what they declared, but the reality is a little different. They keep to themselves.

I wrote this description because someone else is supposed to write to you about other things.

Another important problem is the propagation and organization of legal social activity under the auspices of the Church. I would like to talk to you about that in greater detail. In the meantime, read the note in *Gość Niedzielny* from June 6, 1982, nr. 12. This is an idea worth imitating. I am waiting for further information. Hugs and greetings to all.

August 29

Dear _____ ,

Thank you for all the smuggled information. There is a lot that is new, it's just too bad that it is all so pessimistic. Our assessment of the situation is, unfortunately, similar. I fear August 31, because it seems that both sides are betting a lot on one card, and in this kind of confrontation, the government, of course, has the advantage. The Primate made a nice comparison: he said this was a bullfight, the battle of a toreador with a bull. One has enormous power, and the other goads the bull with a red cape so that he can deal him a cold, precise, and mortal blow. I think that there is small chance that the demonstrations will have any effect. This is not hard to foresee. The decision to have a demonstration on August 31 was a mistake. Many of the internees feel otherwise (the entire fundamentalist fraction including the commander of the legions). You might have noticed traces of disagreement in the letter to the Primate. The letter was a compromise as it was, cut out of the very delicate admission that even we were not blameless in what happened. Such meetings are awful: you think that you are talking to a man, and bam, you hit a wall, a concrete wall, through which the arguments won't penetrate. Our colleagues from

Białołęka have been here only two days, but already they are happy with the change. There they had open cells only three hours daily, shorter walks and visits, everything a lot worse than here. The rest of Białołęka was transported to Darłówek (seven persons), to Zależa (about as many as came here) and to somewhere else, but no one knows where. In Białołęka there was only one prison group (eighteen persons) which was isolated at first (including all those people who left us on December 29: Kuroń, Gwiazda, Wujec, Rulewski, etc.). They drove here fourteen hours in the "refrigerators." In Grudziądz they knocked out an air hole for themselves, and hung a Solidarity flag out of it. All the passers-by stared at the column. We are expecting another transport of forty people, but we do not know from where. Our cell has not changed much (perhaps it is a little dirtier than when you were here). . . .

Try to count how many people have passed through Strzebielinek. Add the internees from Białołęka (I am sending you an earlier list). I marked all the "Americans," that is, the criminal element. After the 31st, I will send you the statistical data. I wonder how certain and safe this channel of ours is (considering the frequency of exchanged information). Perhaps we should consider an emergency channel (think where _____ works). Write about yourself and about your current status. I enclose my warmest greetings as do the others.

· · ·

In the same batch of mail, I got a set of documents pertaining to the brutal beating of forty-five out of eighty-eight internees in the camp in Wierzchowo Pomorskie on July 13, 1982. The military prosecutor in Koszalin had begun criminal proceedings against the perpetrators of this brutal beating, but the case was closed with the decision to drop the investigation and to issue fines. This is what the internees from Wierzchowo who are now in Strzebielinek write about the matter:

Pertaining to the prosecutor's decision . . . The decision to drop the charges brought by the military prosecutor in Koszalin against two prison guards, K. Wronkowski and H.E. Ambryszewski, the direct executors of the July 13 beatings in Wierzchowo Pomorskie, demands considerable additional information. It is true that the bestial beatings were officially admitted, as was the symbolic punishment (blatantly disproportionate to the crime) of the perpetrators of this heinous act, but it also omits many facts connected with it, and which are significant in this matter.

The August 18 decision of the prosecutor mentioned nothing about the conditions of internment in that prison, about the atmosphere which was far from normal, about the facts before July 13 (for example, about the earlier individual beatings), and also about what happened after that day. All of these could point the finger at the real criminals hiding behind the executors of these orders. We warned the prison authorities much earlier about the potential development of such a situation. We mentioned the guards' vulgarity when speaking to us and the ways in which they tried to intimidate us. J. Wiśniewski informed the prosecutor of these facts in letters to the military prosecutor in Koszalin.

The last beating before February 13 took place three days earlier when the internees from Koszalin uncovered a listening device in Cell 2. Other internees found evidence of such devices having been installed and then removed from their cells. In order to find the dismantled parts of the device, the guards turned the cells upside down, and held questionings of the internees at night in the presence of the prison warden, Major M. Gadomski. The questionings were conducted by Colonel Frydrychowicz of Koszalin.

Drunken guards dragged internees out of their cells and beat them. T. Habennan of Koszalin was beaten then, and earlier victims (late January) were J. Witkowski, R. Śnieg, T. Dziechciowski and W. Rudnicki.

Police headquarters in Szczecin and Koszalin decided and knew about every little detail concerning the camp life of the internees. They also confirmed the groups of internees in each cell and whether or not the internees would watch television or take walks. For comparison, it is worthwhile to note that the internees from West Pomerania who had been in the prison in Goleniów felt that in spite of the worse conditions in Goleniów (chamber pots in the cells, 1.75 square meter per person in the cell, first ten days without walks, no television or reading room, bread and margarine for Christmas Eve Supper), they had had a better atmosphere and had been treated better by the guards and *ubeks*. It would have been inconceivable for the beatings to have taken place in Goleniów.

And now specifically: The decision to dismiss the matter was based on the false claim that "the use of physical force against the internees by the prison administrative apparatus in Wierzchowo was not premeditated. Yet everything from early morning on July 13 indicated that something was going to happen: the guards in the watchtowers had reinforcements and there were more people on guard during the distribution of meals. Some of the prison officers, for example our "educator" to the interned, Lubomir

Sikorski, who was dismissed from duty that day, said to our colleague, Leszek Dlouchy, that "this is nothing, greater pleasures await you this evening."

That was true: while beating us the guards shouted: "You fucking Wałęsites," "Jaruzelski gave us clubs so that we could beat you and we have the right to do what we want with you." These "educative" forms were passed over in silence in the prosecutor's report. There are other significant omissions.

The prosecutor writes that in Cell 14, no one was beaten, and the reason for that was that Marian Jurczyk and others members of the Regional Board of Western Pomerania were in that cell. They were told: "Today we will pass up you sons of bitches, but next time it will be different." The guards recognized that the risk of a public uproar would be too great in this case.

Complaints about the beatings were written directly after the fact and often they had to be given to the man who had done the beating. Many of the internees did not believe in the sense and efficacy of the complaints and did not file one. According to the internees' count, forty-five people were beaten. The same with the examinations done by the prison doctor an hour or two after the beatings. The internee was called to go to the doctor by the guard who had just beaten him. Some of the internees thought that this was another trick, and would not go to the doctor.

Also omitted from the report were the actions of two men who did not take part in the beatings, but who indicated the cells or the persons to whom the guards were supposed to "stick it." Here the guards Cap and Maruszewski distinguished themselves.

On Sunday, July 14, Bishop Gałecki came to camp to say mass and was informed by the administration that the internees had taken part in actions which were "contrary to law." It was not until after consultations with the police in Szczecin that the bishop was allowed to say mass. It is worth remembering that the weekly mass was the one opportunity we had to meet together outside of the cells (this remained so until the end of March). The guards frisked the internees who went to mass, and prison personnel observed the mass from the corridor. On that day the visits looked a little different than usual. We were on one side of several tables and our families were on the other. Along the sides were the guards who had worked us over yesterday. At one point, Edward Bałuka took off his shirt and showed the visitors his bruised back, pointing all the while at the people who did this bestial act. The visits were interrupted and a colleague, M. Kłyszka, was charged with insulting an officer of the law.

We organized a hunger strike to draw society's attention to these events. On Tuesday, July 16, we stopped the hunger strike after the visit of Colonel Pawlaczyk from Central Prison Administration, who promised to ease prison regulations and to transfer the most "zealous" of the guards. Many facts pertaining to the beatings were described and confirmed in the prosecutor's statement because we did not know the names of the guards who beat us. Some of them were given to us by their colleagues who were friendly toward us. We also found out that on July 13 someone had called for two ambulances from Złocieniec. They were turned away from the gates, however. We also found out, via leaks from the warden's office, that on the day of the beating, permission for using force against the internees was sent from Warsaw by telex. We have to admit that, thanks to the prepared statement about dropping criminal charges, it was possible to alarm public opinion by referring to this objective description of events.

From the time of the statement, a few colleagues have appealed the decision, as have, apparently, those who beat them.

MONDAY, AUGUST 30

Continuing my journal "in freedom" I am subject to no lesser emotions than those that would overcome me in camp. Suddenly my apartment, so different than before, does not give me a feeling of safety. In order to finish my work, I am constantly hovering around my friends, whom I carefully select. When walking around with my manuscript on the street, I have a feeling which is familiar to me only from films and lectures on the Nazi occupation. I taste life in underground Poland this way. Of course there are many that have been living like this for eight months, and whose faces stare out from wanted posters, their names on lists of the pursued. I have gotten in the habit of shutting off phones in places that I am visiting, of listening to the sound of the elevators, and cars pulling up in front of the house. At the same time, continuing work gives me the feeling of being useful, my colleagues' opinions confirm this, everyone expects us to leave a distinct trace, and a testimony to the present time.

TUESDAY, AUGUST 31

From today's smuggled message (dated August 30):

Today five new internees, detained on Sunday, were brought from Gdańsk (Staszek Burek from the Gdańsk Shipyard was among them). Handing them their bills of internment the officer tried to cheer them up by saying it was only for ten days. All are workers from big factories in the Tri-City area. We have a prison full of guards. They are all garrisoned in the administration building. All night there was nothing but the sound of moving guards and traffic.

. . .

It is night. The city is still being shaken by echoes of bursting petards. The wind blows the rest of the tear gas all the way to the room where I am sitting. Wrzeszcz and Siedlce, two Gdańsk districts, are still fighting, but the flashing is getting less frequent in the Old Town.

I solved the dilemma before noon: I decided that in spite of the risk of repeated internment or imprisonment my responsibility was to be at the shipyard on this day, under the monument. I was there when the Gdańsk Accords were signed and I was there today. Leaving the house, I took a few packages of cigarettes, a notebook, and a pen. We said good-bye to the children longer than usual. In spite of the fact that we have tried to create a protective zone at home for the children, they inevitably feel every single tension.

In order to avoid an i.d. check by ZOMO patrols, I got into a train that runs parallel to the Gdańsk Shipyard. I rode in that tram a few times back and forth. Around 2 P.M., in spite of my fears, I got out at the tram stop closest to the Monument to the Fallen Shipyard Workers. I mixed in with the crowd of people that had gotten out and were waiting at the stop. We were divided from the monument by a police cordon that would not allow people with wreaths to step up to the crosses. We wondered what to do. In the meantime, a large group of a few hundred shipyard workers who had just ended their shift had already gathered under the crosses. Seeing the indecision of the people held back by the ZOMOs, the shipyard workers began to chant: "Every Pole, to the monument!" The chant acted like a spur. We immediately moved forward together from all sides. The police disappeared somewhere, as if the earth had swallowed them up.

A Solidarity poster was pasted onto the monument and greater and greater numbers of people began to shout: "Solidarity! Free Lech!" We look at each other. I try to find familiar faces. There was no script. WRON has caused these protest actions to be spontaneous, unorganized, there is a certain heat to them; people feel the need to express themselves, but their leaders are silent. There is probably no lack of *ubeks* here who would snap up a speaker. That is why instead of an organized program, instead of even the announcement of the statement of the Primate's Council, we can afford only these few chants. More people and a new chant: "All crows to Red Square." This is a signal for the ZOMOs to attack.

Suddenly a column of armed police emerges from the street next to the Liceum. Jeeps, water cannon installed on mud-colored monster-vehicles, buses with barred windows full of armed bands of ZOMOs. I maneuver so as not to get cut off. The people around me do the same. The column forcing its way into Solidarity Square pushes us into the streets surrounding the Shipyard. I back out alongside the ZOMO column.

The people under the monument whistle in protest. Women curse the slovenly band of ZOMOs that jump out of the cars ready to attack. The water cannon, driving onto the square at full speed, blasts the crowds with water. A man next to me pulls out his press credentials, and says something in broken Polish to the ZOMO who is waving a rocket pistol in our direction and who reminds me of a modern Viking in a helmet. His gun is on a rope, and I associate him with desperado foreign legionnaires, hired by dictators to terrorize freedom movements. WRON really has created an ethos of mercenaries who fight against the people for money, bonuses, special treatment, and for being above the law. They are trained in the tactics of breaking up and beating people, and in seizing groups marked in advance, while others are busy preparing prisons and camps. The Sejm, on the other hand, thinks up laws which government propaganda justifies ideologically by controlling the people through press and television. The whole totalitarian machine on one side and we with our idea on the other. The whole arrangement is guaranteed by the army, which takes no direct part in the clashes. People attacked by ZOMOs hide behind the soldiers. Someone shouts: protect us from these thugs. The soldiers say nothing and stand like puppets strung out in columns. The crowd draws the army leaders into conversations. Discussions with soldiers begin at the edge of the slaughter going on on the main thoroughfare along the railroad station and near the Party building. People say to the soldiers: "You swore to protect whom, them or the people?" They ask: "Are you going to shoot us or defend us?" "Do you have orders to use weapons against the people?" The leaders squirm during the conversations. The men are ignored but more and more women surround the leaders and ply them with similar questions. Others say: "These boys aren't to blame, if they are given the orders, they will shoot." One of the leaders is indignant. He explains that whether or not to shoot is a decision made individually by each leader. They also have the right to refuse to give that order if they feel it should not be done.

This is the nature of our conversation on the second anniversary of the signing of the Accords. This is the nature of our Polish dialogue in the eighth month of martial law. I cry, others cry, too, the tear gas is making us cry . . .

It is only at home, when I collect my thoughts, that I see clearly how we let ourselves be drawn into a fight from which there is no exit. It is very convenient for the government to have the idea of Solidarity reduced to street fighting, to have it reduced to clashes with ZOMO thugs, to have it pushed into the underground, where wanted posters are waiting for us, as are decrees, laws, and stiff sentences for underground activities, the distribution of publications, a word or a thought. And we fell for that even though we haven't got a chance in this type of game. It was the government's intention that we should get mixed up in a row with the guards, with the camp warden, with the prison doctor, with the ZOMO van driver, with the *ubek* conducting a search. This crime was committed by a small group of people who made the decision to declare martial law. What followed was only the result of that night.

MONDAY, SEPTEMBER 13

I am copying a few of the camp messages, without comment:

August 8

One hundred twenty-five internees in camp. At 1 A.M. new people—workers—were brought in. At 3 P.M. we held a commemorative ceremony on the second anniversary of the signing of the Accords: the people on the walkways formed a procession. Stanisław Bury, Jacek Merkel and Gabriel Jankowski (*nota bene:* a worker, intellectual, and peasant) led the procession.

We walk once around the square and then we walk between pavilions II and III. Lots of guards, but they do nothing. We sing the hymn and then Bury reads the twenty-one postulates of the Gdańsk Accords. Selected persons shout out slogans demanding an end to martial law, release of the internees, etc. The last one: Long live independent, self-governing Poland! Rota. The end.

September 1

One hundred thirty-six internees in camp. Eleven new ones: two from factories in Gdańsk, three from the Częstochowa hunger strike, and six from Toruń, including three "Americans." With the people from Gdańsk is Jan Eichelberger, the first re-internee from Gdańsk in this camp. He was released before May 1, was a bus driver, and sat in Cell 35.

The hunger strikers (Janusz Walentynowicz, son of Anna Walentynowicz, Andrzej Karut from Gorzów, and Franciszek Winiarski from Nysa) told their story: They began a hunger strike on August 25 at St. Barbara's Church in Częstochowa as an appeal to end martial law and to release the prisoners, and so on. The hunger strike had no planned ending date and twelve people participated (from Gdańsk, Szczecin, Gorzów, Opole, Kraków, and Warsaw), women included (Ala Górnowicz from Gdańsk, for example). Anna Walentynowicz took care of the strikers, but did not take part in the hunger strike herself. The priests asked them to leave the church, and finally the Bishop of Częstochowa served them an ultimatum: either they leave or they will be escorted out. The bishop said that the authorities threatened to cancel all talks with the Church and to withdraw their permission to build more churches if hunger strikes are carried on in churches. After three days, priests escort the hunger strikers out of the church. On August 28 (now there were only eight hunger strikers), they went to Gdańsk and continued their hunger strike in Walentynowicz's apartment. No church in Gdańsk would allow them to strike within its walls, although there might be a chance after August 31. The hunger strikers wanted to hold out until September 17, so that they could cover all the important anniversaries that fall within that period. They were arrested on August 30. Anna Walentynowicz and other persons (Basia Hejcz, for example, who was released from Gołdapia in May) were also taken away. They were taken to Tczew, where they were not given unsweetened tea or vitamins, and some of them had severe pains after being served sweetened tea. Everyone continued the strike. There were neither beds nor blankets, just bare walls and a window with a broken pane. On August 31 they heard noise out in the street, where the demonstrators were trying to free them from police headquarters. The police then had the captured demonstrators run the gauntlet right outside of their window. They could see everything. At night, they heard the shouts of men and women who were being beaten at the police station. Later they found out that 6,000 people had taken part in the demonstrations in Tczew. Three people were take to Strzebielinek on September 1, but what happened to the rest, including the women, no one knows. The hunger strike was interrupted after two days. They were talked out of it by various people. This day ended with a prayer said together for Poland and in commemoration of September 1939.

September 6

Today is the beginning of Strzebielinek's athletic meet. It will last until September 25 and will include tournaments in: volleyball, table tennis, chess, checkers, bridge, long jump, shot put, tug-of-war, the walk, springs, five-lap run, sixteen-lap run, a 4 × 1 lap relay race and a free relay race. Everyone was divided into four regions: Gdańsk, Pomerania (Toruń-Bydgoszcz), Western Pomerania, and Mazowsze (Warsaw and the rest of the regions). Everyone is participating in the meet, it is very well organized, and special diplomas will be awarded to the winners. I will write more about it after it is over. I do not remember if I wrote you that on September 1 our karate courses began. The courses are given by Instructor Mieczysław Kniaź (Szczecin).

September 10

One hundred thirty-nine internees in camp. There was a very long and tempestuous discussion about the text to be drawn up on the subject of political prisoners (especially KOR). Very deep differences have surfaced so that in the end we had to come up with two different texts (see enclosed).

September 12

At midnight we did our ritual banging on the cell doors for ten minutes.

I find out that the problem of whether or not to emigrate to the West has not gone away. I have received two letters on the subject: the first was written from Canada to camp, where it arrived without being censored, and a second letter, which is in answer to the first. In a sense, both of these letters illustrate the problem:

Churchill, July 18, 1982

Dear Friend:
You probably already know the story of my emigration so I will not repeat it. At one point I began to have doubts about the possible success of everything which began to happen in Poland. Because of my education (in economics) and the distinctly "downward" trend in the economy, I decided to emigrate. This was not an easy decision as I had a good job, a lot of free time, and everything that was important to me and my life was in Poland. I felt that time was not working in my favor, and in my perception of what was to come, I did not see a place for myself. But I did not think that things would deteriorate so quickly and I was counting on the fact that the disintegration would last a little longer. Then I decided to forget about everything and with $150 in my pocket, I sailed across the ocean. I was so determined to start a new life that all fear of the new and unknown was completely stifled within me. The beginning of that new life was not very encouraging as is always the case: hard physical work and, well, winter. I am still an unskilled laborer, even though I have been accepted to study economics (the doctoral program) at the university. I will begin my studies in September 1982 or, at the latest, in September 1983. A degree in itself will not solve any of my problems, I will still have to work somewhere, but it

will certainly create opportunities which I would not have had otherwise. The situation of unskilled laborers is pretty grim here. With the recession and changes in the economy it is difficult to find work that pays above the minimum wage (currently $4 an hour) and this state of affairs will last a while. . . . This country is a mixture of émigrés from all parts of the world, so there is no hostility toward newcomers. It is relatively easy to become a Canadian, as tolerance is high and no one demands that you emphasize your background, language, culture, or customs.

Culturally, Canada rates lower than Poland. No one reads too much, and the cultural elite is not as visible so it does not impose its mode of being on the people as is the case in Poland. . . . There are constant rumors in the West that the internees will soon be released. July 22 is mentioned as the possible date of release.

Reply:

September 18, 1982

Dear ——————— :

Your letter made me very happy. In here it is rare to encounter evidence of someone so dear. Letters and visits are the most pleasant things possible in camp. I did not know the details of your emigration. I first heard about it here and thought that your decision to stay was an emotional reaction to December 13. When thinking about you and my other colleagues, who made similar decisions, I am surprised by the regularity of this phenomenon in Polish history. For almost 200 years each new generation pays its dues by the emigration in thousands of, usually young, people. I myself have been familiar with this since childhood. Many of my father's friends stayed in the West after the war and they still write to him, some even come and visit. Now, in turn, my own friends are becoming the new wave of émigrés. There is probably something inescapable in the fact that so many people must emigrate and that so many do not see a future for themselves there where their past is. The size of this phenomenon, and especially the question of whether or not certain potential values are also escaping, muddle the clarity of the picture. Where, O where is that real Poland? Here? Between the Oder and the Bug rivers, in the place where so many things seem to exist but do not and where appearances pass for reality? Or is Poland wherever there are Poles? I think that some of the significant values are contained in the relationship between you and us. In the nineteenth century, Poland was called "a sick man" and currently this condition has gotten even worse. The fact that your decision was not emotional, but rational, testifies to the incurability of that disease. The best, the most needed people, educated people, fine professionals, social pragmatists, talented artists, the entire upcoming generation of modern technocrats and so many others have decided to remain in the West and to break all institutional ties with their country. It is difficult to make value judgments. The reasons must have been important if so many people decided to emigrate. Sociology understands this kind of action as the instinctive defense mechanism of a given social group. Isn't that what it is now: society surrounds itself with various possibilities, including "telling" part of itself to emigrate so that society would not have to bet everything on one card (armed struggle). The examples of Paderewski, Mickiewicz, Narutowicz, Mościcki, etc., show how much this society can gain in the future. Emigration itself, however, will bring about no basic changes in Poland, but it can be a powerful human reservoir, especially an intellectual reservoir which could, in the long run, significantly protect the overall interests of society. . . .

The fact that July 22 was an opportunity that was not taken advantage of by the government, that there was an escalation in mutual hatred on August 31, and that both sides lack a program of action, results in a life here that seems suspended in a void. There is still no light at the end of the tunnel. Someone said that you do not know Poland until you know its prisons. I think that there is some truth to this, although I myself have had only a small dose of prison and a relatively mild one. It is difficult to write about this right now . . . "Wherever we are, that is where our country is."

Your ——————

MONDAY, SEPTEMBER 20

There is more and more rebellion brewing among some of the young Gdańsk workers who were dispersed by ZOMOs during the August 31 demonstrations. In their plans, and for the time being only in their plans, are ideas for some form of physical defense. "Defense" which in the event of its application will immediately have to become terror, in keeping with the irrevocable rules of force. I fear this spiral and I discourage those with whom I have contact from realizing this course of action. People are waiting for justice, because they were beaten. They expect revenge. Martial law is winding its spiral of violence.

This is dangerous, this thinking about constructing slingshots or making metal spears. I think that this kind of thinking is sporadic. I discourage my hotheaded neighbor from the shipyard from taking this route. The authorities want to do this to us, they want to push us to terrorist acts, to commit crimes. The rest is easy. After a few days, my neighbor admits that I am right. "What should I do?" he asks. In the meantime, we are still collecting money to help those dismissed from the shipyard, even though there are also others in need. Wages have gone down, there is no overtime, prices are going up, and people are afraid of the future.

SUNDAY, SEPTEMBER 26

From letters smuggled from camp:

September 20

One hundred thirty-three internees in camp. Today we got news that on September 15 Wojciech Dobrzyński (Mazowsze) escaped from the hospital in Wejherowo. This is the second such incident. The first internee to escape from the hospital was Krzysiek Wyszkowski (August 8). Both, however, are still on the official camp rolls, and for the time being, we have not suffered the consequences of their escapes, neither here nor at the hospital. We all know what a valuable place the hospital is.

September 21

Today Włodzimierz Przybyłko (Zielona Góra) was brought to camp. He had been interned on December 13. He has passed through ten prisons, most recently in Kwidzyn where he took part in the protest action on August 14 (after the infamous beatings of the internees). There he was accused of attacking a prison guard and was charged, after which he was transferred to Elbląg. There he filed a complaint about the decision of the prosecutor, and the charges were dismissed. After six days, he received another bill of internment and they transferred him to Strzebielinek. His case is still open. He claims that the charges are drummed up. . . .

September 23

Presents from the International Red Cross (Danish and Swedish) brought by two very nice women from the Polish Red Cross. These were packages with sanitary products, 75 of them for women. OK. We divided these up and put some aside for new internees. The chaplain from the hospital in Wejherowo sent us some fruit. After we divided it, each cell received a bowlful.

September 24

Two new internees from Grudziądz, Waldemar Borowski and Henryk Bielewski. From them we found out that our colleague, Jurek Przybylski, who was released on September 16, was interned again and put in Kwidzyn. At the same time, he was dismissed from his job.

Apparently it went something like this: on the day when Przybylski returned to his plant (WARMA), he was greeted by some of the workers, who gave him flowers. This happened in the cafeteria during the breakfast break in the morning, and lasted no more than five minutes, after which everyone sat down to eat. After a few days the SB showed up and took away the two who had handed Przybylski the flowers. Each one of the workers was taken separately and each time, the director of the plant and the personnel officer went along to police headquarters. When the *ubek* would say, in the presence of the director and personnel office, that the worker would have to be kept longer for questioning, the personnel officer would pull out a disciplinary dismissal form and hand it to the detained worker.

Doesn't this seem to indicate new pacification methods? It is financially sound (they do not need to maintain the internee on their payrolls), and it frightens the rest of the workers. I wonder how many of us would have refused to sign the loyalty oaths if we had already been dismissed from work and deprived of our salaries? I also imagine that this kind of locking up of two people who simply handed someone flowers, and the reinternment of a man whom people had dared greet publicly, must have made quite an impression on the entire work force and not just on them.

September 25

Today there was a general meeting on the subject of propositions put forth by the warden. A few days ago Major Kaczmarek, after one of the athletic events, invited a few of the organizers to his office and told them three things: first, the women from the Polish Red Cross wanted to give awards to the winners of the meet out of Polish Red Cross funds; secondly, he agrees to move the ping-pong table into the cafeteria for the doubles tournament; and third, would you, gentlemen, agree to play a volleyball match on Wednesday, September 29, with us, the prison personnel? The invited said that they would have to consult with us and that is why today's meeting. The first two matters were taken care of at once: the first, no; the second, yes; but the third one aroused violent emotions. What, play with the guards? But why not? This is a provocation for propaganda purposes! The major is a sports fanatic and just wants to have a game, etc., etc. We concluded with a vote to end the discussion, which means that the match will take place, if there are people willing to play, but it will be a purely private affair. On the pavilion grating we hung up a bulletin board, which for the time being will serve as a tally board for the meet. We are already preparing to change it into a wall newspaper, however, and the first cartoons and bits of poetry have already been put up. Only three events remain in the Strzebielinek meet. Gdańsk is leading hands down.

Minutes and hours pass quickly, but the days and weeks are getting longer and longer and they destroy the rhythm. Life here, from day to day, is more and more strenuous. And this detestable, stubbornly unequivocal, reality. I walk up to the window and look out. I look out and what do I see: prison.

· · ·

Letters smuggled out of camp:

September 30

One hundred thirty-one internees in camp, fifteen in the hospital. A visit from Regional Prison Administration from Bydgoszcz. An older man in the uniform of a colonel visited the cells in the company of the Major. He was all smiles, but he looked into drawers and wherever he wanted. He addressed Bartczak as "You wise guy." The old man likes prisoners and wants to be pleasant.

October 4

Today we sent a collective petition to the Sejm in the matter of the new law regarding trade unions. We could not do this through an official channel because its collective character is against regulations. It went by a different route. Marian Jurczyk and Gabriel Jankowski sent their own letters to the Sejm. I am enclosing everything.

October 5

Gifts from the Gdańsk Curia were brought by Dr. Konopka.

October 6

New arrivals: Artur Bałasz and Stanislaw Wądołowski, who was in Strzebielinek in December. A dozen of the internees from Szczecin are having talks with the merchants. The "Camp Council" has been increased to nine persons. Staszek Wądołowski has replaced Jacek Merkel as the council head. Current members: Wądołowski, Merkel, Bartczak, Jurczyk, Kocjan, Korejwo, Kukuła, Perejczuk, and Jankowski.

October 7

The guards are on alert, that is, their number has been increased. There are more out during the walks and more in the towers. A few dozen more are sleeping in the administration building and there are a lot of new faces among them. Around twenty internees decided to go on a hunger strike in reaction to the expected liquidation of Solidarity. The majority considered this idea unwise, and others decided against it when they found out about the crazy conditions in which it was to be held. I am enclosing related documents.

October 8 (Friday)

The Union is delegalized. The 300th day of internment.

. . .

Knowing the disposition of the Sejm auditorium, I had no illusions as to the result of the vote on the delegalization of Solidarity. Only twelve deputies and almost the whole nation voted against this. That was not enough. I have to force myself to keep writing this diary with the last bit of my energy. It is sad, hopeless, just as if someone close to me had died. On the train platform sits a sad drunkard with an expressive face, croaking: "On December 13 of that memorable year, a crow hatched from a red egg . . ."*

WEDNESDAY, OCTOBER 13

For two days, on the eleventh and twelfth, in spite of the appeal of the underground to hold off on strike action for another month, the Shipyard was shut down. Those workers who called Solidarity to life now expressed their opinion of the Sejm's new law in the birthplace of the Union. A little of the atmosphere of August returned. People began smiling to one another and initiating conversations. The crowd, which had been silent up to now, felt itself the master of its house again. Hope returned. On

---

*The first two lines of one of the camp songs called "Crow," a reference to WRON, the acronym for the military government.

Monday, my neighbor from the Shipyard stopped by, happy and excited, and invited me to his place for a drink. The doorbell rang incessantly, and people kept asking about how the strike in the Shipyard was going. The Shipyard administration and the army commissar asked the strikers what their demands were, but received no answer. The leaders of the strike decided not to show themselves. In reply to the next question, someone from the crowd shouted: "Everyone knows why we are striking." When discussing the strike in the evening, we wondered if the Shipyard would draw the other factories to strike. I was amazed by the success of the first day of the strike, which went on practically without interference from the government. This seemed a little suspicious. I told this to my landlord. Unfortunately, I was right. On Tuesday, using the martial law decree, the strike was broken by militarization of the shipyard. The street that was bustling with freedom yesterday died in mid-gesture. Gdańsk as usual had sent a signal to Poland that it was standing by its commitment to the August Accords.

. . .

Messages smuggled from camp:

October 11

The hunger strike has ended (after five days). As a result of occurrences of jaundice, we have restricted contact between the cells and have introduced inspections to maintain cleanliness.

October 15

A dozen internees from Szczecin are talking to the peddlers. A solemn conclusion to our meet: diplomas were awarded to the winners. The guards have gone off alert.

There are 100 internees in camp. Six are in the hospital in Wejherowo, and ten on leaves.

October 17

The first internee brought to Strzebielinek, Leszek Kaczyński, was released. Leszek had a very thorough cell search and they found all of his well-hidden camp stamps.

October 19

At the meeting we approved the text of the "Letter to Society on the Subject of the New Trade Unions" (main thesis: boycott them). Many felt that only a sober analysis of the regulations should be sent, without emotional interpolations, but the enclosed is what was finally voted on. There were very heated discussions about how the letter should be signed and to this day the matter is not settled. A lot of arguments and insults.

October 21

We received apples from the "city center," that is, from Father Jankowski's parish, where there is a charitable commission that looks after the interned and jailed.

October 27

As of today, a commission of the International Red Cross is in action. The visit will last two days. There are two representatives of the IRC and their doctor (a woman), a representative of and at the same time a translator from the Polish Red Cross, and a major from the Ministry of Justice. It is always the same. Today there was a general meeting and cell visits. Tomorrow there will be individual talks and medical examinations. At the general meeting we voiced the following complaints: (1) our arrested and sentenced colleagues should be placed within the field of jurisdiction of the International Red Cross (answer: in June the International Red Cross made an official request in this matter to which the government has not yet replied, and so it has permission to visit only the interned); (2) lack of hot water, often in the bathroom, always in the cafeteria, where dishes are washed after dinner; (3) free access to the dentist and hospital at all times; (4) to this day, the floor (which we mentioned in an earlier report) in the cells is not fixed; (5) the diet is not balanced; (6) fill the cracks in the wall for the winter; (7) more convenient visiting hours; and (8) allowing the internees to listen to stations other than the one Polish Radio station. As you can see, most of these were of secondary importance, as much had already been taken care of.

A. Stawikowski has been interned again (October 22). This time he ended up in Kwidzyn.

A colleague is preparing to write up the athletic meet. Together with all the documents this will be quite a package. I will try to get it to you through

———— .

I have ordered some materials for you, but this will take a while.

Kaczmarek is on a long holiday, and Biegaj is taking his place which, as you know, is really the same thing. Biegaj has also been promoted to major.

We did a survey on the subject of the future, possible solutions, and especially the justifications for the strike planned for November 10. We are still working on it. I will send you the results.

I have a favor to ask you: if you can, please send ear stoppers.

Keep warm and think about us at least half as much as we think about you.

November 4

I am sending you the most interesting item: the survey. I wanted you to have the survey before November 10. We will try to undertake this work on a larger scale, and we certainly would not be able to manage here without your help. We are having trouble getting the other materials, there are not enough people to help, and a few more internees (involved with your work) have been released. At any rate, I am doing what I can. I draw your attention to the more important matters: Bartczak is in the hospital, Z. Dunowski is out, and another Walentynowicz has been interned (after the strike in the Gdańsk Shipyard), this time Anna Walentynowicz's brother-in-law, Witold. I have to stop because people are rushing me. All of this was prepared at super-express speed during the night and morning, so please forgive the astigmatism of the letter. Damn, there is really no more time, the myrmidons are upon me.

Two days ago Zygmunt Błażek returned from the hospital in Wejherowo after seven months of treatment.   . . .

Zygmunt Błażek, whom the message mentions in one line, was a colorful figure, to say the least. Before he became the Great Patient in Wejherowo, he was the chief of the Union's Poster Brigade, the same brigade which turned Gdańsk and its wall and sidewalks as well as train stations and trolleys into one big newspaper during Solidarity's heyday. This was our Błażek. By the end of its career, the brigade had a red Mercedes minibus, snappy coveralls, and a walkie-talkie network. When at work in the city, the brigade caused a real panic among the police authorities and law enforcement crews. They had a hard time of it with Błażek. He treated his postering and painting of walls, including the Shipyard walls, as the highest vocation; and he carried out not only his assignments, but also his own ideas, impeccably, with great precision and talent. The brigade became extremely good at its work: it took them only a few minutes to paint slogans, giant caricatures, or phrases like "Television Lies!" right across from the Party building. Błażek, as the chief and jack-of-all-trades of the operation, drew in the outlines while the younger people (for whom work with Błażek was one great adventure) filled in the contours with paint. Attempts to stop the brigade or to drag them into a fray of one kind or another always ended unpleasantly for the uniformed police or plainclothesmen. In addition, the brigade had the habit of recording these encounters on tape recorders. All of this made Błażek invincible. The Gdańsk Shipyard stood behind the brigade and valued its work. The Shipyard guaranteed the brigade's safety. Any attempt to eliminate it would have ended in a strike. Almost the whole brigade ended up in the camp in Strzebielinek: Artur Pisarski (The Minor), Andrzej Składowski (Skinny) and others. All of Poland envied Gdańsk its efficient propaganda dissemination. Even the comrades at the special Party congress were worried and appealed to Party officials to do something about the Party's slow and bungling social propaganda. They lamented that Solidarity was heads above them in ingenuity and graphic quality and design. Not to mention something which they avoided to mention: the value of its contents. Błażek's contribution was assessed most accurately by the UB which proposed, after Błażek's internment, that he change sponsors. If he had agreed, he would have been released immediately and could have continued his work on the walls at the UB's dictation. They tried to blackmail him, too. But Błażek chose the hospital. He sat there seven months, beating all previous records. He was an electronics technician by profession and he could adjust a radio receiver in such a way that any old box could get the station you wanted. In the hospital he worked out a color information system and was adored by the the nurses.

. . .

November 10

From today's perspective, the survey which I sent you appears interesting. As much as we can judge at this hour (it is 10 P.M.), the pervasive pessimism of the survey has been confirmed. Today I am sending you, in addition to the regular portion of information, a list from Kwidzyn and an old and current list from Strzebielinek. There are problems with materials, but you will get something next time for sure. Everyone to whom I have turned has been released from Białołęka, and I see literally no one there to help us now. You will get a supplement in the form of a count. I have the intention of sending the survey to all the camps and eventually to all the prisons. The survey would inquire about general positions, choices, visions of the future, etc. This project has been organized. We would need outside help in the form of coordinating the operation, contacts with the camps, collecting the results, and also professional help. Write back about whether or not this is possible to organize. The text would be a standard form that each internee could fill out.

WEDNESDAY, NOVEMBER 10

The underground is appealing for an eight-hour warning strike. It was supposed to confirm the coherence of the Union and society's willingness to support the decisions of the underground . . . Only why was this way chosen to articulate the mood of the people in a situation where they would have to expect a clash with the government, which has long been prepared to deal with this type of action and which is determined to destroy its opponent? It is like having a well-trained heavyweight wait for his opponent, who is stepping into the ring for the first time. That is more or less what our chances are in today's confrontation. And you do not have to be Gallup to know what is going to happen! Yesterday the situation still seemed unpredictable. This morning seems to prove that the people realize that this suicidal approach, which is costly in terms of their losing the most active and most valuable people, needs to be changed. The losses are not in vain, the people in prisons, in detention, in camps and in the cemeteries fill the people's consciousness with a certain determination, and moral force. Everything that has happened up to now has been necessary, but this morning was somehow different. I feel already that this strike will be unsuccessful.

Around noon, I get out of the trolley at the Gdańsk Shipyard stop. SOLIDARITY is written in white chalk on a black background over the LENIN SHIPYARD sign. I hear the Shipyard working from here, however; the crane is operating and there is no strike tension in the air. The Shipyard is militarized and at the extension of Łagiewniki Street and the corner building of the Liceum is ZOMO's armored fist: armored vehicles, water cannon, and heavily-screened vans. They are waiting for the first signs of crowds. It is the same on the square near the theater and in other locations in Gdańsk. Hours pass, there is no traffic. Society understood: Not today.

Around 3 P.M., it is clear that there will be no street demonstrations on a large scale. Combat vehicles drive along Grunwaldzka Street in the direction of Wrzezcz and, mixed with the normal car and street traffic, they seem neutralized and innocuous. They are frightening when they come across dense groups of people, ready to fight. Although there was no strike and demonstration as predicted, I have the feeling that society has won this round. The heavily-armed opponent has been suspended on the ropes . . .

The shipyard workers who return from work comment on WRON's morning maneuvers. They are angered by the waste of paper: each of the workers entering the Shipyard was handed an abridged version of the martial law decree which also contained a list of punishments for violating the regulations of a militarized factory. Military commissars have threatened the workers (via the directors) with immediate dismissals and trials. The more suspicious workers were sent on a vacation and were forbidden to show themselves at the Shipyard. Militarized ZOMO patrols armed to the teeth are surrounded by crowds who do not pay the least attention to them. The appeal from the underground went unheeded. Does this mean that the thread linking the underground to society, and allowing the underground to understand the people's moods and pulse, has been broken? Or does it begin to indicate that the collective genius is seeking other ways of realizing its goals outside of the classic ones blocked by the government? Questions are being asked to which we have no answers as yet.

Our eavesdropping on police radio stations reveals that 129 persons were detained anyway, and that 50 persons had been released by 9:05 P.M.

THURSDAY, NOVEMBER 11

Morning telephone call: Do you know? In a moment, the next call. I meet a familiar priest in the city: Have you heard? How can they say that Poles lack a feeling for the geopolitical situation? All of us know that the death of Leonid Brezhnev, just as the death of the czar in our grandfathers' day, will have a considerable impact on the decisions of the Warsaw government. This sense has not left us for centuries. The shadow of Moscow's throne falls on our Polish reality.

In Gdańsk, the next anniversary: sixty-four years ago Poland regained its independence (1918). The Young Poland Movement has contributed significantly to the revival of this date in the people's consciousness. The young people from the Young Poland Movement have been organizing demonstrations and meetings under the statue of King John III Sobieski (the same statue which is referred to in police communiqués as the "horse" or "mare") on November 11 for the past few years. During demonstrations the police say: "I am sending a battalion of ours into the region of the horse." The chapel of Our Lady of Ostrobrama in the Marian Basilica in Gdańsk was the place where the Young Poland Movement organized prayers for the homeland and later for the release of their colleagues who had been jailed for participation in their patriotic manifestations. This is why a solemn mass will be celebrated today in the Marian Basilica. The Basilica bears the police cryptonym "120." In the afternoon this number begins to sail over the airwaves. Around the church in the Old Town, ZOMO patrols are on maneuvers, on foot and in vehicles. Will all those who take part in today's anniversary return home?

In a certain sense, this is a new society and a new arrangement: the government dismantled Solidarity and built ZOMO in its place. It proposed a new philosophy of force, physical prowess and contempt. The ZOMOs' vocabulary expresses this new element of contempt involuntarily in their radio transmissions. The detained demonstrators are the number 244, as in the Gdańsk cryptonyms. The necessity of neutralizing society's voice is spoken about as a concrete task given to the ZOMOs. The overworked but better and better equipped and armed ZOMOs regularly force back the new waves of society's attacks.

I reach home late in the evening, bypassing the patrols checking i.d.'s. During the mass in the Basilica, at which there were fewer people than I would have expected (there were about 5,000 people), Father Stanisław Bogdanowicz, the pastor of the Marian Basilica, announced Lech's release from the altar. The news was received with a long ovation. This was some sort of unusual sequence of events, beginning with the morning news from Moscow, and ending with WRON's communique about a Sejm session on December 13. Probably to suspend martial law. At the same time, television showed Wałęsa's handwritten letter to General Jaruzelski where Wałęsa signed himself "Corporal Lech Wałęsa." Will the tone which Lechu* found be apt? At this moment I think that it was the only one possible: somewhat with distance to himself and to the whole affair, both accepting the reality and questioning it. So now there is an opening . . .

The letter was dated November 8, two days before the eight-hour strike appealed for by the underground. It would seem that Wałęsa knew that the strike had no chance. Seeing what turn events could take, he decided to write the letter. But what about the underground activists? Is this how he is distancing himself from their decisions, or does he feel the defeat of their idea and so he is trying to save the whole situation? He is playing in a game where WRON is playing its hand, and where entire

---

*Diminutive for Lech.

staffs of people are trying to figure out how to exploit his move in the new circumstances. Will Lech be able to protect himself from the great manipulation, will his instinct deceive him?

MONDAY, NOVEMBER 15

He came home yesterday, at night, after three days of our waiting for him here in Gdańsk, on Zaspa. A few thousand people waiting for him in front of his apartment house, from which he had to speak nineteen times from the window, until he was hoarse. The people who gathered there expressed their opinion of him with the chant: "We elect you our general," in reference to his signature on the letter to Jaruzelski. The people do not want to accept the military order imposed on them by WRON, but if they have to, then they will oppose it by choosing their own general. That is how they see his role. I wonder how he sees it?

What will happen with Wałęsa if WRON decides to go through with its prediction of ignoring him as a possible partner in some new agreement? They have already predicted the end of agreements such as the ones made in August, which were based on such Polish historical traditions. Even then, perverse propagandists were indicating that that government's agreement to those "pacts" with the nation became a source of the Republic's weakness. These themes were probably undertaken for some purpose. So will we be successful in repeating the August scheme in some new form? And what happens if Wałęsa is, in fact, treated like a "private" citizen, the former chairman of the former Solidarity trade union? His strength emanated from the fact that the government went to him, and if Wałęsa had to, he sat at the table with the government. This was part of his strength. He spoke as an equal in our name. And now, after maltreatment at the hands of the government, will he still be able to be great? They showed that they could touch him, even though he was the national flag. We, reeds, had to bend under the imposed force. A perverse force because it was not entirely foreign. The various quickly mounted propaganda fronts in the form of Catholic writers like Jan Dobraczyński; the declarations of pseudo-Catholic groups obedient to WRON; and the new wartime leaders created a lot of confusion in people's minds. WRON, having made up whole series of new laws, also lets the obedient know that it is capable of creating enclaves of freedom, that it can open borders and blocked hard-currency accounts. Promises and threats are also thrown onto the scale, as a counterweight to the ideals of August and the one realistic figure, Wałęsa. He was released at the moment when most of those who had been on the streets shouting "Release Lech!" were in jail. What right does he have to talk to us now? Not all of those who were with him, who treated the defense of the Union as their own personal duty which had to be carried out to the very end, can listen to him. Will he be able to understand this, above and beyond the historical sense of his own person? He will not go down in history if he betrays those people. He was strong because he spoke the truth in our language, the truth which is a bolt of lightning if it is the whole truth. Will he still be able to find a way, a partner, and the listeners to continue his dialogue now, when he is suspended in a void, released by the good graces of the police commander and at a time when no one is allowed to tell the whole truth? Or perhaps this is completely impossible in the Poland of 1982 and 1983? At least for a few years or perhaps even a decade or more . . .

We still do not know who Lechu is today, after his release from Arłamow. After his arrival, during the course of the first talks, he seemed not to realize that the

Union, as an enormous organization, had ceased to exist, that he is directing his gestures to people who are responding, but that Solidarity has lost the power to execute its program. This has been replaced by the "good will" of General Kiszczak or some fraction of army commanders with whom one may take care of this or that in conversations in the corridors. But not the future for millions of people, or the deep reformation of Polish reality, not a new political agreement in a country where the Party monopoly has stuffed itself on everything that could be exploited. All of this falls on a man who for the umpteenth time steps up to the window and whose wife looks at him so full of concern and fear. A wife who knows the realities of martial law and who has been searched and publicly humiliated. Lechu says to us, as before: "We will win." We look at him with concern, not being able to rid ourselves of certain bitter thoughts . . .

· · ·

Messages smuggled from camp:

Strzebielinek, November 14, 1982
Our Dearest Holy Father!
Knowing your great attachment and concern for our homeland and your position on Solidarity, our hope, we allow ourselves to write these few words to you and to ask you to accept these pictures, handmade here in prison.

Dear Holy Father!
In our camp in Strzebielinek, there are 105 internees from several voivodeships (mainly Gdańsk, Szczecin, Warsaw, Toruń and Bydgoszcz); almost half of us have been deprived of freedom since December 13 of last year. Thanks to the help of the Church, the International Red Cross and many kind

people from the whole world, this isolation is a little easier to bear. We worry mainly about what is to come. In Poland recently there have been many laws introduced which paralyze citizens' rights. Perhaps we, as leaders of Solidarity, were incapable of solving many matters well, but the Holy Father knows how difficult it is to get anything done in Poland. It was not possible to lay the problems out and solve them one by one, and we Poles are very impatient and we wanted too much too quickly.

I think that the idea of Solidarity has not been lost even now. It lives and will live in people, not only in Poland, but in the whole world, just as the memory of my meeting with the Holy Father in Rome lives on in me.

In conclusion I send the Holy Father the sincerest greetings from all of the internees, with the request for a speedy visit to Poland.

Stanisław Wądołowski

Together with this letter, there was a collection of the latest iconographic work from camp in the package.

THURSDAY, NOVEMBER 18

I put off pressing the tape recorder button to run the tape. I am afraid of what I will hear. Will Wałęsa be the same as before in his first press conference (November 15)? How would that be possible in a situation in which a decree awaits his every unweighed word, his every superfluous gesture? What an insidious trap, perversely constructed and working automatically from the moment he was released into freedom, which especially for him is no freedom at all. On the other hand there are the people, the press, foreign correspondents: all waiting for the first meeting. A lot depends on him and a lot depends on the nature of the beginning. I hear the words: "I left as a man completely free. I signed nothing, I agreed to do nothing, I joined nothing." He explains about the letter that he wrote to the general and advises the correspondents to read the text slowly. He underscores the fact that each word has its meaning. Together with the signature. Wałęsa created the impression of a man in control of himself and more consistent than before. This is good. New predispositions will be needed for this game. He had time to work on himself. . . .

In the most important matters of program, he emphasizes (in answer to the journalists' questions) that he remains true to the ideals of August. He does not elaborate on this, but it is clear that this is the most important basic point of his "new" program. Instinctively, or perhaps on someone's advice, he has clearly accepted that this is the level on which he can move about. If he leaves it, they will start to attack him. On the next day, the chief of police in the voivodeship of Gdańsk, General Jerzy Andrzejewski (he advanced from colonel to general during martial law), warned Wałęsa in a telephone conversation that he was a private individual and as such he is subject to all the restrictions of martial law. This was the same theme that Jerzy Urban picked up at the last press conference for foreign journalists.

So they are leaving him the stairwell as the last field of Union activity, counting surely that he will either transgress the limits of the so-called law or that he will denigrate his high standing with society, by not satisfying anybody with the necessarily enigmatic elements of his program. The conference and its course indicate, however, in my opinion, that Lechu understood this trap and fortified himself internally to prepare for another round. From the first reactions to his conference, the contents of which circulated in cassette recordings, it seems that he is being well received, together with the intention that he was able to convey at this first meeting.

SUNDAY, NOVEMBER 21

Today in the parish church of the Gdańsk Shipyard, St. Bridget's, a very special ceremony was held. The banner belonging to the Solidarity men's choir from the Shipyard was blessed at 12:30 mass. The choir was formed in that memorable year, 1980, and it was evident that it carries a lot of weight as a symbol. Everyone understood this. About 10,000 people gathered in the church, which created a dense crowd in the church square. There was news that Lech Wałęsa was supposed to be present at the blessing of the banner. It seemed certain because the news was supposed to have come from the pastor, Henryk Jankowski, himself. This would have been Wałęsa's first public appearance outside of his home. Foreign television crews, press correspondents, and photographers were installed in the church. Right before the ceremony began, someone brought the news that Lech would not be there. We treated this information skeptically because we did not think that he would disappoint all those waiting to see him, especially since the ceremony was tied to honoring his own workplace.

The mass was celebrated by Kazimierz Kluz, the Gdańsk suffragan, and two accompanying priests: the Dominican, Father Sławomir Słoma from Gdańsk, and Father Jan Górny from Olsztyn. After the introductory prayers, first Father Jankowski and later Bishop Kluz referred to the expectations of all those gathered. The words of greeting to Wałęsa, who was not present physically but who was here with us, were met by a warm ovation, a very rare thing in Polish churches. From the rumors repeated quietly among the journalists, it seemed that Wałęsa had gone for mass to the catechism center which was being constructed on Zaspa, in his parish. In spite of this, the mass at St. Bridget's had the very lofty and solemn character of a religio-patriotic occasion. After presenting the banner with the emblems of the Gdańsk Shipyard and the word "Solidarity" embroidered in gold, the people sang "God, protector of Poland." Ten thousand hands shot into the air with fingers forming the letter V. Everyone was overcome with emotion. Emotion and hope. Someone next to me said aloud: "They won't break these people." The words "Return to us a free homeland, O Lord" rang out with full force and in one incredible abbreviation contained the thought and the program of Solidarity which the government had officially buried. Nothing had disappeared, nothing had been buried. After the song died out, people began clapping. A giant sign with the word Solidarity unfurled and people shouted "Long live General Wałęsa!" Long, endless applause. Father Jankowski reminded the people of the liturgical character of this gathering and urged us to disperse calmly.

People did not want to disperse. Glowing from inside out, in high spirits, they were waiting for something . . . In the neighboring parish at the Dominican St. Nicholas church, two streets down, conferences of a different nature were being held. The well-known Catholic publicist, Father Jacek Salij, spoke about civil courage in a historical context, in categories of moral imperatives, so desperately needed today, at a time of systematic undermining of character. This Sunday, which was also the feast day of Christ the King, will long remain in my memory.

And now calmly, without emotion: what does Lech's not coming to St. Bridget's mean? . . . Around evening I was positive that he had done the right thing. This was not an accident, but a clear, consistent line of behavior in the new situation. A line without unnecessary exacerbations and theatrical gestures, but which shows that he is gathering strength for the right moment, which will surely come. This proves that Lech is resilient and in a good frame of mind, because it was not easy *not* to come to St. Bridget's. This is another point for Lech after the press conference, which in spite of the great expectations for great words from him, took place quietly as he dictated.

SATURDAY, NOVEMBER 27

Lech Wałęsa. In a sense, he is a man who is "building" himself anew, proving that he understands the situation and showing that he has the elasticity which many of us doubted that he had. We interpreted the long silence erroneously, thinking that his only line would be the unrelenting demand to return to the situation as it was before December '81. A demand that is certainly just, but which, I admit in my heart, is totally unrealistic. He is also building a new team of people with whom he is meeting socially, for the time being, but with whom he is eventually seeking to recreate a picture of the current situation and political tendencies in Poland and abroad.

New faces have appeared. The general tendency seems to be as follows: Lech is looking for people to work with from the so-called "opposition." This is certainly a new quality: building on people who emerged from sectors that opened up to the idea of August and matured during the existence of Solidarity. This is definitely a new, "post-revolutionary" stage of activity, which he had first mentioned at the end of August: a time would come for other people and we will have to make our peace with this. He himself underwent that evolution, but many activists stiffened into the old stereotypical positions that had their genesis in the old opposition. This "oppositionist" position of the Union versus the government caused constant upheavals in the whole social structure. The implementation of this narrow course became more and more dangerous, demanded heroic deeds from the people, a constant throwing of everything into the balance, a constant game of *va banque*. Wałęsa judged accurately that the majority of the people had been exhausted by this tough game. He is seeking a staff which matured during the Union's existence and proved itself during martial law. A staff which will be able to lead the people along a realistic course and avoid the danger of a direct confrontation with the government.

Will he get a chance to return to the scene of the decision-making at the highest level? This depends: The workers from the big factories do not express any resentment towards Lech, they still feel he is one of them. But there are certain unformulated "fluids" of distrust in the air . . . It is a fact that the development of events separated Wałęsa, his fate from the fate of the average Shipyard family. "Their man" became the man of the year in many western magazines. He received doctoral degrees *honoris causa*, and made a brilliant career for himself not just in politics: he became the darling of the international mass media. Some people count his awards, even though everyone knows that almost everything that he has ever received has gone to the Union. The government exploits this thin vein of distrust with insidious observations such as that Wałęsa's living standard differs little from the "prominents" of the Gierek era. It gladly mentions him in the same breath with these characters. Leaflets, slandering Wałęsa and exploiting the most primitive human instincts aggravated by the progressive pauperization of Polish society, have appeared in many Polish cities. Yesterday in the Tri-City train there were more leaflets with the following contents: the leader of the workers got an apartment from the state, furniture from the people and, in addition, has a hard-currency dollar account. In times when everyone is envious of everyone else and watches to see if his neighbor does not have more than he has, this kind of information makes its point. A few days ago on Piwna in Gdańsk, not far from the Old Town police station, a "lost" package was found containing a picture of a pig with Wałęsa's face. It is pretty obvious that the government's entire propaganda attack is moving in the direction of discrediting the chairman. The work is being done systematically, discreetly (no one knows who is doing it) and hits all the sensitive spots.

There is still no frontal attack on his program, there is no real polemic. A Warsaw cafe that disseminates gossip from the "upper strata" is spreading the word that "Wałęsa is sorely mistaken if he thinks that someone will want to talk to him and that he will still play a role of any kind." That is the same formulation that is spread by the government press spokesman, who emphasizes that the released Wałęsa is a private citizen.

What has Wałęsa said about all this? From the various leaks of information emanating from his immediate circle, we get a picture of a new man, a picture that casts some light on the last weeks and days preceding December 13, 1981.

On the second day (December 12, 1981) of National Commission deliberations, Wałęsa had turned to the Gdańsk Communist Party secretary, Tadeusz Fiszbach, and the *wojewoda* of Gdańsk, Jerzy Kołodziejski, with the proposal that there be a legal settlement of matters pertaining to the functioning of Solidarity. Wałęsa understood the intentions of the government propaganda before the martial law crackdown, and knew that the government was especially sensitive in these matters. Wałęsa wanted to outline the areas of competence for Union advisers on whom government propaganda was concentrating, accusing them of steering Solidarity in the direction of "antisocialist counterrevolution." Wałęsa proposed that their roles be outlined clearly and that their influence on the Union's politics be limited. He also proposed that they be deprived of the right to represent Solidarity when appearing outside of Poland. If they do so, it would be on their own responsibility.

This explains his behavior on December 12/13, 1981. Foreseeing what was going to happen, he knew that when the Union was attacked it should try to minimize the number of victims of the crackdown, that it should try to neutralize the force of the attack and accept a posture of passive resistance. The Union should move away from direct confrontation in a position of such great disadvantage. In Konstancin (near Warsaw), Wałęsa proposed that the government allow another special meeting of the National Commission in prison so that it could release the ten million people who had formally committed themselves to defend the Union with a general strike and organized resistance if the Union were attacked from that commitment.

He understood the dimensions of the attack on the Union clearly, down to the government's decision to settle accounts with Solidarity even at the price of bloodshed.

What is being said about the Union from the perspective of an end to martial law? Wałęsa himself did not see the possibility of keeping Solidarity as it was in its final phase. Too many tendencies, too many interests of various sectors, as if there was too much of everything. The ship, to which Walesa liked to compare Solidarity, had steered off course, although the power of the idea was still pushing it forward. Today it is clear that the time has come for breaking down and distributing the task of bringing about change, which Solidarity was supposed to accomplish by itself. Wałęsa thinks that the sowing of ideas must be done by individual social groups. There, in Solidarity, these people came to know their destiny. They came to understand the direction in which they were supposed to move, they learned how to act and organize staffs, and they got to know their own strength. They acquired the skill of independent thinking. With this knowledge, the entire movement enters a new stage. From this angle of approach, the drama of the martial law period is not deprived of certain elements of hope. Next will come the separation of the wheat from the chaff, and the gathered seeds will reap a new harvest. This sounds rather evangelical, but this is probably how it really is. This is not the first time that Wałęsa is seeing into the future, projecting something that is not yet crystal clear, but which accurately interprets those social needs which make up a vision, a vision not deprived of the element that is so vital to life in general: hope.

He obviously has a vision of himself as a man functioning not only now when the Union underground still exists, and the old organizations are still fighting under old slogans, but as someone who can play a vital role in the future. This element appeared clearly in his conversation with the Minister of Internal Affairs, General Czesław Kiszczak, who went to Arłamov in answer to "Corporal Wałęsa's letter to General Jaruzelski."

In the conversation, which had a "manly" course, Wałęsa and Kiszczak each competed to prove that his side represented the real interests of the working class, the real bearer of the idea of socialism. Wałęsa was supposed to have said that he himself is a hundred times more "socialist," by background and conviction, than the general who represents the socialist bureaucracy. He was also supposed to have said that the complete success of WRON's sociopolitical concept, together with its consequences, will be the ultimate defeat of the idea of socialism. Thwarting an original Polish attempt to say something new, and to create a new perspective for this direction of social development in the world, will end in a cataclysm, which no power will be capable of of controlling or steering. General Kiszczak had apparently then said that this is a concern so distant that he personally does not feel responsible for it. There is, however, the matter of the younger generation, the future, for which Poles today take responsibility. In this context, continuing the exchange of opinions, Wałęsa made it understood that he wanted to take on the responsibility for shaping the distribution of power in the future. He admitted that the government could easily destroy him, but at the same time he warned that the destruction of a man acknowledged by workers as their leader would create a situation for the government which would not be controllable if society rebelled. The next social upheaval will oppose the government with its own version of "realistic socialism" and this will arouse a power in a discontented society that will annihilate everything standing in its way.

One has to admit that this is not a modest vision of one's own role. What is true, however, is that after this conversation, Wałęsa was released. There are two possibilities: either the government thought that the Union leader would be incapable of regaining his hold on the masses, or they decided to preserve him just in case. It is doubtful that the government treated Wałęsa as subjectively as he imagines. Time will tell.

What should we do? What should the program for today be? Wałęsa does not have access to the public of mass meetings as he did earlier and it is rare for couriers from the worker, intellectual, or scientific spheres to get through to his immediate circle. A plan of action is being being put together from the fragments of interviews that he has already given, from the snatches of conversations, even though it is not yet entirely clear. It is amazing that equally important to the form of the program is the nature of Wałęsa's future role. These are two unknown factors. When asked about the new unions, he answers "no" right now. Why? Because the atmosphere that accompanies the democratic demands of societal life is nonexistent in Poland today. There is no free press, free organizations have been suspended, and society is still bound and gagged. In these circumstances, in circumstances of mendacity, nothing real can be born. This is how his line of thinking could be formulated. Also characteristic is Wałęsa's faith that even the new unions created at the behest of the government can be treated as a link, which, fortified informally with ideas and concrete solutions that grow out of the needs of the workers, may play a role in the intermediary period. The guarantee, in his opinion, is the people's hunger for truth. If a union member gets two positions, one dictated by the authorities and the other dictated by the need to carry on informal activity (along the lines of the formally nonexistent Solidarity Union), then, in time, he will begin to make the right choices. Today this sounds quite idealistic and murky, but this kind of activity does not provide the government with pretexts for serious confrontations. This would then be a strategy for the intermediary period and would indicate a direction to those who do not want to give up all activity but who do not want to join the new union organizations, either.

On the other hand, an entirely realistic matter, pertaining to Wałęsa himself, is the approaching (and very important) anniversary of December 16. According to his earlier statements, Wałęsa plans to be at the foot of the Monument to the Fallen Dockworkers. This day, before which martial law will probably be suspended, will unveil the stage for events to come. How will Wałęsa be received by the workers? By the government? There are a lot of people who warn him against playing an unreal role, which the propaganda manipulators have prepared for him. They say: who is Wałęsa freed from internment and not leaving his apartment on Zaspa? The head of a Union? Not quite. The Union no longer formally exists, and many of its structures have disintegrated. Is Wałęsa a political figure? What should his role be now? A role which would not arouse doubts, attacks, pretexts to start a fight? Many people expect that Wałęsa will return (after a period of rest at home) to work in the Gdańsk Shipyard which elected him to do Union work. He is advised to spend the entire intermediary period among his colleagues at work. The Shipyard was his strength, from it he drew his authority, knowledge and intuition. There, too, among the workers he was beyond the reach of government attacks. Others advise that he stay at home and "intern himself," that is, seek new ideas, wait for the return of the other internees from camp, wait for those who were sentenced and for those in hiding. They also say that there is no return to the Shipyard, where many members of Solidarity have been deprived of their jobs. Wałęsa is waiting. He feels that December will explain many things and dictate his next steps.

MONDAY, NOVEMBER 29

Letters smuggled out of camp:

(Letter to Lech Wałęsa)
Strzebielinek. November 28, 1982

Dear Lech: I am very happy that you are at home. I was very worried that you had to be interned alone. I cannot imagine how you were able to bear it for so long. I had it a lot better. At first I was sent to Strzebielinek, where I am now, later I was transferred to Goleniów near Szczecin (January 5) where our colleagues from Szczecin are locked up. That was a terrible prison. Next I ended up in Wierzchowo, which was the worst: the guards and their superiors were awful. I was sick and had an operation in a hospital forty kilometers from Szczecin. The hardest thing was getting to the hospital. I was helped by the Church authorities, the International Red Cross, and the Polish Red Cross, not to mention the efforts of my own family. Today I am healthy and in the company of ninety colleagues, although now this number is getting smaller, which makes me happy.

Lechu, your letter created so many expectations that were diminished somewhat later, but most of us do not deny this. In such important matters it is very difficult to make all the decisions. After all, that is how it was even before December 13. Before then many of us criticized, and many of us were strong, but how many of us have remained that way? I, too, had a few propositions to talk, and I agreed under the condition that you would be able to participate, as well as the other members of the presidium, and our lay and ecclesiastic advisers. They did not agree to this condition.

Leszek, I am very worried about the underground, about those who have been arrested and imprisoned, although there seems to be some hope now. This is taken care of by that institution: PRON.* It is important that it do this. Other matters and assignments will certainly be continued with a great amount of energy, and the work we have invested will not go for naught. Individuals are not important here but society is. Society was our strength and our weakness. Lechu, I don't know what they will decide to do with me here, but when I get out, I will drop by to see you. My wife was supposed to have visited you on Saturday, but the train was late and she came directly here. At any rate, keep your spirits up, as you have up to now. I have always believed in

---

Patriotyczny Ruch Obrony Narodowej, the Patriotic Movement for National Defense.

you and still believe in you. If you have more good or bad news, send it back to me.

In closing, I send you and your family the heartiest greetings. Give my best to all of our mutual friends. And one more time, I ask you, don't let it bother you, better days are sure to come. Until we meet again,

Stasiek

Greetings from all your friends here at Strzebielinek.

(Letter to _____)
November 27, 1982

Sincere thanks for the news. . . . We printed and distributed forty-four official thank-you notes (a list is enclosed) sponsored by our Camp Council (currently: Wądołowski, Merkel, Kocjan, Kukuła, Korejwo, Perejczuk, and Starzyński). Slowly we are getting ready to abandon our work, although the news about whether or not someone will remain after December 13 changes constantly as in a kaleidescope and forces us to be ready for all possibilities. The guards devote more time now to things that are leaving than coming in, and we are rushed by the ignorance of whether it is night or day or what time it is. There is a well-justified fear that they could be looking for a pretext in these last weeks to keep someone in here longer. In other words, we are on edge, but this is certainly not the first time. (You probably know how on November 11 the "one more, one more" looked after news of the death of B., and the sharp division after Lech's letter.) One guy bet that the government is backing out of its position and is begging us on its knees for forgiveness. I said that this was impossible, that it is society that is looking for an honorable capitulation. The solution is supposed to surface at the end of the year, but I am, unfortunately, calm about victory. The issue of Wałęsa has very many dimensions. I will not relate my opinions because I think that we are in agreement (it is obvious to me that we cannot lose this trump card). The majority of the internees in camp were very happy about Lech's release, although there were also accusations of collaboration and jokes about the Corporal. Now with the development (or rather the lack of development) of events, the hope that society will take over has been extinguished. People are divided and despondent, and most often simply do not know what they should think. Our defeat or the government's Pyrrhic victory? The heated discussions about Wałęsa have stopped but many people are consumed by regret and even anger toward him. I am convinced that if Lech trips up somewhere seriously, they will blame everything on him and humiliate him as deeply as they elevated him earlier. I am writing to you about all this so that you will be prepared for various developments. This is all nerves. . . . I see so much that still needs to be done that I am happy because, no matter what happens, one can still be optimistic if there is work to do. I think that something useful will come of all these mutual efforts. . . .

P.S. Camp population today: 71 in camp, 9 in the hospital in Wejherowo and 7 on leave. Altogether 87 internees.

FRIDAY, DECEMBER 3

Yesterday things began to move in camp: all of the well-known activists such as Stanisław Wądołowski, vice-chairman of the Union; Stanisław Kojcan, member of the National Commission; and, finally, Andrzej Zarębski, chief of the BIPS bulletin, and former press spokesman for the Union, have been released.

Church sources reported 740 internees at the end of

November. How many of them will be released? A new scenario is being prepared for the period after suspension of martial law. The subjects discussed by Communist Party Secretary Kazimierz Barcikowski, General Florian Siwicki and General Józef Baryła at a consultation of the leaders of the Polish Army on November 16 shed some light on the intentions of the authorities. These points coincide with those worked out by the Poland 2000 Committee. On Monday, Ryszard Kapuściński, the vice-chairman of this Committee, discussed them at a meeting at the Dominicans. The abolishment of martial law that is supposed to take place on December 13 will only be symbolic. The government will still be able to intern people and wartime censorship will still be in effect. The militarized factories and summary courts will still exist. Certain indications that the war vocabulary is being changed to a peacetime one are evident in current methods of "internment." This is mainly in reference to army exercises. This was the maneuver applied on a broad scale before November 10 and 11. It is currently believed that there are about 700,000 men in the army and militarized police. The last army recruitments, especially from the Tri-City area, testify to a new form of repression. The recruits are transported to places far from populated areas. They cannot leave the barracks or correspond with the outside. It was just recently, and only after the first family visits, that information about these "centers" got out. An example is Army Unit 3466 "Z2" in Wygoda near Czerwony Bór in the voivodeship of Łomża. This unit consists of 460 persons between the ages of twenty-four and forty-six. These are mainly men who have never had any army training and who have been classified, for health reasons, as army recruits incapable of doing physical exercises in the war games. As of now, there are nine such "centers." How is one not to believe that the army was told what to do. We can also now add the dissolution of the Association of Polish Artists of Theater, Stage, Radio, Television and

Film (ZASP). So this was the next victim after the Independent Student Union and the Association of Polish Journalists. The next move will probably be against the Polish Writers' Union, which is still suspended.

SUNDAY, DECEMBER 5

Letter smuggled from camp:

December 4, 1982

Dear _____ :

Our situation is still uncertain. No one knows exactly when they will release us or who will stay and when, and there is no sense in repeating the massive speculations on the subject. There are still a lot of us here, today: 61, and 6 on leave, and 5 in the hospital—altogether 72 people. There are twelve camps altogether, and the total number of internees we estimate to be between 600 and 700. On November 10, Wojciech Dobrzyński was caught in Warsaw. He was the one who escaped from the hospital in Wejherowo in August. Apparently he was added to the subject of "management of RKS* in Warsaw." We have the July issue of *Playboy* with Wałęsa's interview (if I have enough time to rewrite it, I will enclose it). I remember how at the first National Commission conference he refused to give those two beautiful women an interview. The interview is lousy.

I am sending you some exhibit items for our future

---

*Regionalny Komitet Solidarności, Regional Committee of Solidarity.

museum through my "brother." Among them are: a Solidarity banner, a May 3 emblem, a "patriotic T-shirt," patriotic curiosities, a map of the grounds, pictures from the exhibit and similar things. You will find posters announcing our literary salon meetings, which will help you figure out the number, dates, and subjects of those meetings. By the way, Hughes's poetry is scheduled for the very next meeting (on Tuesday). I am enclosing materials for the archive on the circle of young internees, a rather informal association, casual and mainly social, but interesting.

THURSDAY, DECEMBER 9

Letter smuggled from camp:

December 8

Dear _____ :

I am sending you immediately the latest results of the Strzebielinek rankings. I am giving you the facts from December 9, as today people from Gdańsk were informed of their release tomorrow. Something new has been introduced: a checkout card. Each internee who leaves has to get confirmation signatures from the doctor, librarian, and warehouse attendant. They have been handing out these cards one day before the release. We have already gotten rid of all of our "transgressions." This is the last bunch. We request information about Lech's second letter and about his collaboration with Staszek. We would really like to know if releasing all of Bydgoszcz also applied to Rulewski and Tokarczuk. We all send you hugs. . . .

FRIDAY, DECEMBER 17

I remember two frames well: one from the evening edition of the television news, still managed by the editor Stanisław Celichowski, a camera shot of the empty square at the Gdańsk Shipyard with the monument of the three crosses and a thin stream of shipyard workers, who are heading straight along Doki Street into the city from the second gate of the Shipyard. Rarely does someone stop for a moment by the monument. The voice off camera praises the wisdom of the workers, emphasizing that they heeded no appeals and "that they go home in peace and dignity." The camera filming this must be up very high, probably on the top story of the skyscraper bordering on Solidarity Square. That is how this moment was registered by the television news.

The second frame, which was not shown but will remain in my memory, was an iron cordon of ZOMOs, with an unprecedented number of water cannon, armored cars, and motorized patrols with gas throwers mounted on jeep roofs. Not to mention thousands of truncheons, helmets, and shields. The city gives the impression of having been methodically divided into quarters and surrounded by police. In the back of the center of expected events: in the region of the building called "the green grocer," at the exit of Doki Street, at the Meeting of Peoples' Square, on the square near the Wybrzeże Theatre and in dozens of other places, are concentrations of armored equipment. In spite of this, right before 3 P.M., a crowd of several thousand people stands on the corners of the streets and looks in the direction of the monument. The people are constantly blocked and shoved in the direction of the city by the ZOMOs. There was only one moment when a large group of shipyard workers suddenly opened one of the gates and about one hundred people headed for the monument. The ZOMOs run away in consternation, thinking that they are being attacked. This is how they were trained, after all, in the gatherings at the Golden Inn, where, day after day, they were methodically trained to attack and disperse crowds under the recreated model of the Shipyard monument and among the ropes and wires recreating the layout of the streets in this part of the city. During this time in the city, a greater and greater crowd of people is pushed into the region of the train station. Above the crowd, a great roar: "Solidarity, Solidarity." The water cannon move into action, the jeeps turn around, and the crowd backs onto the train platforms. The trains carry hundreds of people in the direction of Wrzeszcz.

The frame includes the blockade of Zaspa, the neighborhood where Wałęsa lives. All the entrance roads are manned by police. This is the second day of checkpoints and i.d. checks for all who wish to enter the apartment complex. Before noon on December 16, the ZOMOs flush out all the journalists, foreign correspondents, and photographers from the surrounding entryways. It is only in such "tidied" terrain that a couple of dozen ZOMOs storm the building where Wałęsa had an apartment and drag him out to a waiting car. From the window of the first floor, Danuta Wałęsa shouts "Thugs!" A score of people witness this scene. While ZOMOs are pacifying the city, two Mercedes go up and down senselessly on the two-lane overpass between Gdańsk and Gdynia. In one of the Mercedes, between two *ubeks*, sits Lech Wałęsa. Reinforcements are in the other Mercedes. They will ride like this in a circle until evening, until they get word that the danger of workers' demonstrations has passed. Then around 6 P.M., they return Wałęsa to the door of his apartment. On the stairway halfway up to Wałęsa's apartment, a six-foot *ubek* and a ZOMO guard end their watch. Only the usual network of surveillance remains. Wałęsa's apartment is under constant surveillance and each person who visits Lech's home is reported nonstop on the UKF frequency. Lech Wałęsa's text, prepared for his December 16 appearance, is transmitted by Western radio stations during their evening broadcasts. Order reigns. The PZPR reptile papers such as the Gdańsk *Kontakt*, an organ published by undereducated *politruks** from the Regional Committee, will trumpet: "The street said 'No!'"

THURSDAY, DECEMBER 23

Today's papers report the release of all internees. Not all are released, however: Andrzej Gwiazda (Gdańsk), Seweryn Jaworski (Warsaw), Marian Jurczyk (Szczecin), Karol Modzelewski (Wrocław), Grzegorz Pałka (Łódź), Andrzej Rozpłochowski (Katowice), and Jan Rulewski (Bydgoszcz) are arrested.

---

*Derogatory term from the Russian for "political instructor," i.e. one who indoctrinates.

CHRISTMAS EVE, DECEMBER 24

". . . We are afraid to have you appear, O Star of Bethlehem! What will happen when you flare up, what will happen? . . ."

It did shine . . . from distant Uherce, Michał Mąsior went home. This year he got home in time for Christmas Eve in Rybnik. Tadeusz Mazowiecki and Bronisław Geremek returned to Warsaw from Darłówek. Teresa Remiszewska, the famous yachtswoman, was taken from her home in Gdynia. An August pair, Mariusz Wilk and Bernadeta Stankiewicz, are preparing Christmas Eve supper together in prison on Kurkowa in Gdańsk. Somewhere in a neighboring cell is Maciek Łopiński, the editorial secretary of the former weekly, *Czas.* I wonder if they will be able to share the Christmas wafer.

. . .

From the stories of those leaving Strzebielinek:

On Wednesday, December 22, Bartczak left the Lublin camp. On his way home, he stopped at the hospital in Wejherowo to see Jurczyk. He was told that Jurczyk had been transferred under escort two hours earlier to the prison in Białołęka. He came to Gdańsk with that news, to Lech. Then he went to his parents. The next day, early in the morning, the next internees were released by regions. From Gdańsk, Jacek Merkel, member of the National Commission's presidium; Ryszard Grabowski from BIPS; Roman Pieńkowski from the Gdańsk Shipyard; and Henryk Tarasiewicz from Port Administration in Gdynia (from the hospital). All of these people had been interned from the very beginning. Of the remaining three from the later conscription, Janusz Walentynowicz, Stefan Maciejewski, and Józef Hołownia. From Szczecin, Jerzy Zimowski, Mirosław Witkowski, who had been interned from the very outset, and Zdzisław Konury from the May influx. From Mazowsze: Wincenty Kazańczuk, Józef Taran, the oldest in terms of length of internment, as well as Eugeniusz Madej (July). The last camp was left by Józef Taran, a student from Warsaw Polytechnic, the head of the foreign section of the Independent Student Union.

At the very end of the empty third pavilion on the right hand side in the chapel cell rise the dark outlines of our cross. The cloth that imitates a human figure and drapes down from where the horizontal and vertical beams cross grows more and more faded. The rusty shaft that looks like a spear sticks out from its side. On the back of the cross, where the bark was not removed, there are a couple of hundred signatures of those who were there. Our signatures.

Index

K

Kaczmarek, Franciszek, 26, 48,
53, 58, 72, 95, 103, 106,
110–11, 112, 121, 126, 127, 133,
137, 149, 150, 151, 159, 170,
184, 197, 201–2, 208, 260–61
Kaczmarek, Lech, 56, 156–57, 182
Kaczyński, Leszek, 10, 19, 174,
265
Kapuściński, Ryszard, 175, 180,
181, 292
Karut, Andrzej, 251
Kazańczuk, Wincenty, 299
Keiling, Jerzy, 211
Kinaszewski, Adam, 116
Kisielewski, Stefan, 203
Kiszczak, Czesław, 118, 142,
204, 220, 276, 285–86
Kluz, Kazimierz, 92, 215, 279
Kłyszka, M., 245
Kniaź, Mieczysław, 253
Kobyliński, Zdzisław, 86
Kocjan, Stanisław, 226, 227,
262, 290, 291
Kołakowski, Leszek, 67
Kołodziejski, 15–16, 283
Komitet Obrony Robotników.
See KOR
Konfederacja Polski Niepodległej
(KPN), 74, 123, 193
Konopka, Dr., 262
Kontakt, 196, 297
Konury, Zdzisław, 299
KOR *(Komitet Obrony*
Robotnikow), 29, 74, 123,
188, 190, 191, 192, 193, 196,
253
Korejwo, Stefan, 262, 290
Kowalczykowa, Anna, 174, 238

Kowalska, Anna, 212
Koziatek, Jan, 155
Kozicki, Andrzej, 218
KPN (Confederation of
Independent Poland), 74,
123, 193
Krementowski, Karol, 9
Kruża, Tadeusz, 97
Krystosiak, Aleksandr, 227
Kuberski, Jerzy, 156
Kukołowicz, Romuald, 127
Kukuła (internee), 262, 290
Kułaj, Jan, 168, 179
Kuroń, Jacek, 18, 42, 53, 54, 55,
65, 66, 241
Kutermak, Józef, 155

L

Lapiński, Henryk, 167
Lauer, Wiesław, 173
Le Monde, 105
"Letter to Society on the
Subject of the New
Trade Unions," 265
Lis, Bogdan, 206
Lis, Zbyszek (Zbigniew), 167
Literatura, 136
Łopiński, Maciek, 298
Loyalty oaths, 70, 100, 123, 146,
148, 164, 206, 231
Łuczko (Professor), 232
Łużny, Jan, 77

M

Macedoński, Adam, 179
Macharski (Cardinal), 144
Maciejewski, Stefan, 298
Macierewicz, Antoni, 151

W

Wądołowski, Stanisław
(Staszek), 42, 48, 77, 228,
262, 276–77, 290, 294
Wajda, Andrzej, 90
Walentynowicz, Anna, 10,
251–52
Walentynowicz, Janusz, 251,
298
Walentynowicz, Witold, 267
Wałęsa, Danuta, 16, 174, 187, 296
Wałęsa, Lech, 5–6, 7, 8, 10, 11,
16, 31–32, 42, 53, 59, 61, 67,
79, 105, 127, 173, 178, 187,
189, 201, 218, 223, 277–79,
279–90, 294, 296–97, 298
arrest of, 15
Catholic Church and, 142,
143
letter to Jaruzelski, 273, 274,
285–86, 290–91
Playboy interview, 293
release of, 273–76, 291
Wałęsa, Maria-Wiktoria, 220
WARMA, 259
Warsaw Pact, 198
Wesoły, Szczepan, 142
Wieczór Wybrzeża, 166
Wierzchowo News, 232, 233–34
"Wild-Strawberry Solidarity,"
76
Wilk, Mariusz, 298
Winiarska, Halina, 23
Winiarski, Franciszek, 251
Wiśniewska, Krystyna (from
Department of
Intervention), 23
Wiśniewski, Jerzy, 242
Witkowski, Jan, 243

Witkowski, Mirosław, 298–99
Wojciechowicz, 24
Woroszylski, Wiktor, 179
Wręga, Antek (Antoni), 169
WRON (Military Council of
National Salvation), 13, 14,
34, 60, 61, 64, 75, 76, 112,
117, 118, 121, 130, 141, 142,
162, 165, 176, 177, 178, 185,
203, 209, 218, 224, 239, 248,
271, 273, 274, 275, 285
Wronkowski, K., 242
Wujec, Henryk, 66, 241
Wysocki (Captain), 146
Wyszkowski, Krzysztof
(Krzysiek), 37, 84, 184,
188–90, 258
Wyszyński, Józef, 105–6
Wyszyński, Stefan, 37, 92, 174,
199, 238, 240

Y

Young Poland Movement, 10,
24, 191, 192, 193, 204–5, 272

Z

Żabiński, Andrzej, 79
Zarębski, Andrzej, 225–26, 291
ZASP (Association of Polish
Artists of Theater, Stage,
Radio, Television and
Film), 292–93
Zawadzki, Sylwester, 99–100
Zdanowicz, Zbigniew, 229,
230, 232
Zierka, Wojciech, 38
Zimand, Roman, 179
Zimowski, Jerzy, 234, 298

Złotkowski, Zdzisław, 48
Żołnierz Wolności, 83
ZOMO (Motorized Units of
    the Citizen's Militia), 9,
    11, 15, 17, 24–25, 28, 62, 80,
    87–89, 137, 140, 186, 203–4,
    229, 248–49

at Gdańsk Shipyard, 270–71,
    272–73, 295–97
treatment of internees by,
    37, 83, 100–101, 114–
    15
Życie Literackie, 171
Życie Warszawy, 179